ISLAM

AND PEACEBUILDING

Gülen Movement Initiatives

ISLAM

AND PEACEBUILDING

Gülen Movement Initiatives

Edited by
John L. Esposito
İhsan Yılmaz

BLUE DOME

13 12 11 10   1 2 3 4

Published by Blue Dome Press
244 Fifth Avenue #2HS
New York, NY 10001

www.bluedomepress.com

Library of Congress Cataloging-in-Publication Data Available

ISBN: 978-1-93529-507-5

Printed by
Pasifik Ofset, Istanbul - Turkey

TABLE OF CONTENTS

Part 3
Theology of Dialogue in Comparative Perspective

Part 4
Peacebuilding in Global Action

ACKNOWLEDGMENTS

This volume is the product of three major conferences on the Gülen Movement: Muslim World in Transition: Contributions of the Gülen Movement, House of Lords & School of Oriental and African Studies (SOAS) & London School of Economics (LSE), October 25–27, 2007; International Conference on Peaceful Coexistence: Fethullah Gülen's Initiatives for Peace in the Contemporary World, Erasmus University, Rotterdam, The Netherlands, November 22–23, 2007; and Islam in the Age of Global Challenges: Alternative Perspectives of the Gülen Movement, Georgetown University, Washington, D.C., November 14–15, 2008. We wish first and foremost to thank sponsors and hosts of these conferences.

We must express our deep thanks to the members of the editorial boards of these conferences: Eileen Barker OBE, FBA, Henri J. Barkey, Muhammad Abdul Haleem, George S. Harris, Thomas Michel, Simon Robinson, Zeki Sarıtoprak, David Thomas, Paul Weller, Ian G. Williams, Asaf Hussain, Johnston McMaster, Colin Turner, Tim Winter, Seyyed Hossein Nasr, Akbar Ahmad, John Borelli, B. Jill Carroll, David Cuthell, Sidney Griffith, John Haughey, S.J., Paul Heck, Qamar-ul Huda, John O. Voll, Khaled Abou El Fadl, Jean Michel Cros, Eric Geoffroy, Andreas Kinneging, Paolo Naso, Ton Notten, Klaus Otte, Emilio Platti, Karel Steenbrink, Pim Valkenberg, and Anton Wessels. To all of them we are extremely grateful.

We have received assistance and cooperation from many people while editing this book. We would like to acknowledge the support of all of those individuals whose names we cannot list here. However, they know how grateful we are for their help.

We also wish to give special thanks to Hüseyin Şentürk and Hakan Yeşilova of the Blue Dome Publishing for their cordial, supportive, and especially very patient attitudes in preparing the manuscript. Ruth Woodhall copyedited the manuscript with unusual care and sensitivity, and we benefited and learned much from her bright remarks.

Finally, we are especially grateful to Jean Esposito and Arzu Yılmaz, for their support, understanding and encouragement throughout this project.

Washington, D.C. / Istanbul
John L. Esposito
İhsan Yılmaz

EDITORS

John L. Esposito: University Professor as well as Professor of Religion and International Affairs and Islamic Studies at Georgetown University, John L. Esposito is Founding Director of the Prince Alwaleed Bin Talal Center for Muslim-Christian Understanding in the Walsh School of Foreign Service. Esposito has served as consultant to the U.S. Department of State and other agencies, European and Asian governments and corporations, universities, and the media worldwide. A former president of the Middle East Studies Association of North America and the American Council for the Study of Islamic Societies, Vice Chair of the Center for the Study of Islam and Democracy, and member of the World Economic Forum's Council of 100 Leaders, he is a member of the E. C. European Network of Experts on De-Radicalization and an ambassador for the UN Alliance of Civilizations.

Esposito was the recipient of the American Academy of Religion's 2005 Martin E. Marty Award for the Public Understanding of Religion and of Pakistan's Quaid-i-Azzam Award for Outstanding Contributions in Islamic Studies, and the School of Foreign Service, Georgetown University Award for Outstanding Teaching.

Esposito is Editor-in-Chief of *The Oxford Encyclopedia of the Islamic World* (6 vols.); *The Oxford Encyclopedia of the Modern Islamic World* (4 vols.), *The Oxford History of Islam*, *The Oxford Dictionary of Islam*, *The Islamic World: Past and Present* (3 vols.), and Oxford Islamic Studies Online. His more than 40 books and monographs include: *The Future of Islam; Who Speaks for Islam?; What a Billion Muslims Really Think* (with Dalia Mogahed); *Unholy War: Terror in the Name of Islam; The Islamic Threat: Myth or Reality?; Islam and Politics*; *What Everyone Needs to Know About Islam; World*

Religions Today; Religion and Globalization (with D. Fasching & T. Lewis); *Asian Islam in the 21st Century; Geography of Religion: Where God Lives, Where Pilgrims Walk* (with S. Hitchcock); *Islam: The Straight Path; Islam and Democracy and Makers of Contemporary Islam* (with J. Voll); *Modernizing Islam* (with F. Burgat); *Political Islam: Revolution, Radicalism or Reform?*; *Religion and Global Order* (with M. Watson); *Islam and Secularism in the Middle East* (with A. Tamimi); *Iran at the Crossroads* (with R.K. Ramazani); *Islam, Gender, and Social Change, Muslims on the Americanization Path; Daughters of Abraham* (with Y. Haddad); and *Women in Muslim Family Law*. Esposito's books and articles have been translated into more than 30 languages.

Esposito's interviews and articles have been published in newspapers, magazines, and the media in Europe, Asia, and the Middle East, such as *Wall Street Journal*, *New York Times*, *The Washington Post*, *The Economist*, *The Guardian*, *London Times*, CNN, ABC Nightline, CBS, NBC, and the BBC. A native of Brooklyn, N.Y., he currently resides in Washington, D.C. with his wife, Dr. Jeanette P. Esposito.

* * *

İHSAN YILMAZ: Associate Professor of Political Science at Fatih University, Istanbul as well as the Director of the PhD Program in Political Science and International Relations at the Institute of Social Sciences of Fatih University. He is also the Director of Center for Civilizations Research at Fatih. He received his BA in Political Science and International Relations from the Bosphorus University in 1994 and completed his PhD at the Faculty of Law and Social Sciences, School of Oriental and African Studies (SOAS), University of London in 1999. He then worked at the University of Oxford as a fellow between 1999 and 2001 and taught Turkish government and politics, legal sociology, comparative law and Islamic law at SOAS, University of London between 2001 and 2008. He was also the Deputy Chair of the Centre for Ethnic Minority Studies at SOAS (2003–2008) and the director of the

London Centre for Social Studies (2003–2008). He is the author of *Muslim Laws, Politics and Society in Modern Nation States: Dynamic Legal Pluralisms in England, Turkey and Pakistan* (2005) and co-editor (with Paul Weller) of a forthcoming book *European Muslims, Civility and Public Life: Perspectives On and From the Gülen Movement* (2011). He is a co-editor of the European Journal of Economic and Political Studies (EJEPS). He was the coordinator of the conferences on the Gülen Movement in London and Rotterdam that took place in October and November of 2007. His current research interests are Turkish government and politics; political parties; media and politics; Islamism in Turkey, Central Asia, and the Middle East; faith-based movements; society-law-politics relations; diaspora studies; elites; centre-periphery relations and sociology of Muslim law in the West. He has published his work in international scholarly journals such as *British Journal of Middle Eastern Studies*, *Middle East Journal*, *Journal of Ethnic and Migration Studies*, *Muslim World*, *International Journal of Turkish Studies*, *Journal for Islamic Studies*, *Journal of Muslim Minority Affairs*, *Journal of Caucasian and Central Asian Studies*, *Journal of Economic and Social Research*, *International Law and Politics Journal*, *EJEPS*, and *Insight Turkey*. Dr. Yılmaz is also a regular columnist of *Today's Zaman*, an English language daily published in Turkey.

CONTRIBUTORS

Mohammed Abu-Nimer: Professor, International Peace and Conflict Resolution program at the School of International Service, American University. He is also Director of the Peacebuilding and Development Institute at American University. An expert on conflict resolution and dialogue for peace, Dr. Abu-Nimer has conducted research on conflict resolution and dialogue for peace among Palestinians and Jews in Israel. His work has focused on the Israeli-Palestinian conflict and on the application of conflict resolution models in Muslim communities. Dr. Abu-Nimer has also conducted interreligious conflict resolution training and interfaith dialogue. In the last decade, he has completed many evaluation projects and reports on peacebuilding and development programs. As a scholar/practitioner, he has conducted conflict resolution training workshops and has intervened in many conflict areas around the world, including Palestine, Israel, Egypt, Northern Ireland, the Philippines (Mindanao), and Sri Lanka. In addition to his numerous articles and publications, Dr. Abu-Nimer is the co-founder and co-editor of the *Journal of Peacebuilding and Development*.

* * *

Harun Akyol: Lecturer in the Department of Languages at Suffolk New College, UK. He has taught Turkish language and culture at Suffolk New College since 2002. He received his MA (2002) in Near and Middle Eastern Studies from the University of London (SOAS). He taught sociology at Suffolk College from 2004–2006. He completed a PGCE (Post Graduate Teaching Certificate in Education) through the University of East Anglia (UK) in 2006. His main research interests include the theory of democracy, nationalism, ethnic conflict, Middle Eastern politics, and post structuralism. He is currently engaged in a PhD research project at the University of Essex's Department of

Government focused on the issue of Kurdish national discourse in the struggle for the future status of Kirkuk.

* * *

Philipp Bruckmayr: M.A. in Arabic and Islamic Studies at the University of Vienna (2007) on "The Islamization of Champa;" now preparing his PhD dissertation entitled "Half a Millennium of Muslim Diaspora in Khmer Lands: The Chams of Cambodia." In recent years, he has conducted fieldwork on Arab immigration to the Caribbean in Colombia, Venezuela, and Curacão and on the Chams in Cambodia, Vietnam, and Thailand. He has published articles and book reviews in the *American Journal of Islamic Social Sciences*, *ISIM Review*, *Der Konak*, and *DAVO Nachrichten*, as well as presented papers at international conferences in Austria, Germany, and Turkey.

* * *

David B. Capes: PhD, Southwestern Baptist Theological Seminary, Texas (1990) following a Master of Divinity at Seminary in 1982 and a BA from Mercer University, Atlanta in 1978. He now serves as Chair of the Department of Christianity and Philosophy at Houston Baptist University. In 2000, he was appointed Visiting Fellow of the Faculty of Divinity at the University of Edinburgh where he carried out research on early Christian worship practices. In 1992, Capes published *Old Testament Yahweh Texts in Paul's Christology* (Tubingen: J. C. B. Mohr). Since then he has teamed up with Etty Boochny of Tel Aviv to write *The Footsteps of Jesus in the Holy Land* (Jerusalem: Steimatsky, 1999). He serves with Thomas Nelson as the theological review director of a new Bible paraphrase called the *Voice*. His research interests include Christian origins, Biblical interpretation, Christology, and worship. For years he has been active in Jewish-Christian dialogue in Houston and around the nation.

* * *

Klas Grinell: PhD in the History of Ideas from the University of Gothenburg, where he worked from 1999–2008 as an Assistant Professor of the History of Ideas. Since April 2008, he has served as curator of the Museum of World Culture in Gothenburg. He is also Country Coordinator for Turkey at Amnesty International, Sweden.

Klas Grinell has published in Swedish on the following subjects: images of the other in Swedish tourism abroad; the place of Islam in Hegel's philosophy of history; Ziauddin Sardar, social constructivism and the Islamization of science; al-Suhrawardi and the place of Islamic philosophy in the history of Western philosophy; Orientalism, postcolonial theory, and world systems analysis; the idea of Europe will be fulfilled by Muslim Turkey; justice beyond the reach of reason: comparative analysis of the writings of Said Nursi and Jacques Derrida.

* * *

Mehmet Kalyoncu: He is adviser to Organization of the Islamic Conference's Ambassador to the United Nations in New York. Previously, Kalyoncu worked as a political analyst and reporter for *Zaman US Daily*. He has published scholarly articles in academic journals and op-ed pieces in newspapers and online publications. His writing has appeared in *Balkanalysis, Caspian Business News, Zaman US Daily, Today's Zaman, Zinda Magazine, PINR, American Journal of Islamic Social Sciences, Journal of Central Asia and the Caucasus*, and *Centro Argentino de Estudios Internacionales*. Some of his articles have been republished by the *Al Arabiya*, *India Times*, *Chila Daily*, and *Global Times*; and cited in the *San Francisco Chronicle*, *Jerusalem Post*, and the *Global Media Journal*. His research interests include: Turkish foreign policy, ethno-religious politics, civil society, and social development in countries rich in natural resources. Kalyoncu authored *A Civilian Response to Ethno-Religious Conflict: Gülen Movement in Southeast Turkey* (New Jersey: The Light, Inc., 2008). He holds MS in Management & Administrative Sciences from University of Texas at Dallas with specialization in organization and strategic management (2001–2002); and MA in Eurasian, Russian, and East European Studies from Georgetown University's Edmund A. Walsh School of Foreign Service (2004–2006).

* * *

Turan Kayaoglu: Assistant Professor of International Relations at the University of Washington, Tacoma's Department of Interdisciplinary Arts and Sciences. He teaches international relations, international human rights, and religion and politics. His recent article, "The

Extension of Westphalian Sovereignty: State Building and the Abolition of Extraterritoriality," appeared in *International Studies Quarterly* (September, 2007). Currently he is working on a book manuscript on the emergence of the sovereign state system.

* * *

Karina Korostelina: Associate Professor at the Institute for Conflict Analysis and Resolution, George Mason University and Fellow of the European Research Center of Migration and Ethnic Relations (ERCOMER). Korostelina is a leading expert on identity-based conflicts, ethnic conflicts, the relationships between Muslim and non-Muslim populations, conflict resolution, and peace-building. Her recent interests include the study of civilian devastation, the processes of politicization of history, and the role of history education in conflict and post-conflict societies. She has been a Fulbright New Century Scholar and has participated in the Regional Scholar Exchange Program administered by the Kennan Institute at the Woodrow Wilson Center in Washington, D.C. as well as in the CRC Nationalism session at the Curriculum Resource Center of the Central European University. She has received grants from the MacArthur Foundation, Soros Foundation (Research Support Scheme, Managing Multicultural Communities Project, Renaissance Foundation), the United States Institute of Peace, US National Academy of Education, Spenser Foundation, USDA Bureau of Educational and Cultural Affairs, INTAS, IREX, and the Council of Europe. The results of her research were presented at numerous international conferences in Europe and the US and in publications in international journals. Among her books are: *Social Identity and Conflict* (2007); *Structure and Dynamics of Social Identity* (2003); *The System of Social Identities: The Analysis of Ethnic Situation in the Crimea* (2002); and *The Role of History Education in Conflict and Post-Conflict Societies* (in publication). She is an editor of *Identity, Morality and Threat* (2006) and *Interethnic Coexistence in the Crimea: The Ways of Achievement* (2002).

* * *

Jonathan Lacey: PhD candidate in the Department of Sociology at Trinity College, Dublin, where he completed an MPhil in Ethnic and Racial Studies. Lacey is a part-time research assistant with one of Intel's Senior Ethnographic Researchers, focusing on independent living for older people. His current interests include the sociology of religion, social movements, and global networks.

* * *

Mohamed Nawab Mohamed Osman: MA, Department of History, National University of Singapore. Osman is Associate Research Fellow with the Contemporary Islam Program in the S. Rajaratnam School of International Studies, Nanyang Technological University. He is actively involved in various organizations and regional networks including the Young Association of Muslim Professionals and Southeast Asia Islam and Democracy Workshop. His research interests include: history and politics of South and Southeast Asia, Islamic movements, and Islamic political thought, with fieldwork in Pakistan, India, Malaysia, Indonesia, and the United Kingdom. He has contributed chapters to several books, produced working papers for academic conferences, and articles for various newspapers, including *Straits Times* and *Today's Zaman* (Turkey). He is currently writing a book on the history of Islam in Southeast Asia.

* * *

Richard Penaskovic: Professor of Religious Studies and Former Chair of the University Senate and University Faculty at Auburn University in Alabama. He received his BA in philosophy (the equivalent of an MA in theology) from the University of Wuerzburg, Germany and a doctorate in theology from Ludwig Maximilians University of Munich. He is the author of over 100 publications and has appeared on radio and TV in the US. His latest book, *Critical Thinking and the Academic Study of Religion*, is distributed by Duke University Press. His many articles and book reviews have appeared in such journals as *The Journal of the American Academy of Religion*, *Augustinian Studies*, *Theological Studies*, *The Journal of Ecumenical Studies*, *Louvain Studies* (Belgium), and *The Heythrop Journal* (London). His current research interests include Muslim-Christian dialogue, spirituality, and ecclesiology.

* * *

Douglas Pratt: PhD, St Andrews University (1984); Associate Professor and Chair of the Department of Philosophy and Religious Studies at University of Waikato, New Zealand. Pratt is a member of the advisory board and the UNESCO Chair in Intercultural and Interreligious Relations, Asia Pacific at Monash University in Melbourne. He is also an honorary Interfaith Advisor to the Anglican bishops of New Zealand. Pratt was visiting lecturer at the Centre for the Study of Islam and Christian-Muslim Relations, University of Birmingham (2004); visiting research fellow of Interfaith Relations at Ripon College, Cuddesdon, University of Oxford (2005–06); and associate of the Centre for the Study of Religion and Politics, University of St Andrews. He was recently honored by the Federation of Islamic Associations of New Zealand with a Harmony Award. Among his recent publications on the challenges of pluralism and inter-religious dialogue are *The Challenge of Islam: Encounters in Interfaith Dialogue* (Ashgate, 2005) and *Identity and Interaction: Islam and the Challenge of Interreligious Dialogue* (Adelaide: The Charles Strong Memorial Trust, 2000).

* * *

Zeki Sarıtoprak: PhD in Islamic theology, University of Marmara, Turkey; He also spent several years studying the Arabic language in Cairo while researching his dissertation entitled "The Antichrist (al-Dajjal)." Sarıtoprak is the Bediüzzaman Said Nursi Chair in Islamic Studies at John Carroll University in Cleveland, Ohio. He has researched and taught a range of subjects – Islamic theology, introduction to Islam, world religions, Biblical elements in the Qur'an, Islamic spirituality, classical and contemporary Islamic movements, interfaith dialogue, and notably courses on Islamic personalities such as al-Ghazzali and Bediüzzaman Said Nursi – at Harran University (Turkey), Georgetown University, the Catholic University of America in Washington D.C., and Berry College in Rome, Georgia.

* * *

Irina Vainovski-Mihai: Associate Professor of Arabic Literature at Dimitrie Cantemir Christian University in Bucharest, Romania. After graduating from the Faculty of Foreign Languages and Literatures (Arabic and English) at the University of Bucharest, she spent several years in various Arab countries, publishing travel notes, essays and research on literature and cultural studies, course books, and other academic instruction aids, as well as translating works from Arabic, English, and Hungarian. Her recent publications include: *A Food of Their Kind: The Gastronomic Image of the Eastern Other in a Time of Tensioned Self-Identification* (2006, in English) and *The Wandering European and His Egyptian Guide: On Arabic Story and History-Telling* (2005, in English). She is a founding member of the Center for Arab Studies in Bucharest and of the Romanian Association for Religious Studies.

Part 1 - Introduction

Islam and Peacebuilding: Gülen Movement Initiatives

INTRODUCTION

Islam and Peacebuilding: Gülen Movement Initiatives

John L. Esposito and İhsan Yılmaz

Peacebuilding seeks to consolidate an existing peace and thus is different from peace enforcement. Peacebuilding activities include education, inter-faith and intra-faith dialogue, advocacy, mediation and so on. In the words of a former Secretary General of the United Nations, peacebuilding is "(a)ction to identify and support structures which will tend to strengthen and solidify peace in order to avoid a relapse into conflict" (Boutros-Ghali 1992, 11). An active civil society can create social capital, that is, trust, cooperation over ethnic, religious, and other divisions, inclusiveness, and open debate which is conducive to peace and harmony between sections of society (see Putnam 1992). Interaction over ethnic and religious boundaries and inclusiveness in ways of organizing and associating can serve to prevent violence (Varshney 2002). Civil society can play a positive role in maintaining sustainable peace as civil society is a critical space where diversity and pluralism can be cherished and fostered (Hampson 1996, 7; Peck 1998). A social network of informed and responsible citizens furthers pluralism, democracy and peacebuilding.

Pre-emptive or preventive peacebuilding includes many possible actions in the political, economic and social fields. For instance, community capacity building and fostering collaborative relationships are some of these pre-emptive peacebuilding actions. The need for peace re/building does not exist only at the state level, but also in the social and political spheres, as well as relationships in "everyday life"—those of the basic everyday sociopolitical dynamics, and of the trust that bounds and bridges community together (Brown and Gusmao 2009, 61). Thus, peacebuilding or the positive peace dimension endeavors to create "space for civilian activity to work on the long-term political, economic and cultural dimensions of change in a model of conflict transformation that addresses power asymmetries, poverty and marginalization" (Curran and Woodhouse 2007, 1055).

In an age of post-Westphalian international politics, the state-centrality of peacekeeping has been transcended by Kant's cosmopolitan ethics of caring for the stranger, "grounded in the proposition that humankind is bound together in a community of fate. In such a community, a right violated anywhere is felt everywhere. Such a world engenders an ethos of responsibility and solidarity" (Curran and Woodhouse 2007, 1065).

Transnational religious and faith-based movements can play crucial roles in peacebuilding with their strong faith-based motivation, long term commitment, religious, spiritual and moral authority and ability to facilitate constructive social relations between different groups of population (Stassen 1992, Thistlethwaite and Stassen 2008, Sampson and Lederach 2000, Gopin 1991).

It is not so much religion itself that is influential, but rather the ways in which it has been interpreted and practiced that is influential in religion's orientation toward radicalism, violence, conflict resolution and peacebuilding (Coward and Smith 2004). Thus, it is necessary to elaborate upon what Islam and Muslims have to say about peacebuilding, which we will do below.

Islam and Peacebuilding

Before embarking on a discussion on Islam vis-à-vis peacebuilding, first, we need to understand whether or not Islam is compatible with pluralism and the concept of civil society. As we mentioned above, civil society, pluralist understanding, tolerance, inclusivity and the like play vital roles in peacebuilding. Like all religious traditions, Islamic principles have constantly been reinterpreted. "The result is flexibility of ideas and divergence over time and space" (Eickelman and Piscatori 1996, 16; Esposito 2005, 223). Thus, to understand Islam in the twenty-first century, one needs "an appreciation of the broader struggle for the soul of Islam. As in the past, the religion of Islam, both the faith and its practice, is a complex reality—a multidimensional faith and community" (Esposito 2005, x). As opposed to essentialist claims of both neo-Orientalists and Islamists, "Muslim politics is not predetermined by a template of ideas; it is influenced by a number of factors, which, while including scripturally defined precepts, also include national identities, economic circumstances, and social status" (Eickelman and Piscatori 1996, ix). As a result, "Muslim politics is not monolithic" (Hefner 2005, 4). To appreciate this variety, one needs "to look beyond the categories of Western liberal history and recognize several distinctive concerns of Muslim politics" (Hefner 2005, 5). For instance, in the US context, many Muslim organizations are concerned with improving the condition of all human beings through education and spiritual awareness and some others focus on democratic and human rights issues. With such immense diversity in the American Muslim community, it is difficult to reduce it to a single voice. Instead, there needs to be greater appreciation for the efforts and contributions of Muslims in areas of conflict resolution, interfaith dialogue, peacebuilding, education, political activities, civic work, human rights and women's rights advocacy, legal expertise, and humanitarian efforts" (Huda 2006, 200).

As John O. Voll (1999, 243) observed:

> Humanity is now entering an era where the discussions must go beyond the debates in the context of modernity where religious and secular are seen as opposites. The desecularization of the world does not simplistically refute the ideas of secularization theory; it transcends those ideas. Just as global and local are becoming increasingly interdependent in the processes of globalization, the religious and secular dimensions of contemporary society are coming together in ways that defy the logic of the old conflict between religion and secularism within modernity. In the Muslim world, as in other major faith traditions, articulation of this new relationship takes many different forms that clearly go beyond the main lines of the old assumed polarity between religious and secular.

Most of the binary distinctions or oppositions developed by nineteenth-century social scientists—status/contract, mechanical/organic solidarity, *Gemeinschaft/Gesellschaft*, traditional versus rational-legal legitimization, etc.—simply collapsed into one overall category of artificial constructs traditional/modern after the Second World War (Wallerstein 2004, 3). The fundamental difficulty with modernization theory centers on its sharp but artificial contrast between "modernity" and "tradition," "and the consequent misunderstanding of the entrenched social functions of tradition" (Eickelman and Piscatori 1996, 23). Tradition cannot "be construed in negative terms only. Traditional family and religious networks may in fact facilitate development, and social and political changes are often made possible because they are cast in terms of the traditional framework" (Eickelman and Piscatori 1996, 25).

Two broadly opposed positions exist with regards to Islam's compatibility with pluralism, secularism, and civil society. From an essentialist point of view, pessimists argue that Islam is inherently hostile and "it is unlikely that Muslim societies will embrace democracy and pluralism anytime soon" (Hefner 2005, 2). Very strong evidence exists that many among the world's Muslims have concluded that there is no contradiction between Islam and civil-democratic pluralism (Hefner 2005, 4). The Gallup World Poll of some 35 Muslim countries, stretching from North Africa to Southeast Asia, and representing the voices of a billion Muslims, found that majorities of Muslims admired the West's rule of law, fair political systems, democracy, respect for human rights, freedom of speech, and gender equality. The majority of Muslims, more than 90 percent in Egypt and in Iran, said that if drafting a constitution for a new country they would include "free speech" as a fundamental guarantee. Freedom of assembly and religion were also cited as important.

Admiration for Western democratic values does not, however, translate into support for a Western secular model of government. Most Muslims believe their own religion and values are essential to their progress. (Esposito, J. and Mogahed, D. 2007, 47) As Abdul Aziz Sachedina has observed, recognition of pluralism will "advance the principle of inclusiveness, which would counsel accommodation, not conflict, among competing claims to religious truth in religiously and culturally heterogeneous societies" (Sachedina 2001, 23).

Islam as a religion and as a tradition is replete with teachings and applications about peacebuilding and "provides rich resources for nonviolent values, beliefs, and strategies" (Abu-Nimer 2003, 19). Scholars who have focused on Islam vis-à-vis peacebuilding underline that "Islamic principles of nonviolence and peacebuilding include the pursuit of justice; doing good; the universality and dignity of humanity; the sacredness of human life; equality; the quest for peace (individual, interpersonal, communal, regional, and international); peacemaking via reason, knowledge, and understanding; creativity; forgiveness; proper deeds and actions; responsibility; patience; collaborative actions and solidarity; inclusivity; diversity; pluralism; and tolerance" (Smock and Huda 2009, 8).

Diversity and tolerance of differences are core principles of peacebuilding and thus peacebuilders try "to bring people to the realization that they are different and that such differences should not constitute a basis for discrimination or bias" (Abu-Nimer 2003, 82). Many Muslim and non-Muslim scholars have pointed to Islamic principles and values such as unity, supreme love of the creator, mercy, subjection of passion, and accountability for all actions" (Abu-Nimer 2003, 49). The Qur'anic concept of *ta'lif al-qulub* is an "important socio-legal category of 'those whose hearts are to be reconciled' (Ar. *mu'allafat al-qulub*)' referring to people whose friendship and alliance were to be nurtured. This category of people included new converts to Islam and non-Muslims: Jews, Christians, and even "polytheists" whose goodwill and friendship were deemed as contributing to the well-being of the community. As essential members of the polity they were entitled to the charity (Ar. *zakat*; also *sadaqa*) of Muslims and revenues of the state" (Afsaruddin 2008, 222). Even though this early inclusivist attitude toward non-Muslims was not always given due recognition in the later periods, understanding and interpretation of the Qur'anic verses and practice of the Prophet is important "in the general context of quotidian human relationships and is potentially of special relevance today in the field of religious peacebuilding in our fractious world. It offers a preliminary methodology of effecting reconciliation among adversaries, rooted in love for God that translates (or should translate) into affection and respect for all God's created beings" (Afsaruddin 2008, 224, 226).

Sachedina (2001) argues that pluralism is a major peacebuilding concept in Islam. In his view, there is a need for a new pluralist Muslim paradigm in dealing with the other and he calls for the rediscovery and promotion of Islamic moral concern for peace and justice (Sachedina 2001, 6). This discourse, based on pluralism, nonviolence and peace is the cornerstone for inter-religous and intercultural dialogue (Abu-Nimer 2003, 40).

Social justice is one of a number of values that relate Islam to peace and peacebuilding. Empowerment of the weak, the needy and the oppressed through *ihsan* (doing what is beautiful) and *khayr* (doing good) is an important path to social justice in the

Islamic tradition (Abu-Nimer 2003, 55). Islam has a "deep commitment to empower the weak, and it remains a religion of dynamic social activism in terms of individual duties and sense of social responsibility" (Abu-Nimer 2003, 55). As doing good "deeds and individual responsibility are so central to Islam, involvement in community life becomes the most visible channel for meaningful deeds. Therefore, Muslims are urged to improve their communal life, to support one other, and to combat poverty" (Abu-Nimer 2003, 71). It must be noted that these are related to a vibrant and well-functioning civil society, which can play crucial roles in peacebuilding. Islamic peacebuilding "can promote objectives such as an increase of solidarity among members of the community: bridging the gap of social and economic injustice; relieving the suffering of people and spare human lives; empowering people through participation and inclusivity; promoting equality among all members of the community; and encouraging the values of diversity and tolerance" (Abu-Nimer 2003, 83).

Muslim peacebuilders today are engaged with work in areas of civil rights, human rights, interfaith dialogue, education, charity, public diplomacy, political activism, and other religious and secular activities. Many of those peacebuilders "believe that interfaith dialogue with Christians and Jews on both local and national levels is critical to understanding their religion within a monotheistic tradition" (Huda 2006, 189).

The Gülen Movement and Peacebuilding

Fethullah Gülen is an Islamic scholar, thinker, writer, and poet. His teachings and efforts have resulted in the emergence of the Gülen Movement and inspired many in Turkey to establish educational institutions that combine modern sciences with ethics and spirituality. The actual size of Gülen's millions of followers and sympathizers is not exactly known. But it is agreed that it is the largest civil movement in the country, an "apolitical communitarian movement" (Fuller 2008, 56).

Gülen's model draws together belief in God, science and the Turkish nation, and is "an attempt to synthesize tradition and modernity, religion and science" (Koyuncu-Lorasdaği 2010, 221). Gülen regards the Movement as a cultural activity whose essence is based on the voluntary cooperation of many people who may not know each other, have no organic ties or mutual acquaintances but who all share the faith of Islam. On these grounds he always insists on keeping his distance from any political claim which he thinks could threaten to corrupt Islam as well as from any (worldly) political post" (Koyuncu-Lorasdaği 2010, 225). "As a combined *ulama*-intellectual persona, Gülen not only preaches inner mobilization of new social and cultural actors, but also introduces a new liberative map of action. His goals are to sharpen Muslim self-consciousness, to deepen the meaning of the shared idioms and practices of society, to empower excluded social groups through education and networks, and to bring just and peaceful solutions to the social and psychological problems of society" (Yavuz 2003, 19).

The Gülen Movement began in Turkey at the end of the 1960s "through Gülen's teachings at the Kestanepazarı Qur'anic School in Izmir, where he worked as a state imam. It expanded through schools that were opened in the Turkic republics after the fall of the Soviet Union and with the emergence of the Central Asian Turkic republics and the Balkans in the early 1990s (Koyuncu-Lorasdaği 2010, 225). "Gülen directed businessmen who were sympathetic to his cause to invest in there construction of these Turkic republics and provide financial support for the schools. In the 2000s, Gülen's educational network spread to countries all over the world, from Azerbaijan to Ukraine, Albania to Macedonia, the Netherlands to Canada, Australia to the South Africa, and Japan to Taiwan... The reputation and success of these schools can be explained by the high-quality education they provide and top-notch students selected on the basis of their success" (Koyuncu-Lorasdaği 2010, 226).

Habermas' (1984) theory of communicative reason (or rationality) includes an argument called universal pragmatics, that human beings possess the communicative competence to bring about "mutual" understanding. Habermas, as a believer in dialogue, is an optimist who criticizes the Frankfurt School and postmodernist thought for excessive pessimism. In Gülen's thought and praxis, we find a similar belief in mutual understanding, dialogue and optimism, in contrast to the Islamists' pessimism. Gülen's optimism and belief in dialogue, coupled with his intellectual-*alim* self-confidence, make it easier for him to be a border transgressor.

Gülen pioneered the establishment of the Journalists and Writers Foundation in 1994, well before the significant increase in dialogue activities in the post-9/11 world. Starting from 1995, "he was intent on promoting dialogue and tolerance among all strata of the society in Turkey and elsewhere. In the context of the Inter-cultural Dialogue Platform, Gülen has held talks with many religious leaders and institutions, such as Pope John Paul II (1998), Greek Ecumenical Patriarch Bartholomew (1996), Sepharadic Chief Rabbi of Israel Eliyahu Bakshi Doron (1999), as well as a number of Turkish non-Muslim religious leaders" (Gözaydın 2009, 1224). Gülen's dialogue and peaceful coexistence discourse was also replicated in institutions abroad, like the Dialogue Society established in London and the Rumi Forum established in Washington, D.C. in 1999. There are now hundreds of interfaith and intercultural dialogue associations and charities all over the world founded by the Gülen Movement's Muslim and non-Muslim volunteers, engaging in interfaith and intercultural dialogue with people of different faiths, backgrounds, and cultures (Gözaydın 2009, 1224).

Gülen holds an inclusive, universalist and transcending Islamic conception. He does not claim ownership to a monopoly of truth, and the Movement is not an ideological movement, thus it is inclusive as opposed to exclusivist Islamist ideologies. As Turam (2003, 185) states, the Gülen Movement "aims to revitalize faith in secular regimes and not against them." In Gülen's view, the faithful can reside comfortably in secular environments. He makes reference to an Anglo-Saxon understanding of passive secularism and argues that within the boundaries of this type of secularism, Islam and secularity of the state could be compatible.

Gülen's theology of peace is based on the integrity of the individual regardless of ethnic or religious background and approach to peacebuilding, therefore, is one of "bottom-up" social change (Sarıtoprak 2010). Scholars of peacebuilding consider forgiveness essential for peacebuilding, and in Gülen's theology of peacebuilding, there is no place for revenge (Sarıtoprak 2010).

In Gülen's worldview, there are three major enemies of not only Muslims, but also humanity as a whole: ignorance, poverty and disunity. As opposed to so-called "Islamism"'s simple but abstract assertion that surrendering to the ancestors, i.e. returning to the golden age of pristine Islam, will solve all problems of Muslims, the movement espouses a concrete socio-economic and cultural analysis of the current spatio-temporal context and based on this analysis offers concrete solutions to tackle the challenges Muslims face rather than insisting on abstract rhetoric. If ignorance is one of three major enemies, then the Movement's offer would be education at different levels, not only at school or through religious education. The Movement's educational projects cover almost all major stages of life. It is not only confined to the mosque, nor is it solely confined to secular schools. It also includes family education, child upbringing, educating religious scholars, educating by example and not only in classrooms etc. If poverty is the second enemy of Muslims, then the Movement's offer would be to establish poverty relief and humanitarian aid charity organizations in addition to education, to raise people's socio-economic status (see in detail Michel 2008). If dissension or internal conflict is the third major enemy, then, dialogue, tolerance and mutual understanding are the remedies to tackle this conflict. As can be seen, the Movement's major projects all focus on one of these three areas and the Movement's media organizations also play supporting roles in this global civil activism (see in detail Yılmaz 2008). Today in Turkey, Central Asia and many other parts of the world, the Movement's educational institutions contribute to the education of people from different religions and ethnicities. They have "already contributed, through educational endeavors, to the building of peace in many areas of conflict, including the Balkans, northern Iraq, Northern Ireland, and the Philippines" (Sarıtoprak 2007, 636).

The Movement has been able to convert its social network and spiritual capital into creative and educational projects from nursery to university level, for boys and girls (Küçükcan 2007, 187). Investment in general education represents a "critical support for a pluralizing Muslim politics" (Hefner 2005, 26). "In its diverse specializations, its encouragement of innovation, its (relative) gender equality, and its culture of civility-in-plurality higher education is shimmering example of all that is best about modern freedom and civic decency" (Hefner 2005, 27). Educational institutions can foster sustainable development by bridging international values with local values and cultures; by capacity-building, preparing professionals to foster a sustainable future and by creating public spaces through civil society associations (Vargas 2000, 377–396). The Movement provides intermediary networks that contribute to the integration of individual citizens and the state (Özdalga 2005, 433).

The Movement does not only give priority to poorer countries like Kyrgyzstan, but also to areas where ethnic and religious conflicts are escalating, such as Albania, Kosovo, Macedonia, the Philippines, Banda Aceh, Northern Iraq. These schools are believed to "have played remarkable roles in decreasing levels of conflict in these areas" (Sarıtoprak 2005, 423). During the civil war in the region that was formerly known as Yugoslavia, children from different ethnicities were being sent to a school that was formed by the Movement in Skopje, Macedonia. These children were being educated peacefully under one roof while their parents were at battle (Sarıtoprak 2007, 637). The Movement has established schools in Bosnia where the community is "composed of Muslim Bosnians,

Christian Serbs and again Christian Croats. Despite their common ethnic identity, and more or less, similar political cultures due to their common Yugoslavian background, these three different communities had as recently as a decade ago engaged in the bloodiest conflict due to nationalistic aspirations. Their religious differences had exacerbated, if not caused, their nationalism-driven conflict" (Kalyoncu 2007, 604).

Afghanistan is another example of a community which is highly diversified with various ethnic groups such as Pashtun, Tajik, Hazara, Uzbek, Aimak, Baluchi, Kyrgyz, Turkmen, Nuristani and Pamiri, among other small ethnic groups. Yet, this is another country that hosts several schools that have been set up through the Movement, including all-girls schools (Kalyoncu 2007, 603–604). Another country where these schools operate is the Philippines, which is an example of a community stigmatized by an enduring Muslim-Christian battle (see in detail Michel 2003). Minority Moro Muslims in the Philippines are populated in the autonomous region of Mindanao in Southern Philippines. After the end of colonialism in the Philippines, the conflict in the country has transformed into an enduring one between the Muslim minority and the Christian majority. The schools bring together both Christian and Muslim students under the same roof. The schools which are associated with the movement do not take part in "the conflict. Instead, they prefer to identify common grounds where they get together and cooperate to tackle their common problems" (Kalyoncu 2007, 605).

In the African context, field research on Kenya's Turkish "schools suggests that the schools have been functioning not only as a secular alternative to religious, Christian missionary schools and Islamic schools, but also as barriers to potential ethno-religious conflict between Kenya's local Christian tribes and its politically empowering Muslim minority" (Kalyoncu 2008, 350). Similarly, the Movement's "civil society initiatives in Uganda seem to have introduced the local Ugandans with a pragmatist approach to development by seeking to instill in them the notion of relying on their own resources instead of international aid" (Kalyoncu 2008, 350).

Previous studies have suggested that societies where women have higher social and economic status and greater political representation are less likely to become involved in conflict (Gizelis 2009, 505). Thus, the Movement is contributing to peacebuilding, albeit indirectly, by providing education to girls in several countries ranging from Afghanistan to Kenya. As the Movement rejects extremism and violence of any kind, stating that they are incompatible with the true message of Islam, the schools and other institutions affiliated with the Gülen Movement emphasize "the development of tolerance among religious communities" (Fuller 2008, 58). Various Turkish organizations all over the world promote the teachings of tolerance and pluralism advocated by Gülen (Smock and Huda 2009, 8). These activities could also be called "peacebuilding by conduct" even though the Movement does not boast that they are engaged in peacebuilding. "Young people from different religions, languages, and cultures study, are educated, and admired in the same educational institutions. Loving and understanding each other is the main principle" (Sevindi 2008, 75). When asked, "You have schools where there are no Muslim Turks. What do you expect from them?" Gülen replied that we hope that Turkish culture, and our conception of tolerance, will alleviate them and create the foundation for a living dialogue (Sevindi 2008, 102). On another occasion he explained that enmity becomes figurative once there is true love in one's heart. Love requires that we not look at the bad characteristics in someone we love. Since this aspect is not properly understood, people imagine that Muslims lining up on one side and hating the 'other', while being consumed with feelings of jealousy. They imagine that this is a religious requirement (Sevindi 2008, 107).

Islam and Peacebuilding: Gülen Movement Initiatives is divided into four parts: Part I Introduction; Part II Globalization and Gülen as a Border Transgressor; Part III Theology of Dialogue in Comparative Perspective; Part IV Peacebuilding in Global Action and Conclusion.

Part I is compromised of our introduction followed by chapter 1, "Gülen's Ideas on Freedom of Thought, Pluralism, Secularism, State, Politics, Civil Society, and Democracy," in which we present a succinct account of Gülen's ideas on these issues, as these are crucial with regards to Islam and peacebuilding. In chapter 2, "Islamic Resources of Peacebuilding: Achievements and Challenges." Muhammed Abu-Nimer and İhsan Yılmaz summarize Islamic peacebuilding studies and present a concise theory of Islamic peacebuilding. The focus then shifts to how Gülen and the movement named after him could provide resources for Islamic peacebuilding.

Part II "Globalization and Gülen as a Border Transgressor" is comprised of four chapters. In chapter 3, "Border Thinking: Fethullah Gülen and the East-West Divide," Klas Grinell shows that Gülen's message of dialogue departs from the bordering practice of modernity that creates dichotomies and trenches between *us* and *them*. Through the concept of border thinking, Grinell argues for the special double vision Gülen holds, thanks to his Turkish experience of modernistic Kemalism and Islamic traditions. In Grinell's view, Gülen shows that today we are all living in borderlands, where no one can live a life sheltered in one tradition only; we therefore need to engage in dialogue. For dialogue to be possible, there must be difference as well as a belief in our ability to understand each other despite these differences. The bordering modernity has only seen difference and dichotomies. The concept of civilization is explored in this chapter to differentiate between a border building huntingtonian concept of civilization and Gülen's insistence that we are all fundamentally of the same make. In chapter 4, "The Dialogue as a Source for Peaceful Co-existence between Muslims and Christians," Karina Korostelina considers the role of dialogue in the formation of common secular identity (national or regional) as a tool for the development of peaceful coexistence between Muslim and non-Muslim groups in a secular context. Such dialogue aims to develop a new dual identity, one that is connected to religious identity and the other which reflects membership in a secular nation. Korostelina describes the role of interfaith dialogue in developing tolerance and a common secular identity with respect to religious identity. Chapter 5, "Gülen on Healing the Rift between Islam and the West," by Richard Penaskovic argues that Gülen may be a bridge toward better understanding between Islam and the West because of his views on peace, tolerance, and interfaith dialogue and because of his optimistic view of the future relations between the two aforementioned blocs.

Part III "Theology of Dialogue in Comparative Perspective" has four chapters. Chapter 6, "Preachers of Dialogue: International Relations and Interfaith Theology," by Turan Kayaoglu compares the approach of three monotheistic religious leaders to dialogue of civilizations and interfaith using their respective scholarly works including Rabbi Jonathan Sacks' *The Dignity of Difference*, the late Pope John II's *Crossing the Threshold of Hope*, and Gülen's *Advocate of Dialogue* (edited by Alphonse Williams and Ali Ünal). Kayaoglu argues that Islam's emphasis on diversity and the Qur'an's accommodation of earlier religious traditions put Islam and Fethullah Gülen in the best position for offering religious justifications that will accommodate the value and cherish the dignity of followers of other religions Irina Vainovski-Mihai's in chapter 7, "The Limits of the Otherness in Fethullah Gülen's Dialogic Methodology for Interfaith Encounters," examines Fethullah Gülen's teaching on interfaith encounters, highlighting his dialogic methodology proposed to a globalized world in which Samuel Huntington's idea of the "clash of civilizations" is still prominent. Zeki Sarıtoprak focuses on Gülen's theology of peacebuilding in chapter 8, "Fethullah Gülen's Theology of Peacebuilding." Sarıtoprak examines the concept of peacebuilding through Gülen's writings and activities with reference to the main sources of

Islam and Gülen's commentary on them. Sarıtoprak examines a sampling of Fethullah Gülen's theological views on peace and peacebuilding, and the roots of these views in the Qur'an. In focusing on Gülen's activities, the chapter emphasizes the work of the Washington D.C. based Rumi Forum for Interfaith Dialogue (of which Gülen has served as honorary president), and its contribution to peacebuilding through interfaith activities. In chapter 9, "Islamic Prospects for Inter-religious Dialogue: The Voice of Fethullah Gülen," Douglas Pratt argues that Gülen is a strong voice from within Islam seeking to proclaim the Muslim priority for peaceful and harmonious relations with the wider world, including relations with religious neighbors. Pratt looks at the issue from a Christian scholar's perspective and seeks to understand the prospects and appropriate contexts for dialogue: what enables, and what hinders, good interfaith relations? He also briefly addresses the issue of Islamic paradigms for inter-religious relations and dialogue, then he analyzes and critically discusses the views of Fethullah Gülen. In chapter 10, "Tolerance in the Theology and Thought of A. J. Conyers and F. Gülen," David B. Capes compares the theologies of a Christian theologian and Fethullah Gülen with regard to the concept of "tolerance." Capes discusses in this chapter the significance of authentic tolerance based on humility, and the notion of "*hoşgörü*, or what is roughly translated as "empathetic acceptance" in the writings of Gülen, advocated by Conyers.

Part IV "Peacebuilding in Global Action" has five chapters. Chapter 11, Philipp Bruckmayr's "Phnom Penh's Fethullah Gülen School as an Alternative to Prevalent Forms of Education for Cambodia's Muslim Minority" argues that the thought of Fethullah Gülen is valuable for the Cambodian Chams in several aspects, including their coexistence with the Buddhist Khmer majority, intra-community harmony, and their quest for both empowerment and the preservation of their identity through education. The latter factor is practically and exemplarily related to the Zaman International School in Phnom Penh, whose particularity for the Cambodian Chams' case is likewise discussed. In chapter 12, "Investigating the Contribution of Fethullah Gülen through the Activities of a Gülen-inspired Religio-cultural Society based in Ireland," Jonathan Lacey illustrates how Fethullah Gülen's principles are practiced in a European context. This chapter focuses on a Gülen-inspired society based in Ireland, namely the Turkish Irish Educational and Cultural Society (TIECS), which provides a range of inter-faith and intercultural activities. Lacey argues that TIECS and the Gülen community practices "Turkish Islam," which has Sufi principles at its core, promotes tolerance and reason as the keys to peaceful coexistence. Mehmet Kalyoncu, in chapter 13 is titled "Building Civil Society in Ethno-religiously Fractured Communities: the Gülen Movement in Turkey and Abroad," analyzes the impact of educational and socio-cultural activities that are carried out by civilian initiatives in reducing the popular support for terrorist organizations, such as PKK and Hezbollah. In chapter 14 titled "Towards a Middle Way: Islam in Southeast Asia and the Contributions of the Gülen Movement", Nawab bin Mohamed Osman demonstrates how the Gülen Movement is relevant in developing a counter-trend to extremist ideology and enhancing inter-religious discussion in the Southeast Asian region. The chapter examines case studies of organizations inspired by Gülen in Singapore and Indonesia and how these organizations utilize his ideas to enhance inter-religious dialogue and provide an alternative to the legalistic discourse on Islam. Finally, Harun Akyol, in chapter 15 "The Role of Turkish Schools in Northern Iraq in Building Trusting Cross-Ethnic Relationships," discusses the role and effectiveness of the Turkish schools affiliated with the Gülen Movement in preventing trans-national ethnic conflict. The main argument of Akyol is that Turkish schools inspired by Fethullah Gülen have prepared and set up the preconditions for understanding each other's needs, and that in so doing they are able to build confidence between antagonistic parties.

References

Abu-Nimer, M. 2001. "Conflict Resolution, Culture, and Religion: Toward a Training Model of Interreligious Peacebuilding." *Journal of Peace Research,* Vol. 38, No. 6, 685–704.

———. 2003. *Nonviolence and Peace Building in Islam: Theory and Practice*. Gainesville, FL: University Press of Florida.

Abu-Rabi, I. M. 2008. Editor's Introduction to Nevval Sevindi, *Contemporary Islamic Conversations: M. Fethullah Gülen on Turkey, Islam, and the West*. Edited by Ibrahim M. Abu-Rabi'. Translated by Abdullah T. Antepli. Albany, NY: State University of New York Press. vii–xiv.

Ackermann, A. 2003. "The Idea and Practice of Conflict Prevention." *Journal of Peace Research*. Vol. 40, No. 3. 339–347.

Afsaruddin, A. 2008. "Taking Faith to Heart: Reconciliation and Peacebuilding in Islam." Ibrahim M. Abu-Rabi, ed. *Spiritual Dimensions of Bediuzzaman Said Nursi's Risale-i Nur*. Albany, NY: SUNY, 2008. 213–229.

Annan, K. 1999. *Toward a Culture of Prevention: Statements by the Secretary-General of the United Nations*. New York: Carnegie Commission on Preventing Deadly Conflict.

Brown, M. A. and A. F. Gusmao. 2009. "Peacebuilding and Political Hybridity in East Timor." *Peace Review*. Vol. 21, No. 1. 61–69.

Burton, J. 1990. *Conflict: Resolution and Prevention.* New York: St Martin's.

Coward, H. and G. S. Smith, eds. 2004. *Religion and Peacebuilding*. Albany, NY: State University of New York Press.

Curan, D. and T. Woodhouse. 2007. "Cosmopolitan Peacekeeping and Peacebuilding in Sierra Leone: What Can Africa Contribute?" *International Affairs*. Vol. 83, No. 6, 1055–1070.

DeRouen, Jr, K. R. and S. Goldfinch. 2005. "Putting the Numbers to Work: Implications for Violence Prevention." *Journal of Peace Research*, Vol. 42, No. 1, 27–45.

Eickelman, D. L. and J. Piscatori. 1996. *Muslim Politics.* Princeton, NJ: Princeton University Press.

Esposito, J. L. 2005. *Islam: The Straight Path.* Revised third edition with an epilogue. New York: Oxford University Press.

Esposito, J. L. and J. Voll. 1996. *Islam and Democracy*. New York and Oxford: Oxford University Press.

Esposito, J. L. and D. Mogahed. *Who Speaks for Islam? What A Billion Muslims Really Think*. Gallup Press, 2007.

Fuller, G. 2008. *The New Turkish Republic: Turkey as a Pivotal State in the Muslim World*. Washington D.C.: United States Institute of Peace Press.

Galtung, J. 1969. "Peace, Violence and Peace Research." *Journal of Peace Research*. 6: 167–191.

Gizelis, T. 2009. "Gender Empowerment and United Nations Peacebuilding." *Journal of Peace Research*. Vol. 46, No. 4, 505–523.

Gopin, M. 1991. "Religion, Violence, and Conflict Resolution." *Peace and Change* 22 (1):1–31.

Gözaydın, İ. B. 2009. "The Fethullah Gülen Movement and Politics in Turkey: A Chance for Democratization or a Trojan Horse?" *Democratization*, Vol. 16, No. 6, 1214–1236.

Habermas, J. 1984. *The Theory of Communicative Action*. Boston: Beacon Press. First published as *Theorie des Kommunikativen Handelns, Band 1: Handlungsrationalitat und gesellschaftliche Rationalisierung,* 1981 by Suhrkamp Verlag, Frankfurt am Main.

Hampson, F. O. 1996. *Nurturing Peace. Why Peace Processes Succeed or Fail.* Washington D.C.: USIP.

Heck, P. L. 2007. "Turkish in the Language of the Qur'an: *Hira'*." İhsan Yılmaz et al (eds.) *Muslim World in Transition: Contributions of the Gülen Movement.* London: Leeds Metropolitan University Press. 643–649.

Hefner, R. W. ed. 2005. Introduction: Modernity and the Remaking of Muslim Politics. *Remaking Muslim Politics: Pluralism, Contestation, Democratization.* Princeton and Oxford: Princeton University Press.

Huda, Q. 2006. "Conflict Prevention and Peace-Building Efforts by American Muslim Organizations following September11." *Journal of Muslim Minority Affairs*. Vol. 26, No. 2, 187–203.

Kalyoncu, M. 2007. "Building Civil Society in Ethno-Religiously Fractured Communities: The Case of the Gülen Movement in Turkey and Abroad." İhsan Yılmaz et al (eds.) *Muslim World in Transition: Contributions of the Gülen Movement*. London: Leeds Metropolitan University Press. 597–607.

———. 2008. "Gülen-inspired Schools in the East Africa: Secular Alternative in Kenya and Pragmatist Approach to Development in Uganda." *Islam in the Age of Global Challenges: Alternative Perspectives of the Gülen Movement* (conference proceedings), Georgetown University, Washington, D.C., November 14–15, 2008, Washington D.C.: Rumi Forum. 350–373.

Koyuncu-Lorasdaği, B. 2010. "The Prospects and Pitfalls of the Religious Nationalist Movement in Turkey: The Case of the Gülen Movement." *Middle Eastern Studies*. 46: 2, 221–234.

Küçükcan, T. 2007. "Social and Spiritual Capital of the Gülen Movement." İhsan Yılmaz et al (eds.) *Muslim World in Transition: Contributions of the*

Gülen Movement. London: Leeds Metropolitan University Press. 187–197.

Lund, M. S. & A. Mehler. 1999. *Peace-Building & Conflict Prevention in Developing Countries: A Practical Guide*. Ebenhausen: Stiftung Wissenschaft und Politik; Brussels: Conflict Prevention Network.

Miall, H. 2000. "Preventing Potential Conflicts: Assessing the Impact of "Light" and "Deep" Conflict Prevention in Central and Eastern Europe and the Balkans." Lund & Rasamoelina Lund, Michael & Guenola Rasamoelina (eds.) *The Impact of Conflict Prevention Policy: Cases, Measures, Assessments*. SWP–CPN Conflict Prevention Network Yearbook 1999–2000. Baden-Baden: Nomos. 23–45.

Miall, H., O. Ramsbotham & T. Woodhouse. 1999. *Contemporary Conflict Resolution*. Cambridge: Polity.

Michel, T. 2003. "Fethullah Gülen as Educator." M. Hakan Yavuz and John L. Esposito (eds.) *Turkish Islam and the Secular State: The Gülen Movement*. Syracuse: Syracuse University Press. 69–84.

———. 2008. "Fighting Poverty with Kimse Yok Mu?" *Islam in the Age of Global Challenges: Alternative Perspectives of the Gülen Movement Conference Proceedings,* Georgetown University, Washington, D.C., November 14–15, 2008, Washington D.C.: Rumi Forum. 523–543.

Özdalga, E. 2005. "Redeemer or Outsider? The Gülen Community in the Civilizing Process." *The Muslim World.* Vol. 95. No. 3. 429–446.

Peck, C. 1998. *Sustainable Peace: The Role of the UN and Regional Organizations in Preventing Conflict*. London: Rowman and Littlefield.

Putnam, R. D. 1992. *Making Democracy Work: Civic Traditions in Modern Italy*. Princeton, NJ: Princeton University Press.

Sachedina, A. 2001. *The Islamic Roots of Democratic Pluralism*. New York: Oxford University Press.

Sampson, C. 1997. "Religion and Peacebuilding." *Peacemaking in International Conflict: Methods and Techniques*, W. Zartman and L. Rasmussen (eds.) Washington D.C.: United States Institute of Peace Press, 273–316.

Sampson, C. and J. P. Lederach, eds. 2000. *From the Ground Up: Mennonite Contributions to international Peacebuilding*. New York: Oxford University Press.

Sarıtoprak, Z. 2005. "An Islamic Approach to Peace and Nonviolence: A Turkish Experience." *The Muslim World*. Vol 95. 413–427.

Satha-Anand, C. 1987. *Islam and Nonviolence*. Tampa, FL: University of South Florida.

Schrodt, P. & D. Gerner, 2000. "Cluster-based Early Warning Indicators for Political Change in the Contemporary Levant." *American Political Science Review*. Vol. 94, No. 4. 803–817.

Secretary-General of the United Nations. 2001. *Prevention of Armed Conflict, Report of the Secretary-General.* New York: United Nations.

Sevindi, N. 2008. *Contemporary Islamic Conversations: M. Fethullah Gülen on Turkey, Islam, and the West.* Edited by Ibrahim M. Abu-Rabi'. Translated by Abdullah T. Antepli. Albany, NY: State University of New York Press.

Smock, D. R. ed. 2002. *Interfaith Dialogue and Peacebuilding.* Edited by David R. Smock. Washington, D.C.: United States Institute of Peace.

Smock, D. R. and Q. Huda. 2009. "Islamic Peacemaking since 9/11." *USIP Special Report*. No. 218, January 2009. Washington D.C.: USIP.

Stassen, G. 1992. *Just Peacemaking: Transforming Initiatives for Justice and Peace*. Louisville, KY: Westminster/John Knox.

Thistlethwaite, S. and G. S. Stassen. 2008. *Abrahamic Alternatives to War*, Washington D.C.: USIP Publication.

Turam, B. 2003. "National Loyalties and International Undertakings in Kazakhstan." M. Hakan Yavuz and John L. Esposito (eds.) *Turkish Islam and the Secular State*: *The Gülen Movement*. Syracuse: Syracuse University Press.

Vargas, C. M. 2000. "Sustainable Development Education: Averting or Mitigating Cultural Collision." *International Journal of Educational Development*, Vol. 20, No. 5. 377–396.

Varshney, A. 2002. *Ethnic Conflict and Civic Life: Hindus and Muslims in India*. New Haven, CT: Yale University Press.

Voll, J. O. 1999. "Renewal and Reformation in the Mid-Twentieth Century: Bediuzzaman Said Nursi and Religion in the 1950s." *The Muslim World*. Vol. 89, No. 3–4. 245–259.

Wallerstein, I. 2004. "World-System Analysis." George Modelski, ed. *World System History*, *Encyclopedia of Life Support Systems* (EOLSS). Developed under the Auspices of the UNESCO.

Yavuz, M. H. and J. L. Esposito, eds. 2003. *Turkish Islam and the Secular State: The Gülen Movement*. Syracuse: Syracuse University Press.

Yılmaz, İ. et al. 2007. *Muslim World in Transition*: *Contributions of the Gülen Movement*, London: Leeds Metropolitan University Press.

Yılmaz, İ. 2008. "Beyond Post-Islamism: A Critical Analysis of the Turkish Islamism's Transformation toward Fethullah Gülen's Stateless Cosmopolitan Islam." *Islam in the Age of Global Challenges: Alternative Perspectives of the Gülen Movement Conference Proceedings,* Georgetown University, Washington, D.C., November 14–15, 2008, Washington D.C.: Rumi Forum. 859–925.

CHAPTER 1

Gülen's Ideas on Freedom of Thought, Pluralism, Secularism, State, Politics, Civil Society and Democracy

John L. Esposito and İhsan Yılmaz

GÜLEN'S CRITICAL ENGAGEMENT WITH MODERNITY AND THE WEST

Fethullah Gülen's self-confident positive view of the world stands in sharp "contrast with Wahhabism, Tablighism, and Jihadism. It is embodied in the form of Sufism advanced by the Gülen movement has a positive view of the world entire. The internal workings of the universe—science, history, politics, art and culture, philosophy—are not something Muslims should fear or stuff into an Islamized box but rather engage positively in view of the spiritual insight of Islam" (Heck 2007, 645). Gülen does not turn his face away from the East: "We must cling to the East as the West," but he puts that "at present there appears to be little to elevate in the East. Tolerance is such a bridge, one that can provide an exchange between people and civilizations. I regard integration with Europe as necessary" (Sevindi 2008, 48). He believes that "(a)unification with the West in one way or another is most important. Integration with the West will bring separate benefits" (Sevindi 2008, 45). Gülen's "acceptance of the two Turkish identities—European and Islamic—as complementary rather than contradictory was innovative at a time when both secular and Islamist identities totally rejected this duality. Gülen's national-security identity encourages Turkish foreign-policy decision makers to remain fully on track with EU membership. As a leader of a significant Islamic movement, he gave his approval to this policy goal. Many Turkish Islamists joined him later, unloading the Islamic element in the anti-EU camp. Yet Gülen also defends the argument that the success of Turkish diplomacy in the West lies with its success in the East" (Kösebalaban 2003, 182). "Gülen's pro-Western attitude has played a key role in the domestication and softening of other Islamist groups' anti-Europe and anti-U.S. positions. Although many Islamists eventually came closer to embracing this idea, a majority of them initially criticized Gülen for his pro-European views. He was one of the first Islamic leaders to embrace the idea of EU membership at a time when Islamists in general regarded it as a threat to Turkish security and Islamic culture" (Kösebalaban 1999, 176).

Gülen does not see the world in political terms and does not draw imaginary boundaries. His frequently used term *dar al-hizmet* (abode of service to others for the sake of God) reflects his border transgressing vision (Yılmaz 2003, 234). By employing *ijtihad*, he bases this border transgressing understanding on – and also extends it to- Islamic jurisprudence (*fiqh*). He does not divide the world by employing mutually exclusive concepts of *dar al-harb* (abode of war) and *dar-al Islam* (abode of Islam, peace) but sees it as an almost coherent place, as it were, that needs to be served continually by utilizing the concept *dar al-hizmet* (Yilmaz 2007, 35). Gülen stresses that wherever a Muslim is, even outside a Muslim polity, he or she must obey the law of the land, respect others' rights and behave justly. He or she must also disregard discussions of *dar al-harb* and *dar al-Islam* (Yilmaz 2003, 235). In Gülen's understanding, *ummah* is a transnational socio-cultural entity, not a Utopian politico-legal one (Yilmaz 2003, 235).

Even though Gülen is open to dialogue and does not maintain the idea of the "Constitutive Other," his discourse is strict and not very accommodating. He holds principles, especially with regards to individual/private practices of religion, and follows Islam's fundamental principles. It must be noted, however, that Gülen is involved in critical engagement with the world around him, modernity and the West.

As Klas Grinell explains in this volume, Gülen's critique is directed at both sides of the civilizational border. In his view, "the East's and West's civilizations existed separated from each other. This separation, which should not have occurred, was based on the former's retiring from intellect and science, while the latter retired from spirituality, metaphysics, and eternal and invariable values. As a result, the last centuries of this millennium have witnessed disasters that are hard to believe. The border set up between East and West is a false one, he says. To say that science is Western and spirituality Eastern is just a symptom of the bordering mentality. The separation should not have occurred, Gülen says. It was an invention. As all inventions it had a purpose connected to its time and place of invention."

Although Gülen's discourse is critical, it is a constructive engagement which is compatible with modernity and the West. "There is no such thing as modernizing only in the Western way" (Sevindi 2008, 73). He argues that if the West "can see that Western culture too has its own prejudices and socially empty beliefs, global communication will be much easier. Prejudices carried by the Western world, especially during times of war and conflict, result in vehement and uncivilized primitive reaction" (Sevindi 2008, 52). He keeps his critical distance and opposes an unconditional assimilation to Western culture and values: "Walking together with Europe within reasonable parameters, the result of establishing our own conditions, might portend good things for our future" (Sevindi 2008, 85). He also warns that: "Leaving our identity to the side, however, and chasing after a European identity, as was the case, would mean rejection and humiliation" (Sevindi 2008, 85).

Gülen on Freedom of Thought, Pluralism, Secularism and Democracy

Reason and a diversity of interpretations of Islam are integral to the development of Islamic law and tradition. "The very diversity of reading found in the schools and manuals of Islamic law reflect the influence of reason, differing cultural contexts, and changes in the history of the community" (Esposito 2005, 248, see in detail Yılmaz 2005). Pluralism and democratization have vernacular roots in Muslim societies, "[a]lthough Islam has jurists and religious scholars, it has no pope, sacerdotal priesthood, or ecclesiastical hierarchy to coordinate their actions" (Hefner 2005, 7). Thus, "religious authority in the Muslim community as a whole tended toward a fissiparous pluricentrism" (Hefner 2005, 8). Many Muslims state that Islam is compatible with pluralism and democracy thanks to "longstanding Islamic concepts of consultation (*shurah*), consensus (*ijma*), and independent interpretive judgment (*ijtihad*)" (Esposito and Voll 1996, 27).

According to Fethullah Gülen, freedom and the intellect are first and foremost in Islam. He unequivocally states that "[i]t is the intellect that makes mankind human, but immediately after intellect, Gülen lists freedom" (Sevindi 2008, 6; 31). He reiterates that "[t]hinking is one of the most important characteristics of man" (Sevindi 2008, 31). For Gülen, freedom of thought and expression is vital: "There should not be any pressure; human beings should be able to express themselves" (Sevindi 2008, 84). He argues that "[t]he biggest problem facing Islamic countries are poverty and lack of freedom: not having individual and social freedom, not having a liberal way of life, these things being hindered" (Sevindi 2008, 70). He gives special emphasis to human dignity and underlines that "[e]ach individual is a species with regard to other individuals" (Sevindi 2008, 44). In contrast, oppressing people will cause a number of their talents to wither on the vine, and hatred for the oppressor from below will begin to increase (Sevindi 2008, 87).

When Gülen speaks of freedom, pluralism, tolerance, freedom of choice, and democracy, he speaks from an Islamic perspective. Although not compromising the fundamentals of these attributes, attitudes and characteristics, he does reinterpret the original Islamic sources and concepts in accordance with the temporal and spatial contexts (see in detail Yılmaz 2003, Yılmaz 2005). This can be seen in his understanding of the five major purposes of Islamic law *(al-maqasid al-shari`a)* as developed by al-Shatibi (see in detail Al-Raysuni 2005; Masud 1998): the protection of life/self/person (*nafs*), intellect/reason (*'aql*), generation/procreation (*nasl*), property (*mal*) and religion (*din*). As can be seen, these are related to fundamental human rights and freedom. Protection of the intellect has tremendous ramifications with regards to freedom of thought, expression, religion, and also pluralism and democracy. The importance of the intellect in Islamic law is also apparent in the requirement that to be a responsible Muslim, a person has to be sane and of age to make certain decisions (i.e. pubescence). Moreover, the Islamic belief that humans are here in the world so that they can be tested in addition to knowing, appreciating and worshipping the Creator, and are thus given free will, the right to choose between good and bad, coupled with the legal maxim (also a verse in the Qur'an) that "there is no compulsion in religion" shows the importance given to the intellect, individual choice, and freedom of expression.

Gülen summarizes the theological reasons why Islam considers the individual responsible for his own fate and thus governance:

> Islam considers a society to be composed of conscious individuals equipped with free will and having responsibility for both themselves and others... The Qur'an (13:11) says: "God will not change the state of a people unless they change themselves [with respect to their beliefs, worldview, and lifestyle]." In other words, each society holds the reins of its fate in its own hands. The prophetic tradition emphasizes this idea: "You will be ruled according to how you are." This is the basic character and spirit of democracy, which does not conflict with any Islamic principle. As Islam holds individuals and societies

> responsible for their own fate, people must be responsible for governing themselves (Gülen 2006, 16).

He also underlines that Islam has room for democratic thought as witnessed by the fact that "The first Muslims to establish a parliament were the Ottomans. Turks also were first to use the word Republic" (Sevindi 2008, 70). Gülen also addresses the sometimes contested concepts of divine and popular sovereignty:

> The phrase, "Sovereignty belongs to the nation unconditionally," does not mean that sovereignty has been taken from God and given to humans. On the contrary, it means that sovereignty is entrusted to humans by God; that is to say it has been taken from individual oppressors and dictators and given to the community members. To a certain extent, the era of the Rightly-Guided Caliphs of Islam illustrates the application of this norm of democracy. Cosmologically speaking, there is no doubt that God is the sovereign of everything in the universe. Our thoughts and plans are always under the control of the power of such an Omnipotent. However, this does not mean that we have no will, inclination or choice. Humans are free to make choices in their personal lives. They are also free to make choices with regard to their social and political actions (Gülen 2005, 453).

In speaking of the relationship of Islam to democracy, Gülen emphasizes that Islam is a religion and thus is more than a political method, system or ideology: "On the issue of Islam and democracy, one should remember that the former is a divine and heavenly religion, while the latter is a form of government developed by humans" (Gülen 2005, 451–452). Thus, there is no single model of governance; Islamic principles can support diverse forms of government, "Islam does not propose a certain unchangeable form of government or attempt to shape it. Instead, Islam establishes fundamental principles that orient a government's general character, leaving it to the people to choose the type and form of government according to time and circumstances" (Gülen 2006, 14; see in detail Yılmaz 2008). Fundamental principles Islam prescribes, according to Gülen, are social contract and election of a group of people to debate common issues (Gülen 2006, 17). He also puts that "[i]t is not possible to maintain intelligence, judgment, justice, equity, and law in a place where problems are solved on the basis of power alone" (Sevindi 2008, 41). "Power that is not based on equity and justice deviates into oppression, and thus prepares its own ending" (Sevindi 2008, 61).

Gülen's understanding of majority rule does not permit a tyranny of majority: "Members of minority communities should be allowed to live according to their beliefs. If these sorts of legislations are made within the norms of international law and international agreements, Islam will have no objection to any of these. No one can ignore the universal values that the Qur'an and the *Sunnah* have presented with regard to the rights mentioned above" (Gülen 2005, 451).

Secular law-making, in Gülen's view, is neither necessarily antithetical to nor prohibited by Islam:

> In Islam, the legislative and executive institutions have always been allowed to make laws. These are based on the needs and betterment of society and within the frame of general norms of law. On domestic issues in the Islamic community and its relationship with other nations, including economic, political and cultural relations, Muslims have always developed laws. The community members are required to obey the laws that one can identify as "higher principles" as well as laws made by humans. Islam has no objection to undertaking *ijtihad* (independent reasoning), *istinbat* (deductive reasoning), and *istikhraj* (derivation) in the interpretation of *Shari'ah* principles (Gülen 2005, 450).

Gülen Movement vis-à-vis Politics and State

Though not an advocate for statism, yet Gülen shows a major concern for the rule of law. "In Islam, ruling means a mutual contract between the ruler and the subject and it takes its legitimacy from the rule of law, and from the principle of the superiority of the law. Accordingly, the law is above the ruler and the subject" (Gülen 2005, 449). While some have interpreted his preference for state stability over anarchy as sanctifying state, he strongly opposes it:

> I have always stipulated that "even the worst State is better than no State" whenever I voiced my opinion in words such as "the State is necessary, and should not be worn down." I have never sanctified the State as some people have done. This preference is a necessity for me, because if the State were not to occupy a certain place, it is certain that anarchy, chaos, and disorder would dominate there. Then, there would be no respect for ideas, freedom of religion, and our consciences would be violated; justice would be out of the question. In the past, there were times when our nation suffered from the absence of the State. Therefore, I regard supporting the State also as a duty of citizenship... this is our preference (to support the State); although we are aware of certain mistakes, we bury this in our hearts. I never had such thoughts as, "the State is innocent, it is as infallible as a Prophet; whatever it does is to the point, it is never mistaken." They too can be mistaken (like anyone else).[1]

Even though some undemocratic authoritarian forces in some past Turkish governments opposed Gülen's activities, he never allowed state pressure to stop him or to curtail the activities of the movement. His position avoided the extremes of sanctifying a state or trying to disestablish it. Some have described the Gülen Movement as: "a perfect example of 'participant resistance,' which is not stated but underlies the writings of Antonio Gramsci on ideological struggle" (Bilici 2006, 17 and Gürbüz 2007).

Critics have argued that the Movement is not apolitical as it is able to influence society. "There is no doubt that the movement quite explicitly aspires to transform society through transformation of the individual, a process that could ultimately lead to collective calls for the creation of national and social institutions that reflect belief in a moral order. In a very loose sense, it is possible to call this a political project if we consider any attempt to transform society to be a political project. But I would argue that it is just as much a social and moral project. Indeed, the term "political" loses its meaning if applied equally to all efforts to transform society, regard-

1 http://gulenmovement.net/press-room/mehmet-gundems-interview/1918-gulen-qeven-the-worst-state-is-better-than-no-stateq.html (accessed on 21 April 2010).

less of means. Promotion of change through teachings, education, and information does not really become political until it formally and institutionally enters the political process" (Fuller 2008, 59).

In contrast to many Islamists who advocate an Islamic system of government, Gülen believes that Islam can be practiced and the issues facing Muslims in the 21st century can be addressed without resorting to politics. He advocates a total separation between religion and the state and opposes religiously based political parties, "believing that they end up compromising or contaminating religion and that they only serve to create social strife damaging to the position of religion in society" (Fuller 2008, 58). Indeed, he rejects the totalizing ideology of Islamism:

> This vision of Islam as a totalizing ideology is totally against the spirit of Islam which promotes the rule of law and openly rejects oppression against any segment of society. This spirit also promotes actions for the betterment of society in accordance with the view of the majority (Gülen 2005, 452).

He rejects those Islamists who claim what they advocate is indeed the true, authentic, original and pure Islam:

> When those who have adopted Islam as a political ideology rather than a religion in its true sense and function, review their activities and attitudes they claim to be based on Islam, especially political ones, will discover that they are usually moved by personal or national anger, hostility, and other similar motives... It would not be a correct understanding of Islam to claim that politics is a vital principle of religion and among its well-established pillars. While some Qur'anic verses are related to politics, the structure of the state, and the forms of ruling, people who have connected the import of the Qur'anic message with such issues may have caused a misunderstanding. This misunderstanding is the result of their Islamic zeal, their limitations of their consideration solely of historical experiences, and their thinking that the problems of Islamic communities can be solved more easily through politics and ruling. All of these approaches within their own con-

> texts are meaningful. However, the truth does not lie in these approaches alone (Gülen 2005, 455).

He explains that:

> ...in Islam it is not possible to limit the concept of governance and politics into a single paradigm, unlike the principles of faith and the pillars of Islam. History shows us that in the Islamic world, since the time of the Prophet, there have been many types of states... I have to note that these differences were the result of the aspects of religion that are open to interpretation and related to the field of independent reasoning (*ijtihad*) (Gülen 2005, 454).

Even though Islamic politics are frequently described as in some way combining "religion and politics," in the words of many Islamists, Islam is *din wa dawla* (religion and state), from the era of the Umayyads and the Abbasids, important non-state structures and institutions developed (Esposito and Voll 1996, 4). The existence of independent *ulama* and the development of Islamic schools of law (*madhhab*s) autonomous from the state were important parts of the early Muslim experience. Later, Sufi brotherhoods also emerged as important civil institutions for popular religious life, "autonomous and separate from the state, and sometimes in conflict with the state institutions" (Esposito and Voll 1996, 4, see also Yılmaz 2005). Trying to re-invent this tradition, Gülen has argued that in this age, Islam does not need state support, which is a new *ijtihad*. Thus, he does not oppose the idea of mutual autonomy of state and Islam: "[i]f a state... gives the opportunity to its citizens to practice their religion and supports them in their thinking, learning, and practice, this system is not considered to be against the teaching of the Qur'an. In the presence of such a state there is no need to seek an alternative state" (Gülen 2005, 451) Establishing an Islamic state is not a religious duty for Muslims who, in this age civil society, can independently maintain Islamic beliefs and practices even where Muslims are not the majority.

We understand from the Turkish Islamic scholar and intellectual Ali Bulaç's conversation with Gülen that on the issue of Muslim minorities vis-à-vis establishment of an Islamic state, Gülen is unambiguous. Bulaç writes that:

> There was a question in my mind for a long time. I used to ask myself: What is the ultimate aim of Muslim endeavors both as individuals and also as a society in this life? I have thought that there are two aims of jihad: 1) To have a free medium and environment where a Muslim could live his life in accordance with God's pleasure, staying away from the forbidden and to practice permissibly; and 2) To have freedom of speech with appropriate opportunities, power and instruments so that s/he would be able to transmit Islamic truths to others. But, if such a political, social and legal medium is present where Muslims are a small minority, is it absolutely necessary to wage an independence war? Is it an indispensable obligation of religion that every small Muslim minority has to establish an independent nation-state? For instance, is it absolutely necessary for the little Muslim island Chechens in the sea of 150 million Russians to have a war for an independent state? The 1994 agreement [with Russia] gave them a strengthened autonomy so that they were able to apply Islamic law. They had their own sources, no one was imposing on them [anything negative] in terms of language and culture; they had only to be dependent to Russia in foreign affairs. Conditions of the agreement could be improved. As known, there was an attack on [neighboring] Daghestan and [Chechhens] resorted to weapons to reach their stated [Islamic] aims. Since that day, tens of thousands of people have lost their lives; a generation has perished; civilians have been killed. Was this the right strategy? ... Could not an important number of conflicts and wars that Muslims are engaged in the other parts of the world be considered in the same framework? I asked this question to Hodjaefendi [Fethullah Gülen] to test my thoughts' virtue. He concurred with me and of course gave long explanations. I was very glad with this.[2]

In Gülen's understanding, establishing an Islamic state is not a religious duty for Muslim individuals and this is more so as far as Muslims living as minorities are concerned. To him, in this age civil society can independently maintain Islam even where Muslims are not in the majority as long as democratic standards and conditions

2 Ali Bulaç, "Hocaefendi'ye Sorular," *Zaman*, 23 November 2005.

are met and satisfied. It seems that Gülen's approach reflects what Alexis de Tocqueville observed in the early nineteenth century in America. Tocqueville's conclusion was that congregational Christianity was a vital element in the democratic culture and that the American separation of church and state took the state out of the business of coercing conformity, but it did not take religion out of public life; religion remained one of the most important institutions in American civil society (Tocqueville 1969, cited in Hefner 2001, 493). Like Alexis de Tocqueville's analysis of America, Jurgen Habermas' (1989) concept of a public sphere highlights that democratic life does not only depend on formal structures and relations but also on informal resources, relations and dispositions operative in society. Throughout Islamic history, nonstate actors and structures with important functions operated. The emergence of the *ulama* as distinctive group within Muslim society, and the development of Islamic schools of law (*madhhab*s) autonomous of state were important parts of the Islamic experience. Moreover, Sufi brotherhoods had also emerged as part of public religious life, independent of state control. These institutions and social structures were not "churches," but they were autonomous and separate from the state and even sometimes in conflict with state (Esposito and Voll 1996, 4). In this sense, it could be said that Gülen is simply engaged in a re-interpretation and renewal of an Islamic tradition where religion and state were autonomous of each other to a great extent, interacting mainly in the public sphere.

In conclusion, it is obvious that the most significant aspect of Gülen's "approach is the re-signification of an Islamic orientation and its attachment to key norms also found in Western liberal thought – democracy, justice and individual freedoms" (Atasoy 2009, 181). Gülen is not a socially inactive thinker and practitioner who formulates a discourse and then only passively observes if people discover and emulate it; he seeks to actively, if critically, engage with this world by teaching and presenting his *weltanschauung* and its praxis as documented in the following chapters.

References

Al-Raysuni, A. 2005. *Imam Al-Shatibi's Theory of the Higher Objectives and Intents of Islamic Law*. Herndon, VA: International Institute of Islamic Thought.

Atasoy, Y. 2009. "Islamic Engagement with European Universalism: The State Transformation in Turkey. Yıldız Atasoy (ed) *Hegemonic Transitions, the State and Crisis in Neoliberal Capitalism*, London: Routledge, 166–185.

Bilici, M. 2006. "The Fethullah Gülen Movement and Its Politics of Representation in Turkey." *The Muslim World*. Vol. 96. 1–20.

Bulaç, A. 2005. "Hocaefendi'ye Sorular" (Questions to Hocaefendi). *Zaman Daily*, 23 November 2005.

Eickelman, D. L. and J. Piscatori. 1996. *Muslim Politics*. Princeton, NJ: Princeton University Press.

Esposito, J. L. 2005. *Islam: The Straight Path*. Revised third edition with an epilogue. New York: Oxford University Press.

Esposito, J. L. and J. Voll. 1996. *Islam and Democracy*. New York and Oxford: Oxford University Press.

Fuller, G. 2008. *The New Turkish Republic: Turkey as a Pivotal State in the Muslim World*. Washington D.C.: United States Institute of Peace Press.

Grinell, K. 2007. "Beyond East and West: Fethullah Gülen and 'Border' Thinking." İhsan Yılmaz et al. (eds.) *Muslim World in Transition: Contributions of the Gülen Movement*. London: Leeds Metropolitan University Press, 203–214.

Gülen, F. 2000. *Advocate of Dialogue*. Compiled by Ali Ünal and Alphonse Williams. Fairfax, VA. The Fountain Press.

———. 2005. An Interview with Fethullah Gülen – translated by Zeki Sarıtoprak and Ali Ünal. *The Muslim World, Special Issue, Islam in Contemporary Turkey: The Contributions of Fethullah Gülen*. Vol. 95. No.3. 447–467.

———. 2006. *Essays–Perspectives–Opinions*. Second revised ed, 3rd impression. Somerset, NJ: The Light, Inc.

Gürbüz, M. 2007. "Performing Moral Opposition: Musings on the Strategy and Identity in the Gülen Movement." İhsan Yılmaz et al. (eds.) *Muslim World in Transition: Contributions of the Gülen Movement*. London: Leeds Metropolitan University Press. 104–117.

Habermas, J. 1989. *The Structural Transformation of the Public Sphere: An Inquiry into a Category of Bourgeois Society*. Tr. by T. Burger with F. Lawrence. Cambridge: Polity Press.

Heck, P. L. 2007. Turkish in the Language of the Qur'an: *Hira'*. İhsan Yılmaz et al (eds.) *Muslim World in Transition: Contributions of the Gülen Movement*. London: Leeds Metropolitan University Press. 643–649.

Hefner, R. W. ed. 2005. Introduction: "Modernity and the Remaking of Muslim Politics." *Remaking Muslim Politics: Pluralism, Contestation, Democratization*. Princeton and Oxford: Princeton University Press.

Kösebalaban, H. 2003. "The Making of Enemy and Friend: Fethullah Gülen's National-Security Identity." M. Hakan Yavuz and John L. Esposito (eds) *Turkish Islam and the Secular State: The Gülen Movement*. Syracuse: Syracuse University Press. 170–183.

Masud, M. K. 1998. *Shatibi's Philosophy of Islamic Law*. Islamabad: Kitab Bhavan.

Sevindi, N. 2008. *Contemporary Islamic Conversations: M. Fethullah Gülen on Turkey, Islam, and the West*. Edited by Ibrahim M. Abu-Rabi`. Translated by Abdullah T. Antepli. Albany, NY: State University of New York Press.

Tocqueville, A. de. 1969. *Democracy in America*. Ed. by J. P. Mayer, tr. by G. Lawrence. Garden City, N.Y.: Doubleday.

Turam, B. 2003. "National Loyalties and International Undertakings: The Case of the Gülen Community in Kazakhstan." M. Hakan Yavuz and John Esposito (eds.) *Turkish Islam and the Secular State: The Gülen Movement*. Syracuse, New York: Syracuse University Press. 184–207.

Yavuz, M. H. and J. L. Esposito, eds. 2003. *Turkish Islam and the Secular State: The Gülen Movement*, Syracuse, New York: Syracuse University Press.

Yılmaz, İ. 2003. "*Ijtihad* and *Tajdid* by Conduct: The Gülen Movement." M. H. Yavuz and J. L. Esposito (eds.) *Turkish Islam and the Secular State: The Gülen Movement*, Syracuse, New York: Syracuse University Press, 208–237.

———. 2005. "Inter-Madhhab Surfing, Neo-Ijtihad, and Faith-Based Movement Leaders." Ruud Peters, Frank Vogel and Peri Bearman, (eds.) *The Islamic School of Law: Evolution, Devolution and Progress,* Cambridge, MA: Harvard University Press

———. 2007. "Social Innovation for Peaceful Coexistence: Intercultural Activism from Rumi to Gülen." İhsan Yılmaz et al (eds.) *Peaceful Coexistence: Fethullah Gülen's Initiatives in the Modern World*. London: Leeds Metropolitan University Press, 25–41.

———. 2008. "Beyond Post-Islamism: A Critical Analysis of the Turkish Islamism's Transformation toward Fethullah Gülen's Stateless Cosmopolitan Islam." *Islam in the Age of Global Challenges: Alternative Perspectives of the Gülen Movement Conference Proceedings,* Georgetown University, Washington, D.C., November 14–15, 2008, Washington D.C.: Rumi Forum. 859–925.

Yılmaz, İ. et al. eds. 2007a. *Peaceful Coexistence: Fethullah Gülen's Initiatives in the Contemporary World,* London: Leeds Metropolitan University Press.

———. 2007b. *Muslim World in Transition: Contributions of the Gülen Movement.* London: Leeds Metropolitan University Press.

Chapter 2

Islamic Resources for Peacebuilding: Achievements and Challenges

Mohammed Abu-Nimer and İhsan Yılmaz

Introduction

In its fourth decade of development, the field of peacebuilding (conflict resolution and peace studies) has gained significant growth and recognition in both academic institutions and professional organizations. Hundreds of undergraduate and graduate programs have been created which grant degrees in this field of study, and thousands of nongovernmental organizations around the world focus their work on promoting peace and conflict resolution practices on all social and political levels. Within this context, a new emerging field of religion and peace has also gained momentum; this field is evidenced by a proliferation of academic programs focusing on the role of religion in peacebuilding that are being launched in various academic institutions.[1] For the last two decades,

1 The volume on religion and peace edited by Johnston and Sampson (1994) has functioned as a main reference in this regard, arguing for the need for institutionalizing religious approaches to peace in the political process. Since its publication a number of institutions have emerged as leaders in the field of religion and peacebuilding in North America, including the American University's Peace and Conflict Resolution Program; George Mason University's Center for Religion and Diplomacy; the Kroc Institute at Notre Dame University; Emory University's Center for East and West; Harvard University's Divinity School; and the United States Institute of Peace's Religion and Peacemaking Program.

many Christian scholars and theologians have led the way in contributing to the development of a religious peacebuilding subfield within the fields of peace studies and conflict resolution (Stassen 1992, Thistlethwaite and Stassen 2008, Sampson and Lederach 2000, Gopin 1991). Muslim scholars and practitioners have also engaged in similar efforts to systematically explore and articulate principles and methods of peacebuilding based on Islamic theology and tradition.

This article focuses on two questions: What are the current debates and challenges facing Muslim scholars and practitioners of peacebuilding in their efforts to develop a religious and cultural peacebuilding framework based on religious and cultural sources? Second, what roles can the Gülen Movement play in this process?

Justifying Violence and Peace

Scholars examine issues of violence and its use in the Islamic context under two main headings: (1) offensive groups: war and violence; (2) defensive groups: just war theorists. There are thousands of books and articles (especially by non-Muslim scholars) that focus on the first category and a large proportion of the literature is aimed at proving the argument that Muslim teachings mainly support violence and aggression (Satha-Anand 1987, 1994, 1996; Said and Funk 2002); Sa'id 1993, 1997, 2000).[2] The second category of studies, on just war or the use of defensive violence, is reflected by the thousands of books and articles (especially by Muslim scholars) that articulate the conditions for engaging in war and violent conflict (Kelsay and Johnson 1991; Tibi 1996). Compared to these works, academic work on nonviolence is the least developed field. However, in the last two decades there have been many studies published in support of the hypothesis that nonviolence, peace, acceptance of diversity, pluralism, and interfaith and intercultural dialogue are central to the teaching of Muslim theology and studies

2 See many references in support of these categories in Abu-Nimer (2003, 20–30).

in this category reject the use of violence in pursuit of justice and peacc.[3]

When examining these studies, it is clear that an Islamic framework for peace and nonviolence has emerged and is being systematically developed and applied in various Muslim and non-Muslim communities.

Pursuit of Peace in Islam Based on Justice and Nonviolence

Scholars have identified Muslim values and rituals of peace and nonviolence that constitute a solid base for a theoretical framework. Muslim values of peace include concepts such as *ihsan* (perfect goodness, healing, reconciliation), *samah* (forgiveness), *sabr* (patience), *adl* (justice), *taqwa* (piety), *aml al-khayr* (good deed), and a collective sense of communal peacemaking and human solidarity (*ummah*). These concepts are common to all Muslim communities and have been emphasized by all Muslim prophets (peace be upon them). Muslim processes of peace and conflict resolution have also been identified and documented by learned and experienced scholars and practitioners. These processes include Muslim approaches to mediation, arbitration, and dialogue. In supporting these practical methods of peacemaking researchers have re-examined the practices of peacemaking in Islam such as the Prophet's behavior and intervention as mediator in cases such as the Ka'bah incident (the moving of the black stone by Qurayshi tribes with the intervention of the Prophet); the Treaty at Hudaybiyah (a treaty that fellow Muslims saw as humiliating, but is evidence of Islam's desire for peaceful coexistence with those of other faiths); the liberation of Mecca from Qurayshi tribes; the Prophet's preaching and life in the thirteen years in Mecca; the Medina constitution and other treaties; and the concept of ceasefire or truce (*hudnah*) as prac-

3 There are many studies in this category, see Said (1996; 2007); Crow (1997); Abdalla (2000); Abu-Nimer (1996a, 1996b, 2003).

ticed by Arab tribal communities and its Muslim adaptation. In addition, many scholars have recognized *sulhah* (reconciliation) as a Qur'anic peacemaking method.[4]

When examining Islamic peacebuilding studies in the last two decades, it is obvious that scholars have made a solid theological and sociological case for the presence of an Islamic peacemaking framework.[5] More than fifteen books and hundreds of articles have been published in the last decade that propose a Muslim peacebuilding framework.[6]

Bridging the Gap between the Ideal and the Real

A major challenge that faces scholars and practitioners of Islamic peacebuilding is to translate their newly constructed framework into relevant practices or mechanisms that can be utilized by various Muslim and non-Muslim professionals, as well as the average person in their daily life. This need becomes even more relevant and pressing when Western conflict resolution techniques and frameworks are packaged through training programs and publications by Western governments, corporations (forces of globalization), and non-governmental organizations. Such methods are introduced with their cultural assumptions of materialism, rationalistic cost–benefit analysis, individualism, and a strong emphasis on contractual relationships. Such cultural values do not necessarily fit collectivist and relationship-oriented communities. In addition, many of these conflict resolution models assume that the core problem in

4 See the many studies documenting the procedures of *sulhah* and traditional dispute resolution mechanisms in Muslim communities, including Irani (1998) and Irani and Funk (1999); Kadayifci (2003); and Abu-Nimer (2003).

5 It should be noted that the overwhelming majority of these studies rely heavily on Sunni perspectives and resources. There are few studies that utilize Shi'a perspectives and sources in constructing a case for Islamic peace and nonviolence.

6 See Nonviolence International (http://nonviolenceinternational.net/?page_id=25, last visited on 2 February 2010) for a complete list of these references on Islamic Peace (compiled by Karim Crow in 1998).

any given conflict is mainly in communication and perceptions. This often results in simplistic analysis of the conflict and failure to address the asymmetric power structure or institutional discrimination and oppressive policies that characterize many of the social and political conflicts in Muslim community contexts.

Islamic peacebuilding approaches have not yet produced practical methodologies to compete with the governmental and nongovernmental agency approaches mentioned above that constantly conduct training in order to market conflict resolution methodologies in the Muslim world. Adopting such peace and conflict resolution approaches that are disconnected from the reality of the Muslim masses is problematic and ineffective. By the same token, the problems facing the average Muslim who lives in a deeply divided society such as Iraq or Sudan are not the same as those to which Ibn Taymiyyah, al-Ghazzali, Rumi, or other great scholars were responding when they wrote about peace and war. While the problems lie in the social, cultural, economic, and political systems, Islamic peacebuilding frameworks, as defined by intellectual, legal, theological, and philosophical debates, remain theoretical and generally speaking have little connection to real-life issues. The question remains: Can Islamic peacebuilding approaches develop relevant and effective methods for the average Muslim to utilize in confronting these systems?

Confronting Violent Interpretations of Islam

The events of September 11, 2001, unleashed a dangerous and violent force in some marginal Muslim extremist groups and individuals, while overwhelming majority of Muslim condemned both 9/11 attacks and the US occupation of Iraq and Afghanistan. Al-Qaeda ideology was unintentionally strengthened among some Muslim circles by the violent attacks launched by Europeans and Americans on Afghanistan, Iraq, Palestine, Lebanon, Chechnya, Yemen, and so on. This colonial legacy and reality of imperialism have fueled those voices that support the defensive use of violence in responding to injustice. In this context, the Islamic peacebuilding framework has contributed to moving the scholarship and practice beyond the already well established narrative of defensive Islam, and strengthening Muslim conflict resolution as a frame of reference upon which non-violent interpretations of Islam can be justified.

The main discussion in most of the studies published on Islamic peacebuilding has been framed within a defensive mode of thought in which authors defend the hypothesis that Islam has sufficient resources for peace, or they respond to those who argue that Muslim values promote a "violent, jihadist culture." Post-9/11 policies have intensified the need to clarify and show Western governments and the wider public the fact that Islam as a religion does not preach violence or terrorism. Scholars have also produced some literature in response to those who support the "clash of civilizations" hypothesis, proving that Islam as a religion and tradition is not inherently violent or supportive of aggression (Paige et al 1993). In addition, several Muslim scholars, including Gülen, had already answered the question of how Islam promotes peace, pluralism, and interfaith dialogue well before 9/11.

Scholars and practitioners have made significant progress in the development and publication of the framework of Muslim peacebuilding and nonviolence in the last two decades. These scholars, as mentioned earlier, have managed to articulate the rich and diverse Muslim theological sources that support an Islamic nonviolence and peacebuilding hypothesis. Research, in this initial phase, has focused on some basic questions:

> What principles of conflict resolution are reflected in the Qur'an? What techniques and strategies for dealing with conflict are described in the Qur'an? Are there different techniques and procedures for approaching family, community, and state conflicts? (Abu-Nimer 1996a, 37).

The same research methodology has been applied to examining Islamic sources on dialogue and pluralism. Scholars addressing these questions in relation to pluralism have published books on sources of interfaith dialogue and pluralism according to the Hadith and Qur'anic sources. In addition, new courses have been developed in academic institutions to teach about religious sources for peacebuilding in Islam. Seminars and workshops are being offered on a continual basis by various Muslim organizations around the world to bring this framework to both Muslim and non-Muslim audiences.[7]

An Islamic Peacebuilding Framework and Root Causes of Conflict

Despite the above achievements and rich historical experience which is filled in many ways with exemplary incidents of peaceful coexistence, toleration, and dialogue, the research and practice of an Islamic framework for peacebuilding and nonviolence today appear to have become trapped in an initial phase of extracting Qur'anic verses and statements from Hadith in support of the hypothesis. The overwhelming majority of books and articles on this topic repeatedly return to the Holy Qur'an and list those verses that support peace and nonviolence. Muslim and non-Muslim readers have been repeatedly exposed to these religious teachings but this repeated exposure has not produced practical results. Movements such as the Gülen Movement have the ability to add a practical element to these Muslim teachings by investing in more than simple doctrinal defensiveness, but rather bringing a new understanding of "discourse by conduct" of nonviolent action.

7 These organizations include several Gülen Movement intercultural dialogue institutions all over the world, such as the Rumi Forum in Washington DC, and the Dialogue Society in London. The Center for Global Peace at American University has developed six graduate courses on Islamic Peace and has put together a Global Islamic Peace curriculum for peace.

The Islamic peacebuilding framework is an important formulation of a social and cultural narrative or discourse to counter radicals and marginal pro-violence individuals and groups in Muslim communities. Having an Islamic peacebuilding framework for resisting oppression and pursuing justice leaves less space for Muslims to be complacent about a situation in which marginal fanatical interpretations are imposed by a minority of scholars or militant activists.

Introducing an alternative discourse is a first step in confronting militant and pro-violence interpretations of Muslim teaching; however, participants in peacebuilding workshops often point out that the real problems and challenges facing Muslims are not in the theological debate, but in dealing with the root causes of the conflicts in their communities.

Some of the macro factors that continuously generate violent conflicts, however rare and marginal, in Muslim societies include:

- A reality of economic deprivation: The majority of the population of Muslim societies, in which often small economic elite controls more than 70 percent of the national wealth,[8] lives in economic deprivation. These extreme differences in wealth increase tension and instill a sense of despair and hopelessness in some Muslim communities. Several scholars and analysts have attributed the continuing growth of pro-violence radical Islamist movements to this reality (see Laqueur 2003).
- Muslims' inability to deal with the effects of global cultural invasion on rural and urban Muslim communities: In some cases, Muslim religious leaders have either fully co-opted the global trends or fully merged with consumerist culture, or they have withdrawn to marginal, out-dated and out-of-context Muslim interpretations to counter twentieth- and

8 For more information on the economics of Arab society, see Barakat (1993). See also Laqueur (2003).

twenty-first-century globalization trends. Very few leaders have, like Fethullah Gülen, managed to formulate an authentic Muslim response which is in tune with the classical and traditional Muslim sources to handle globalization forces in healthy and productive ways.[9] In several Muslim countries, due to the weak and fragile central state systems of government, the political elites have not developed any authentic tools or mechanisms to handle globalization and its consequences on their societies' religious and cultural identity.

- Authoritarian political regimes rule many Muslim countries with little space for opposition groups to express their dissent. The masses are under constant surveillance and pressure to conform to the ruling regimes' various ideologies or discourses. These "security states or regimes" promote a culture of violence which has nothing to do with Islam through their sheer existence and daily practices in repressing individual and collective rights.[10] Muslim teachings that aimed to liberate Arab Muslims from their tribal mentality in the early Muslim period have been manipulated in several cases to perpetuate the tribal and authoritarian mentality in twentieth- and twenty-first-century reality.[11]
- In some Muslim societies there is little space for reinterpretation of Qur'anic teachings or Muslim history and tradi-

9 In the context of Arab society, Amr Khaled is among the few young, Arab preachers who have been formulating new teachings to help the younger Arab Muslim generation to deal with the contradictions resulting from modernization and globalization trends (see www.amrkhaled.net).

10 A quick review of the fifty-six Muslim countries reveal that the overwhelming majority of these regimes lack any comfortable space for the opposition (individual or collective) to express their political views or participate in a democratic process of governance. Under such regimes, elections are often manipulated by one party or the royal family, political prisoners are held without trial, the interior security forces impose an environment of terror on opposition groups, and media outlets are heavily censored.

11 Iraqi, Afghani, Saudi, and Pakistani tribal and clan loyalties are examples of how deeply this primordial tribal identity remains ingrained in Muslim societies blocking the emergence of more egalitarian community structures.

tion. Certain religious leaders in those countries have acted as gatekeepers in defending the process of recycling certain outmoded understandings and interpretations and opposing or delegitimizing new *ijtihads* and interpretations that break commonly espoused myths. Thus, religious myths are being recycled and sustained by these "gatekeeper scholars" who resist renewalist interpretations. Some of these myths relate to the role of violence in settling internal and external disputes involving Muslims; spreading a sense of superiority over other nations and religions; continuing to impose harsh limits and restrictions on Muslim women by disseminating certain cultural, traditional and customary rules.

- Even though Muslim teaching, when originally spread in the tribal Arab context, aimed at liberating and enhancing the rights of women, there persists a dominant patriarchal system in which male identity (especially older males) sits on the top of the social and cultural system, with specific norms and values to systematically maintain that identity. This reality has produced wide institutional gender gaps (in economic, political, educational, cultural, religious, and all other systems).[12] Women in the Arab world especially are still denied equality of opportunity despite the fact that their disempowerment is a critical factor crippling the Arab nations' quest to return to the first rank of global leaders in commerce, learning and culture, according to a new United Nations-sponsored report released recently.[13]

12 See the United Nations Development Agency report on the gender gap in the Arab World.

13 The report not only calls for all Arab women to be given equal access to essential health, education, and all types of activity outside the family, but also urges temporary adoption of affirmative action to expand such participation, thus allowing centuries-old structures of discrimination to be dismantled. "Full participation and empowerment of women, as citizens, as producers, as mothers and sisters, will be a source of strength for Arab Nations and will allow the Arab World to reach greater prosperity, greater influence and higher levels of human development," said UN Development Programme (UNDP) Administrator Kemal Dervis, whose agency

- In some Muslim societies there is a legitimacy crisis facing the religious establishment since most religious leaders are co-opted by the undemocratic and usually authoritarian political elite and/or state. This alliance of the religious and political elites has produced a reality in which the masses are torn between this co-opted religious leadership and dissenting militant, radical and, in some cases, pro-violence, however marginal, interpretations of Islam. In this context, the mainstream and traditional Rumian third discourse is rarely heard.
- Educational institutions in some Muslim countries continue to promote a superficial, conformist, authoritarian, and submissive type of education. Self-examination and self-critique are not encouraged or absent from the teaching curricula and pedagogy of many Muslim societies. Public education systems often promote shame and honor codes that reduce creativity and critical thinking skills. Such systems become effective tools in the maintenance and control of certain political, ethnic, and religious elites.[14] Fandy (2004) has argued that Muslim intellectuals have struggled for decades to institute a pedagogical "software" that would encourage students to critically engage with the West and take up the challenge of reforming their customary cultures

---

sponsored the Arab Human Development Report 2005: Toward the rise of women in the Arab world. http://www.peacewomen.org/news/International/Dec06/GenderEquality_ArabWorld.html, visited on 2 February 2010)

14 There are many sources in support of this hypothesis; however, more importantly, there are recent attempts to address these characteristics in Muslim education. "We as leaders of the Muslim world need to take responsibility for ourselves and our citizens," said Sheikh Saud bin Saqr al-Qasimi, the crown prince and deputy ruler of Ras al-Khaimah, a part of the United Arab Emirates. "We need to make sure that our young people can find jobs." Shortfalls in education in Muslim countries "make people vulnerable to misinformation." See "Can the Muslim world be re-branded?" by Thomas Fuller, International Herald Tribune, May 28, 2007, a report on an Indonesia- and Malaysia-led conference to counter these trends in the Muslim world. (www.nytimes.com/2007/05/28/world/.../28iht-forum.1.5894814.html, visited on 2 February 2010).

> from within to make them compatible with modern, global society. For reasons of political expediency, however, some governments have allowed and even encouraged another version of "educational software" that nurtures student resentment and hostility toward the non-Muslim world, as well as toward progressives and intellectuals within Muslim societies.

At this point it should be noted that political and nationalist motives are the major factors behind violence and terrorism; contrary to popular assumptions, religious beliefs are much less pivotal, if at all. In most cases, religions are either hijacked by marginals or are abused by radicals who have political agendas. According to a recent research conducted by Professor Robert Pape of the University of Chicago, "there is little connection between suicide terrorism and Islamic fundamentalism, or any one of the world's religions. In fact the leading instigators of suicide attacks are the Tamil Tigers in Sri Lanka, a Marxist-Leninist group whose members are from Hindu families but who are adamantly opposed to religion. … Rather, what nearly all suicide terrorist attacks have in common is a specific secular and strategic goal: to compel modern democracies to withdraw military forces from territory that the terrorists consider to be their homeland" (Pape 2005, 4). As a matter of fact, as majority of the chapters in this edited volume have produced solid evidence, both Muslim teachings in general and the Gülen philosophy and tradition in particular support acceptance of diversity, pluralism, nonviolence, peacemaking and alliance of civilizations. Gülen was already advocating alliance of civilizations in mid-1990s and Journalists and Writers Foundation of which Gülen is the honorary chairman organized conferences on these themes.

Due to the heavy reliance of militant Muslim organizations (such as al-Qaeda) on narrow and exclusive Wahhabi interpretations of Muslim sources, it is essential for Muslim and non-Muslim communities to be exposed to an alternative narrative and perspective on these issues of war, violence, and relations to the other. This book about the Gülen Movement is another step in confronting these exclusivist interpretations. In order to understand how the Gülen Movement contributes to Muslim peacebuilding, we will now look closely at how Gülen evaluates the Other, East–West relations, and intercultural and intercivilizational dialogue.

Gülen on the Other, East and West and the Movement's Peacebuilding

Gülen does not pursue an identity politics and does not define himself by the Other. In other words, he does not have a constitutive other. In his discourse, "(o)therization and the adversary component is weak" (Kömeçoğlu 1997, 86); it is not reactive but proactive, not having a coarse *us* versus *them* schism. To put it differently, "unlike the confrontational New Social Movements, the Gülen Movement has engaged in 'moral opposition,' in which the movement's actors seek to empathize with the adversary by creating (what Bakhtin calls) 'dialogic' relationships" (Gürbüz 2007, 104).

This is also a reflection of Gülen's not seeing the world in terms of Muslims versus others. Because of his views on the disunity of the Muslim world, he also does not think that trying to revive the caliphate is feasible: "I would say that the revival of the caliphate would be very difficult and making Muslims accept such a revived *khilafah* would be impossible. The perception of the modern world regarding the revival of *khilafah* must be considered" (Gülen 2005a, 457). It is not only realistic considerations that make Gülen think along these lines but he also looks at the issue from a perspective of Islamic jurisprudence:

> Is there anything that suggests "that a state which is not represented by the title of caliphate is not legal"? To what degree was the matter of the caliphate regarded… was it thought that "it is indispensable"?... What matters is the meticulous practice of Islam. It would not be correct to emphasize historical subjects that are of secondary importance in order to cause polemics; these are always open to debate... If some fellow Muslims put

> an emphasis on this issue, I don't know who they are incited by. Can you say that there was a Caliphate in the real sense of the word during the Umayyads and Abbasids, did Yezid or Walid represent the Caliphate properly, allowing us to argue over it now? Deliberately or not, the creation of such debates can be something done by those who don't practice Islam in order to cover up their own flaws (Gülen 2005b).

He rejects the idea that a clash between the "East" and "West" is necessary, desirable or unavoidable. In Gülen's view an abstract West is not the enemy of Muslims but ignorance, poverty and disunity are:

> Unlike many Islamic revivalist movements, the Gülen Movement shaped its identity against the perceived threat of a trio of enemies, as Nursi named them a century ago – ignorance, disunity, and poverty. This perception of the opposition is crucial to understanding the apolitical mind-set of the Gülen Movement's followers (Gurbuz 2007, 104).

In line with Nursian thought, Gülen looks at the West more analytically, following Nursi's declaration that "Europe is two," one positive and the other negative:

> It should not be misunderstood: Europe is two. One follows the sciences which serve justice and right and the industries beneficial for the life of society through the inspiration it has received from true Christianity; this first Europe I am not addressing. I am rather addressing the second corrupt Europe which, through the darkness of the philosophy of Naturalism, supposing the evils of civilization to be its virtues, has driven mankind to vice and misguidance (Nursi 1995, 160).

Gülen states, "I don't see any harm in joining the West and Western thought on points where it's necessary and where there's no danger. I don't see any harm in taking things the West developed" (Gülen 2000, 191). He has been supportive of Turkey's accession to the European Union (Gülen 2000, 189). "Gülen's pro-Western attitude has played a key role in the domestication and softening of other Islamist groups' anti-Europe and anti-US positions. Although many Islamists eventually came closer to embracing this idea, a majority of them initially criticized Gülen for his pro-Europe views. He was one of the first Islamic leaders to embrace the idea of EU membership and at a time when Islamists in general regarded it as a threat to Turkish security and Islamic culture" (Kösebalaban 2003, 176).

In contrast to Islamism's simple but abstract assertion of surrender to the ancestors, that is, that returning to the golden age of pristine Islam will solve all the problems of Muslims, Gülen attempts a concrete socio-economic and cultural analysis of the current spatio-temporal context and based on this analysis offers concrete solutions to tackle Muslims' enemies (i.e. ignorance, poverty, disunity and anarchy) rather than insisting on abstract rhetoric.

If ignorance is one of the three major enemies, then the Gülen project's offer is education at different levels, not only at schools and not only religious education. Gülen's educational project covers life. It is not only confined to the mosque nor is it only confined to secular schools. It also includes family education, child upbringing, educating religious scholars (Atay 2007), educating by example (*tamsil*) and so on.

If poverty is Muslims' second enemy, then the Gülen Movement's offer is to establish charity organizations (such as Kimse Yok Mu?) in addition to education's indirect help to raise people's socio-economic status.

If dispute or internal conflict is the third major enemy, then dialogue, tolerance and mutual understanding are the remedies for this conflict.

As can be seen, the Gülen Movement's major projects all focus on one of these three areas, and the Movement's media organizations also play supporting roles in this global civil activism that aims in the long run to eradicate the root causes of conflict.[15]

---

15 Needless to say, instead of constantly blaming Muslims, non-Muslim interlocutors of Muslims should question how they can contribute to the process by taking these root causes of conflict into account.

In addition to its economic, intercultural and poverty eradication and aid activities, the Movement contributes to conflict prevention and peacebuilding in four major ways.

First, the Gülen Movement enhances the Islamic framework as another venue to produce new interpretations of Muslim sources that support justice, conflict prevention and peaceful mobilization. With its activities in more than 120 countries, this process has already started.

Second, the Gülen Movement's wide appeal to all Muslims with a universal set of values rooted in Muslim teachings empowers the existing Islamic framework for peacebuilding in its attempts to challenge tribal ethnocentric cultural traditions that have been justified as an integral part of Muslim teachings and practices in many parts of the world.[16] It also contributes to the negation and isolation of other oppressive cultural norms, values, and habits that certain Muslim societies have adopted or developed.

Third, Gülen's teachings about individual and collective responsibility are based on self examination, acknowledgment that one's self is responsible for one's own conditions, and that constantly blaming others is a faulty attitude. In addition, Gülen's focus on tolerance and acceptance of differences contributes to the development of an Islamic peacebuilding framework that is explicitly counter to certain militant so-called "Islamist" discourses promoting exclusion, intolerance and even violence. The Gülen Movement carves an essential space for dialogue among Muslims on such issues. This internal conversation on how Muslims can (communities and individuals) engage in a constructive process of self help is essential for any awakening project. Through this process of internal dialogue, Muslims in such movements can stand and act against

16 This universal perspective is rooted in Gülen's unequivocal acceptance of the assumption that Judaism, Christianity, Buddhism, Hinduism, and other world religions basically pursue the same goals, and, as a result, typify Gülen's own emphasis that any religion reflects the universality of religion, which is "a system of belief embracing all races and all beliefs, a road bringing everyone together in brotherhood" (Gülen 2000, 243).

those within the community who use violence internally and externally in a brutal and terrorizing way.

Fourth, reaching out to non-Muslims has become a condition for cultural and economic survival for many Muslim minorities in the western world. The Gülen Movement, with its emphasis on peaceful coexistence, reaching out to the other, and redefining the meaning of the other (as described above and in several chapters in this book), provides an example for Muslims in such diverse societies on how to engage with non-Muslims. It also counters fears spread by certain Muslim groups who are against interfaith dialogue and social or personal engagements with non-Muslims.

Gülen's approach to diversity is essential for an Islamic peacebuilding framework that relates to non-Muslims without apologies or defensiveness, but with constructive social, cultural, economic and educational initiatives. Non-Muslims can learn more about Islam and its history through these pluralist principles rather than dogmatic preaching. What is more, these Gülen initiatives will challenge and refute—by conduct—both the prejudices and the Islamophobia widespread in some non-Muslim circles.[17]

Conclusion

The ongoing construction of the Islamic peacebuilding framework and practices can contribute to several necessary developments and changes in the process of engaging and mobilizing social and political change agents in Muslim communities. With its deep scholarly and intellectual roots and links to the Sufi tradition (first- and second-century Muslim mystics, Rumi, al-Ghazzali, ibn Arabi, etc.) the Gülen Movement offers a significant contribution in support of the hypothesis that Muslim nonviolent social mobilization and

17 The hundreds of economic development projects (schools and other poverty reduction programs) are a crucial aspect of the Gülen Movement's approach in many Muslim communities around the world. Such emphasis enhances and empowers the local Muslim capacity and assists in developing a new community discourse that is not based on victimhood.

peacebuilding values and norms can be the central lens for all Muslim communities in dealing with their internal and external conflicts and interactions. Gülen's approach—and its application on the ground in many Muslim countries—is an important force in this process.

In addition to being influential in Turkey, Gülen's understanding of Islam, one can expect, will also be influential in the wider Muslim world in parallel with the increasing influence of both Turkey and the Movement on a global scale. As Voll (2003, 247) noted, "In the clashing visions of globalizations, Fethullah Gülen is a force in the development of the Muslim discourse of globalized multicultural pluralism. As the impact of the educational activities of those influenced by him attests, his vision bridges modern and postmodern, global and local, and has a significant influence in the contemporary debates that shape the visions of the future of Muslims and non-Muslims alike" (Voll 2003, 247). Major developments in Turkey are already followed with considerable interest by the Muslim media, thinkers and activists. The Movement has also increased its activities in the non-Turkish Muslim world. In addition to operating several schools in major Muslim countries such as Pakistan, Bangladesh, Malaysia and Indonesia, it has recently been opening schools, hospitals and also universities in Africa and wherever permitted in the Middle East.

Moreover, the Movement, being aware of the need to situate itself and publish its ideas within the wider *ummah*, started publishing *Hira* magazine in 2005 (Heck 2007, 643). The magazine "is chiefly intra-Muslim in its aims and aspirations. The magazine is published in Arabic and features articles written by both Turkish and Arabic writers; a lead article by Fethullah Gülen opens and sets the tone of each issue. The magazine acts to bring the intellectual outlook of the Gülen Movement to the Arab world, serving as a cultural bridge between Turks and Arabs, as a forum in which pressing issues in contemporary Islam can be aired and treated by leading Muslim thinkers, and as a tool for the global Muslim community to consolidate a renewed vision of its relation to the intellectual and socio-political realities of the modern world" (Heck 2007, 643). Furthermore, in 2006, the "Movement, which has been criticized not paying enough attention to the Muslim World... invited intellectuals from the Middle East including Arab, Jewish and Turkish to discuss the future of the Middle East. And... in February 2007, the [Abant] platform co-organized a meeting in Egypt with the prominent Al-Ahram Institute to discuss Turkish and Egyptian experiences with democracy, modernization and secularism" (Ugur 2007, 158).

In short, the Gülen Movement, with its theological and practical responses to real challenges facing Muslim communities in the twenty-first century, is gradually becoming a central force in actively facilitating, engaging, and mobilizing certain segments of the Muslim community in their quest to institute much needed constructive changes in their economic, cultural, political, and social realities.

References

Abdalla, A. 2000. "Principles of Islamic Interpersonal Conflict Intervention: A Search within Islam and Western Literature." *Journal of Law and Religion* 15:151–184.

Abu-Nimer. M. 1996a. "Conflict Resolution in an Islamic Context: Some Conceptual Questions." *Peace and Change* 22 (40):22–40.

———. 1996b. "Conflict Resolution Approaches: Western and Middle Eastern Lessons and Possibilities." *The American Journal of Economics and Sociology* 55(1):35–55.

———. 2003. *Nonviolence and Peacebuilding in Islam: Theory and Practice*. Florida: University Press of Florida.

———. and S. A. Kadayifci-Orellana. 2005. "Muslim Peace Building Actors in Africa and the Balkans." *Salam Institute for Peace and Justice Report*. Washington DC.

Atay, R. 2007. "Reviving the Suffa Tradition. *Muslim World in Transition: Contributions of the Gülen Movement*, ed. İ. Yılmaz et al. London: Leeds Metropolitan University Press, 459–472.

Barakat, H. 1993. *The Arab World: Society, Culture, and State*. Los Angeles: University of California Press.

Chittick, W. C. 1990. "Theological Roots of Peace and War according to Islam." *The Islamic Quarterly* 34 (3):145–163.

Crow, K. 1997. "Divided Discourse: Muslim Discussion on Islam and Peace." *Nonviolence International*, unpublished paper. Washington DC. July.

Donner, F. M. 1991. "The Sources of Islamic Conceptions of War." *Just War and Jihad: Historical and Theoretical Perspectives on War and Peace in Western and Islamic Traditions*, ed. John Kelsay and James Turner Johnson, 31–69. New York: Greenwood Press.

Easwaran, E. 1984. *A Man to Match His Mountains: Badshah Khan: Nonviolent Soldier of Islam*. Petaluma, California: Nilgiri Press.

Fandy, M. 2004. *Educational Crisis in the Muslim World*. June. United States Institute for Peace, Senior fellow report. (http://www.usip.org/fellows/reports/2004/0610_fandy.html)

Gopin, M. 1991. "Religion, Violence, and Conflict Resolution." *Peace and Change* 22(1):1–31.

Grinell, K. 2007. "Beyond East and West: Fethullah Gülen and 'Border' Thinking." *Muslim World in Transition: Contributions of the Gülen Movement*, ed. İ. Yılmaz et al (ed.). London: Leeds Metropolitan University Press, 203-214.

Gülen, F. 2000. *Advocate of Dialogue*. Compiled by Ali Ünal and Alphonse Williams. Fairfax, VA. The Fountain Press.

———. 2004. Nuriye Akman's interview with Fethullah Gülen. *Zaman Daily*. http://en.fgulen.com/press-room/nuriye-akmans-interview/1726-no-islamic-world-exists-today, visited on 2 February 2010.

———. 2005a. An Interview with Fethullah Gülen – translated by Zeki Sarıtoprak and Ali Ünal, *The Muslim World, Special Issue, Islam in Contemporary Turkey: The Contributions of Fethullah Gülen*, 95(3): 447–467.

———. 2005b. *Mehmet Gündem's interview with Fethullah Gülen in Milliyet Daily*, http://en.fgulen.com/press-room/mehmet-gundems-interview/1928-the-subject-of-reviving-the-caliphate.html, last visited on 2 February 2010.

Gürbüz, M. 2007. "Performing Moral Opposition: Musings on the Strategy and Identity in the Gülen Movement." *Muslim World in Transition: Contributions of the Gülen Movement*, İ. Yılmaz et al (ed.). London: Leeds Metropolitan University Press, 104–117.

Heck, P. L. 2007. "Turkish in the Language of the Qur'an: *Hira'*." *Muslim World in Transition: Contributions of the Gülen Movement*, İ. Yılmaz et al (ed.). London: Leeds Metropolitan University Press, 643–649.

Irani, G. 1999. "Islamic Mediation Techniques for Middle Eastern Conflicts." *MERIA (Middle East Review of International Affairs) Journal* 3(2) at http://www.bui.ac.il/SOC/meria/journal/1999/issue2/jv3n2a1.html (June).

Irani, G. and N. Funk. 1998. "Rituals of Reconciliation: Arab-Islamic Perspectives." *Arab Studies Quarterly* 20(4): 53–73.

Johansen, R. C. 1997. "Radical Islam and Nonviolence: A Case Study of Religious Empowerment and Constraint among Pashtuns." *Journal of Peace Research* 34(1):53–71.

Johnston, D. M, and C. Sampson, eds. 1994. *Religion: The Missing Dimension of Statecraft*. New York: Oxford University Press.

Kadayifci-Orellana, S. A. 2003. "Religion, Violence and the Islamic Tradition of Nonviolence." *Turkish Yearbook of International Relations* 34.

Kelsay, J. and J. T. Johnson. 1991. *Just War and Jihad: Historical and Theoretical Perspectives on War and Peace in Western and Islamic Traditions*. New York: Greenwood Press.

Kömeçoğlu, U. 1997. *A Sociologically Interpretative Approach to the Fethullah Gülen Community Movement*. Istanbul: Boğaziçi University.

Kösebalaban, H. 2003. "The Making of Enemy and Friend: Fethullah Gülen's National-security Identity." M. H. Yavuz and J. L. Esposito (eds.) *Turkish Islam and the Secular State: The Gülen Movement*, Syracuse, New York: Syracuse University Press, 170–183.

Laqueur, W. 2003. *No End to War*. New York: Continuum International Publishing Group.

Malik, I. H. 1998. "Islamic Discourse on Jihad, War and Violence." *Journal of South Asian and Middle Eastern Studies* 21(4): 47–78.

Moulavi C. A. 2000. "War and Peace: Popular Jihad." *Contemporary Debates in Islam: An Anthology of Modernist and Fundamentalist Thought*, ed. M. Moaddel and K. Talattof. New York: St. Martin's Press.

Mousalli, A. S. 1997. "An Islamic Model for Political Conflict Resolution: *Tahkim* (Arbitration)." *Conflict Resolution in the Arab World: Selected Essays*, ed. Paul Salem. Beirut: American University Press.

Nursi, S. 1995. *The Flashes Collection*. Translated by Şükran Vahide. Istanbul: Nur Publishers.

Paige, G. D. et al. 1993. *Islam and Nonviolence*. Honolulu, Hawai'i: Center for Global Nonviolence.

Pape, R. 2005. *Dying to Win*. Random House, New York.

Sa'id, J. 1993. *The Doctrine of the First Son of Adam: The Problem of Violence in Islamic Practice*. (Fifth Edition). Damascus: Dar al-Fikr.

———. 1997. "Peace—or Nonviolence—in History and with the Prophets." Paper written for conference Islamic Values for Change. Trans. Dr.

Abduhu Hammud al-Sharif, revised with notes by Dr. Karim Crow. Syria: Bi'r Ajam, Qunaytra.

———. 2000. "Law, Religion and the Prophetic Method of Social Change." *Journal of Law and Religion* 15(1&2): 83–149.

Said, A. A. and N. C. Funk. 2002. "The Role of Faith in Cross-cultural Conflict Resolution." *Peace and Conflict Studies* 9(1):37–38.

———. 2001. "Peace in the Sufi Tradition: An Ecology of the Spirit." *Peace and Conflict Resolution in Islam: A Global Philosophy.* Said, Abdul Aziz, Nathan C. Funk, and Ayse S. Kadayifci (eds). Lanham, New York Oxford: University Press of America, 2001. 247–262.

Salem, P., ed. 1997. *Conflict Resolution in the Arab World: Selected Essays.* Lebanon: American University of Beirut.

Salmi, R. H., C. A. Majul, and G. K. Tanham. 1998. *Islam and Conflict Resolution: Theories and Practices*. Lanham: University Press of America.

Sampson, C. 1997. "Religion and Peacebuilding." *Peacemaking in International Conflict: Methods and Techniques*, ed. W. Zartman and L. Rasmussen. Washington DC: United States Institute of Peace Press, 273–316.

Sampson, C. and J. P. Lederach, eds. 2000. *From the Ground Up: Mennonite Contributions to International Peacebuilding*. New York: Oxford University Press.

Satha-Anand, C. 1987. *Islam and Nonviolence*. Tampa, FL: University of South Florida.

———. 1994. "Core Values for Peacemaking in Islam: The Prophet's Practice as Paradigm." *Building Peace in the Middle East: Challenges for the States and Civil Society*, ed. Elise Boulding. Boulder, CO: Lynne Rienner Publishers.

———. 1996. *Nonviolent Crescent: Two Essays on Islam and Nonviolence.* Alkmaar, Netherlands: International Fellowship of Reconciliation.

———. 2001. "The Nonviolent Crescent: Eight Theses on Muslim Nonviolent Action. *Peace and Conflict Resolution in Islam: Precept and Practice*, ed. Abdul Aziz Said, Nathan C. Funk, and Ayse S. Kadayifci, 195–211. New York: University Press of America.

Stassen, G. 1992. *Just Peacemaking: Transforming Initiatives for Justice and Peace*. Louisville, KY: Westminster/John Knox.

Thistlethwaite, S. and G. S. Stassen. 2008. *Abrahamic Alternatives to War*, Washington DC: USIP Publication.

Tibi, B. 1996. "War and Peace in Islam." *The Ethics of War and Peace: Religious and Secular Perspectives*, ed. Terry Nardin. New Jersey: Princeton University Press.

Ugur, E. 2007. "Religion as a Source of Social Capital? The Gülen Movement in the Public Sphere." *Muslim World in Transition: Contributions of the Gülen Movement*, İ. Yılmaz et al (eds.). London: Leeds Metropolitan University Press, 152–162.

Voll, J. O. 2003. "Fethullah Gülen: Transcending Modernity in the New Islamic Discourse." M. H. Yavuz and J. L. Esposito (eds.) *Turkish Islam and the Secular State: The Gülen Movement*, Syracuse, New York: Syracuse University Press, 238–247.

Yılmaz, İ. 2003. "*Ijtihad* and *Tajdid* by Conduct: The Gülen Movement." M. H. Yavuz and J. L. Esposito (eds.) *Turkish Islam and the Secular State: The Gülen Movement*, Syracuse, New York: Syracuse University Press, 208–237.

———. 2007. "Social Innovation for Peaceful Coexistence: Intercultural Activism from Rumi to Gülen." *Peaceful Coexistence: Fethullah Gülen's Initiatives in the Modern World*, İ. Yılmaz et al (eds.). London: Leeds Metropolitan University Press, 25–41.

Yılmaz, İ. et al. 2007a. *Muslim World in Transition*: *Contributions of the Gülen Movement*, London: Leeds Metropolitan University Press.

———. 2007b. *Peaceful Coexistence: Fethullah Gülen's Initiatives in the Contemporary World,* London: Leeds Metropolitan University Press.

PART 2

Globalization and Gülen as Border Transgressor

CHAPTER 3

Border Thinking: Fethullah Gülen and the East–West Divide

Klas Grinell

INTRODUCTION

East is East and West is West. We have heard it many times. Kipling said they shall never meet, Huntington that they will always clash (Huntington 1993). In his "Ballad of East and West" Kipling went on to state that when two persons meet face to face there is neither any border, nor any East or West.

Today Huntington is more widely read than Kipling, and those using Kipling's refrain quote only the first line, not bothering with the following lesson of how borders might be overcome. Huntington is far from alone in imagining an uncrossable border between East and West. He is merely an all-too-ordinary representative of Western modernity, and bordering is a fundamental practice of modernity. In this article I will discuss Fethullah Gülen as a critic of modernity who departs from bordering practices and offers an alternative of civilizational dialogue.

This opening section is scattered with opaque and problematic entities—East, West, modernity, civilization. Everything said in such broad generalizing terms is bound to be rather superficial. Distinctions will be made along the way.

Modernity as Border Building

I will begin by sketching an ideal type of modernity that fits the intention of this paper. As stated above, the practice of creating borders is a fundamental aspect of modernity. The border can be seen as a political and epistemological invention of European modernity, politically established with the peace of Westphalia in 1648 and spread around the world with imperial colonialism, epistemologically maybe most influentially articulated by René Descartes in the same era (Mignolo 1999, 60; *International Studies Review* 2000). In different fields dichotomies and trenches were created between *us* and *them*—this state and that state, mind and body, civilized and barbarian, either–or, and so on.

One aspect of this was developed in the Cartesian theory of science in which an object could only have one essence, a cause only one effect. The burning of coal, for example, created heat and energy. That was the essential outcome. Other effects could only be interpreted as side effects; pollution was thus not essential. In the long term, however, we might see that pollution will kill everyone that the coal could warm and produce energy for. From that perspective the energy effect can be seen as only a temporal gain from a deeply destructive process.

This very simplified example serves to show that matters are more complicated than the border building, either–or thinking modernists could see. The over-confident belief in science dominant in positivistic modernity is related to what Gülen has often criticized under the name of materialism: "Enlightenment movements beginning in the eighteenth century saw human beings as mind only. Following that, positivist and materialist movements saw them as material and corporeal entities only" (Gülen 2004a, 79).

If we take modernity to be what the staunchest modernists wanted it to be, as I have done so far, we run the risk of simplifying life lived in modern society. Modernization did not make the world modern in the way the modernists expected. But in my use of the term, modernity is the ideology and practice of the modernists; the borderland is a place where its shortcomings and abuses become visible. Another way of stating that modernist modernity never has been hegemonic can be found in the sociological concept of multiple modernities: there have always been many different ways of being modern (Göle 2000). From a sociological perspective I find that concept fruitful, but from a more philosophical perspective modernity is useful as a marker for the ideology and practice of Western expansionism.

Gülen as a Border Transgressor

But Gülen is not merely a critic of *them* on the other side of the civilizational border. His critique is directed at both sides:

> The East's and West's civilizations existed separated from each other. This separation, which should not have occurred, was based on the former's retiring from intellect and science, while the latter retired from spirituality, metaphysics, and eternal and invariable values. As a result, the last centuries of this millennium have witnessed disasters that are hard to believe. (Gülen 2004a, 28)

The border set up between East and West is a false one, he says. To say that science is Western and spirituality Eastern is just a symptom of the bordering mentality. The separation should not have occurred, Gülen says. It was an invention. Like all inventions it had a purpose connected to its time and place of invention. I would argue that one important purpose of the invention was to prove the West's superiority. Its time has run out, and there is no room for it today.

> Borders are set up to define the places that are safe and unsafe, to distinguish *us* from *them*. A border is a dividing line, a narrow strip along a steep edge. A borderland is a vague and undetermined place created by the emotional residue of an unnatural boundary. It is a constant state of transition. The prohibited and forbidden are its inhabitants. (Anzaldúa 1999, 25)

In the words above Chicana feminist Gloria Anzaldúa is claiming the borderland as a place to have a full identity, not accepting all those that say that purity and belonging to only one side is essential for a qualitative identity. In her writings the borderland becomes a place for a new understanding of traditions, heritage and identity. She is from the indigenous Mexican mestizo population of south Texas that came under US rule after the wars between the United States and Mexico in the middle of the nineteenth century. Her borderland is Anglo-Spanish-Aztecan. Her story is tied to her very special biography, but her example can be inspiring in the analysis of many other places.

Turkey as a Borderland

Turkey is often called a bridge between East and West, a place where they meet and intermingle. Tourist guides are full of that kind of wording. We could, to sound more academic, call it a borderland instead, a borderland where East and West are wrapped in layer upon layer that makes it impossible to say what is what: Hittite, Greek, Roman, Byzantine, Seljuk, Ottoman, Turkish, Central Asian, Kurdish, Muslim, Sunni, Alevi, Balkan, Middle Eastern, Mediterranean, European, and many other layers. If Turkey is a borderland, Fethullah Gülen can be called a person who has developed and preached a border gnosis that takes us beyond the confrontational understanding of East and West—I will return to the concept of border gnosis later.

Turkey is not the only borderland, however, maybe just a more obvious one. At least in a metaphorical way today we are all living in borderlands, a global border village where no one can live a life sheltered by one tradition only. If we could only escape from the comfortable self-absorption of fixed identities and instead live in the multilayered present, we might see that bordering is a modernistic and even unnatural practice. Many on each side of the imagined East–West divide, be it a Sayyid Qutb or a Hindutva man, or a Donald Rumsfeld or a staunch Kemalist, will, of course, cling frenziedly to the fixed identities guarded by the border and its barbed wire. They want to stay safe and only have to mingle with those who are one of *us*.

Fethullah Gülen, on the other hand, has devoted much of his time and made many efforts to mingle with *them*, and it could be said that he has seen the borderland as a place to meet *them* and dialogue with *them*. Since the borderland is an undetermined place it is a place where something new can come into being. The bright future of the new millennium that Gülen speaks about so often is for him not a return to something pure and forlorn within the established borders, it is something new and transgressive. "Giving up their centuries-old clashes, these two worlds should come together for a happier, more peaceful world" (Gülen 2000a, 58). For Gülen religion will be the foundation for a new and happier world; the revelation sets parameters for it. So even if Gülen is an advocate of dialogue and a spokesman for everyone's place in a global civilization of love and tolerance, he still has a firm normative ground for his message. Religion, in an inclusive understanding, is the answer (Gülen 2000a, 241).

> "Religion reconciles opposites that seem to be mutually exclusive: religion–science, this world–the next world, nature–divine books, the material–the spiritual, and spirit–body. Religion can erect a defense against the destruction caused by scientific materialism, put science in its proper place, and end long-standing conflicts among nations and peoples... The goal of dialogue among world religions is not simply to destroy scientific materialism and the destructive materialistic worldview; rather, the very nature of religion demands this dialogue. Judaism, Christianity, and Islam, and even Hinduism and other world religions accept the same source for themselves, and, including Buddhism, pursue the same goal." (Gülen 2000a, 241–42)

Gülen on the Western Side of the Border

Gülen has special experiences that make him able to be transgressive and inclusive. His Turkish experience of modernistic, westernistic Kemalism and a deep rooted and familial Islamic tradition gives him a double vision: "We have one side in common with Europe and one side in common with the Muslim world" (Gülen 2000a, 189; Sevindi 2008). He uses that double belonging to argue for his cause from both sides. He is as firm in his critique of the lack of intellect and science in the Islamic tradition as of the materialistic denial of the spiritual in the Western tradition. He shows that there is a Western counterpoint to the materialistic strand and tries to argue for a different and truer Western canon in contact with Platonist and Christian thinking. In this non-materialistic canon he places thinkers like Plato, Descartes, Pascal, Leibniz, Kant, Hegel, Bergson and Heisenberg. With this broadened Western tradition he can argue against the materialist imitators of the West, who, he says, are always more radical in their borrowed modernist attitudes (Gülen, 2004c, 148). The Westerners in the East are thus trying to imitate a fake image of the West.

So what role do European thinkers play in Gülen's message? Here and there in his writings he invokes their names to strengthen his point against those who believe that science must equal materialism and atheism. "The worldly allusions derive their specific meaning through their existence within the sacred universe of God and the Ultimate Truth that stands at its centre," one could say (Sunnemark 2001, 215). The quote is taken from an analysis of Martin Luther King's rhetoric. To me, Gülen's and King's use of the Western non-theological canon are very similar. As Fredrik Sunnemark argues in his analysis of King's rhetoric, it is hard to find any detailed content in the references made to the authorities of the modern canon. They are not building blocks for the argument. It might seem as if King's use of literary references simply has the function of ornamentation, but that is an oversimplified understanding, Sunnemark says. The allusions are a method of legitimizing the civil rights movement's claim to righteousness, but it is not a philosophical method; it is a preacher's method. The allusions are significant and important, but they are part of a rhetorical establishing of a theological argument formed without their participation.

Materialistic conclusions drawn from European philosophy and European scientific developments are not only contrary to the message of the Qur'an, but they are not scientifically valid or representative of the major philosophers of European modernity such as Descartes, Leibniz, Kant and Hegel, Gülen states in a passage in *Toward a Global Civilization of Love and Tolerance* (Gülen 2004c, 149); these thinkers are mobilized as religious and anti-materialistic. It is not clear what it is in their work, however, that has led Gülen to this conclusion.

Gülen's Theory of Science

Not all of Gülen's use of the Western tradition is rhetorical. Science is one of the most important subjects in Gülen's message. Science is something that in the last couple of hundred years has been developed in the West. To get rid of its compartmentalized and materialistic conceptions of reality, Gülen says, it needs to be conducted within the spiritual and moral frame of Islam: "There is no reason to fear science. The danger does not lie with science and the founding of the new world it will usher in, but rather with ignorance and irresponsible scientists and others who exploit it for their own selfish interests" (Gülen 2005b, 233).

His discussions of science are often in tune with contemporary strands in the theory of science field gathered under the name of science and technology studies (STS).[18] Here, however, the relationship is rather different from the one with the classical philosophers. Here Gülen does not mention any names. It is thus difficult to know whether his arguments stem from readings of this field, or if he has come to similar conclusions from a different angle. He very strongly emphasizes that "none of the findings of scientific research are ever absolute" (Gülen 2005a, 105). To support this claim he

18 STS works from the understanding that social, political, and cultural values affect science and technology innovation, and that they in turn affect society. It is richly presented in Jasanoff 1995.

refers to the majority of scientists, without giving any references. Also, without mentioning names he distances himself from those who try to see simple correspondences between today's scientific results and verses in the Qur'an: "The great volume of articles and books produced in this vein in recent times will be open to ridicule in the future" (Gülen 2005a, 105).

The wisdom of the Qur'an does not need any external support, Gülen stresses. In this respect his position on the relation between Islam and science is similar to that of the British Muslim writer Ziauddin Sardar. However, a big difference is that Sardar makes many references to the contemporary debate among theorists of science in the STS tradition such as Thomas Kuhn, Jeremy Ravetz and Donna Haraway (Sardar 1989, 2002; Stenberg 1996).

> What we must, and do, reject is that the truth of Qur'an and hadith should be made to depend on verification and confirmation by scientific data which are, as explained above, incomplete, disconnected from the meaning and purpose of life as a whole, and vulnerable to change as the borders of human ignorance change. (Gülen 2005a, 107)

Gülen criticizes Darwinism for being too certain of the truth of its claims. His argument that the theory of evolution is just a theory that leaves many things unexplained is a rather standard one from religious critics, and hard to reconcile with his rhetorical and broad approval of the importance of scientific knowledge. But Gülen does not approve of the theory of intelligent design; it is a debate in the wrong arena, trying to beat the opponent in his own field with scientific arguments, rather than trying to transgress the dichotomy and see the explanations as incommensurable.[19]

19 Thomas Kuhn saw theories as incommensurable if there is no common theoretical language that can be used to compare them, and since there is no place outside the paradigms, different paradigms will, from their own perspectives, judge the other's theory as flawed. There is no absolute way to decide which theory is better (Kuhn 1970). Gülen's argument is in line with Kuhn's, but as I have said, since there are no references, I cannot know if Gülen is influenced by Kuhnian perspectives. The stand point is also well in line with Islamic traditions.

Border Gnoseology

Gülen can be seen as a border thinker, as a producer of border gnosis, but what does that mean?

Argentinean philologist Walter Mignolo has theorized about the border and developed the concepts of border thinking and border gnoseology. It might seem pure post-modern jargon, but according to Mignolo it is often necessary to change the terms in order to change the content of a discussion. I will argue that there are certain affinities between Mignolo's and Gülen's critical ambitions, or, maybe more to the point, that Gülen can be seen as a representative of the break with modern/colonial epistemology that Mignolo is trying to encourage and develop.

Mignolo develops the concept of gnosis as an alternative to episteme. They are both Greek words for knowledge, but in modern international academic language, gnosis has been connected with Gnosticism and the search for knowledge of God.[20] The rational knowledge revered by modernity's major philosophers such as Descartes, Kant and Husserl is episteme, which is connected with empiricism and rationalism. Mignolo argues, however, that the division was made not only in the interest of philosophy and science, it also excluded a lot of local, non-Western knowledge that

---

20 In explaining the concept of *ma'rifa* (Turk. *marifet*) the English translator Ali Ünal uses the term *gnosis* as a synonym for the Turkish word *marifet*. "A traveler who is completely closed to all else save God, who has resisted all corporeal desires and impulses in order to be carried by the tides of peace, has reached the stage of *ma'rifa*. One who travels around this point is called a traveler to *ma'rifa*; one who has reached it is called an *'arif* (a Gnostic, or one who has spiritual knowledge of God). The differences found in commentaries on *ma'rifa* are based on the temperaments and schools of thought or levels of the Gnostics." (Gülen 2004b, 147). This opens the very interesting question of translation, and transmission of knowledge. Here the translator has inserted a rather Christian concept to explain to readers in English what the Arabic *ma'rifa* is. In Gülen's exposition of the Turkish *marifet* (Gülen 2001, "Marifet"), there is no such connection, instead we find a reference to ibn Hanbal, al-Ghazzali and al-Daylami that is omitted in the translation. Now it seems as if accessibility is chosen before accuracy, and therefore it is hard to tell if the message might be somewhat altered in the translation process.

was articulated in different, maybe non-textual, ways and therefore was not recognized as epistemic knowledge by modernity (Mignolo 1999, 10). A lot of important local knowledge was thus lost forever, but it is still possible to reactivate some of it.

As stated in the earlier quote from Gülen, episteme was reserved for the West and gnosis for the East. That was of course a simplification, but a simplification that in time became productive in the sense that the two sides of the dichotomy came to reproduce themselves in line with it. Gnosis was non-Western and therefore not wanted in the West. Episteme was Western and therefore not understandable or useful to the East. So the prejudice and empty phrase that "East is East and West is West" was born. It implied that we should stick to our respective fields of expertise and learn to live with the fact that we cannot understand each other. For the hardliners it meant that the others should be conquered and ruled over or even that they had no right to live.

It is very important to note that the reverence for episteme and the contempt for gnosis grew hand in hand with colonial expansion. Among the radical propagators of epistemic fundamentalism were those Gülen criticizes as scientific materialists and whom Bediüzzaman Said Nursi called students of philosophy and positivists (Gülen 2005b, 228; Said Nursi 2004, 561–69). Mignolo rather calls them propagators of colonial knowledge, to emphasize that this knowledge was used to gain control over nature and other peoples by suppressing other ways of knowing. To escape from this version of colonial modernity Mignolo want to resurrect the concept of gnosis with a meaning covering both episteme and doxa and use it so that Western philosophy no longer will be allowed to stand in judgment over other forms of knowledge (Mignolo 1999, 10).[21]

---

21 *Doxa* means belief or opinion, and has often been regarded as the opposite of *episteme* (knowledge). An interesting project would be to develop this concept of gnosis in relation to the Islamic concept of *'ilm*. I think this could help us to further free the understanding of knowledge from the limitations upheld by the Western philosophical tradition. (Rozenthal 1970) Following Suhrawardi, Western philosophy can still be seen as discursive philosophy (*hikma bathiyya*), Mignolo's opening to doxa might be

Instead, different ways of knowing can suit different times and different places, and there is no need for a totalizing system of all knowledges where they are put in boxes and hierarchies.

Border thinking, or border gnosis, is thinking and knowledge produced from the borders of colonial modernity, knowledge that recognizes the colonizing aspects of what has been seen as true knowledge (episteme) in mainstream modernity, and uses local resources to confront and alter that knowledge in order to know the particularities of life lived in that setting better.

The first criterion for a border thinker is that she or he cannot be an unproblematic part of the centre, nor entangled only in a local tradition. Fethullah Gülen fits very well into Mignolo's description, even if Gülen comes from a different background and position than the authors Mignolo deals with.

Intersectionality and Border Thinking

The concepts of border thinking and borderland should be read deconstructively. All thinking is in some way border thinking. There are no uncomplicated national identities, and there are always cultures living without care for national borders. It is a myth that there are people that have ever felt themselves altogether at home in European rational modernity. To understand this we can make broad use of the concept of intersectionality.

Intersectionality is a concept developed within feminist theory, at first by women of color as a way to show how mainstream feminists have tended to universalize the experiences and conditions of white middle-class women in theories of gender oppression. To stress the fact that there are factors besides gender that make up the

---

said to correspond to the illuminationist concept of intuitive philosophy (*hikma dhawqiyya*). One way of arguing for the validity of localized knowledge would be to articulate it as knowledge by presence (*'ilm al-huduri*). There is no way that objective definition can override the knowledge gained in direct contact (Suhrawardi 1999). Taking this into a human realm could also provide us with an argument for the importance of dialogue as a means for understanding between people.

specific way any person is limited by her situation, feminists of color developed the concept of intersectionality. Categories like gender, race and class are simultaneous and intersecting, and any one of them cannot be said to be prior or more fundamental. They always intersect in any particular and localized situation. Many of those who use the concept of intersectionality also stress that categories aren't fixed—the understandings of gender or race are always construed in complex relation to other factors. The different factors in play always constitute each other. A broader use of the concept of intersectionality has been criticized because it often fails to acknowledge that the concept was used to analyze oppression and power. It is a concept with which to see and analyze the intersections of different power structures, not merely a metaphor for multicultural identities (Mohanty 1989–90; Gillman 2007, 119).

I want to use the concept to bring power in as a factor in the analysis of the borderland. Along some axes Gülen speaks from above, along others from below. He is male and partakes in a patriarchal discourse from the dominant perspective, but he is Muslim and as such from the unprivileged side of Turkish official identification. Very few persons are privileged in all sections; a binary opposition between *in* and *out* is too coarse, and an underdog perspective on one axis cannot be universalized as a representation of the oppressed as such. This application of the concept of intersectionality is not altogether true to its feminist intentions; the gender axis is too invisible in this article. With that acknowledged, I still think the concept is important to highlight the power relations in the borderlands.

Universalism and border thinking

Mignolo's insistence on different ways of knowing calls universalism into question. If there is no universally valid knowledge, can there be any universal values? If border thinking is opposed to universalism, then Gülen can hardly be a border thinker. His message is definitely universalistic. Also, in this analysis we have to release ourselves from an over-dichotomous understanding of a choice between absolute universalism and absolute particularism. The opposite of universalism is situatedness, rather than particularism (Haraway 1991). There might be universal values, but every attempt to express them will be tied to the time and place where the attempt takes place; it will be colored by what Mignolo calls its *loci of enunciation*. German sociologist Ulrich Beck has coined the concept *contextualized universalism* to describe a similar position (Beck 1992).

The emancipatory power of border thinking lies in the double vision it upholds, the border thinker is more prone to see this situatedness of every expression. Thinking made in the borderland might still spring from universal values, but it will be aware of the impossibility of speaking for everyone. Therefore, the border thinker will need to dialogue with others to see, and show respect towards, other localized understandings of the universal values.

Border dialogue

A dialogue must start with difference (or we will have monologue) and a belief in the possibility that we can understand each other. We must break with the empty phrase that East is East and West is West. First and foremost, we are human beings of the same make. In Western epistemology there has been a dominant tradition to separate the understanding of non-Westerners off into special fields such as anthropology. In anthropological philosophy, a branch of philosophy discussing the possibilities of understanding other peoples, it has been common to state that it is nearly impossible to understand a person or a custom from another tradition. For example, it might be hard for me as a Swedish historian of ideas to try to relive the thoughts of Aristotle, but to try to understand an African sage is utterly impossible since we do not share the same *we*, which Aristotle and I are assumed to do (Clack 1999; Motturi

2003).[22] Such a view makes true dialogue impossible and therefore meaningless. That is the stance of those protecting borders.

There are of course representatives of a similar position from Eastern countries, but I am not the most fit to give examples. To them Gülen says, "Islam is the religion of the whole universe. That is, the entire universe obeys the laws laid down by God, so everything in the universe is 'Muslim' and obeys God by submitting to His laws" (Gülen 2004a, 18; 2004c, 223). His message goes out to all humanity. We are all of the same make and therefore we can understand each other. The differences are only on the surface; essentially we are all the same.

Another requisite for dialogue is that we do not think that a person or a tradition can only speak for themselves. Walter Mignolo might be called a post-colonial critic. One of the main aims of post-colonial critique is to show that the urge to gain knowledge of non-Westerners has often been used to conquer, rule and diminish them (Gandhi 1998). It is easy to jump to the conclusion that any attempt to seek knowledge about another person or culture is a way of suppressing them. The next logical step is to say that no Western orientalist or Islamologist can understand Islam, that only a Muslim has the right to talk about Islam. However, the just moral imperative that everyone should have the right to speak for themselves does not imply that everyone can *only* speak for themselves. This would lead to a position holding that we cannot represent someone else's rights and thus take away the possibility of engagement for others and of humanitarian solidarity. Those who are too oppressed to be heard cannot gain any rights if that view is put into practice. It would lead to an egoistic and cynical world.

---

22 A way to make it possible for me to understand Gülen within these axioms would be to argue that Aristotle is as Muslim as he is Western European. For example, in Gülen's discussion of proofs for God's existence we can see the strong Aristotelian legacy in Islam (Gülen 2000b). We have the same philosophical ancestors, and thus we can understand each other. But that would only serve to argue for a more exclusive Abrahamic dialogue.

Gülen, however, is no advocate of that kind of misguided respect for the other. As we have seen he takes the right to argue from both sides of the border, a must in a real dialogue.

Civilizations?

What are these "sides of the border"? What are "East" and "West"? What is a civilization? Both Gülen and Samuel Huntington speak of civilizations. If we are not to assume they are comrades in arms, it is important to see the differences in their understanding of what the term civilization denotes.

The word civilization (Turkish: *medeniyet*) has more than one meaning. According to English dictionaries the main meanings are (1) the state of being civilized, (2) culture, (3) a cultural entity. In Turkish *medeniyet* covers roughly the same meaning of being civilized and, as the *Redhouse* dictionary puts it, "the sum of those qualities that give a society its particular character." In both languages it is connected with the root *civic* or *medeni* used in concepts like *civil law*, or *medeni hukuk*.

A major problem with talk about civilization is that the different meanings often are intermingled, and the descriptive use of civilization for different cultural entities in the world often becomes linked to an understanding of a hierarchy according to those entities' different levels of civilization. The scale for that leveling is, of course, often Western civilization's most chauvinistic self-image of itself as being guided only by liberty, equality, reason, and democracy. Only in the West is there Culture. Only in the West is there true civilization.

One of the major proponents of the importance of civilizations in understanding the present state of the world was the infamous Samuel Huntington. In the context of my discussion it is not so important whether one accepts his argument for the inevitable clash of civilizations or not; it is more important to scrutinize his definition of civilizations. In my view he would be just as mistaken even if his thesis was "the peaceful coexistence of civilizations." That is because he is committed to the East–West dichotomy, to the barbed wire border.

Every civilization has its own unique core values and we cannot understand each other, he says. It is the same stance as that of anthropological philosophy. Even if Huntington were not militaristic, his definition of civilization could never lead to understanding or real dialogue. The most positive option within that conception of civilizations is some kind of exoticizing interest in those whom we can never understand. As we can see, this is far from Gülen's stance. His concept of civilization cannot be the same as Huntington's, but what is the content of his concept? Unfortunately, it is not easy to find out since he apparently uses the term civilization in a rather broad and undistinguished way.[23] Gülen's concept of global civilization seems to refer to the state of being civilized, but also that the world will come together in one civilization, one culture and cultural entity. This is possible because we already are essentially one and living under the rules of God, our creator, according to Gülen.

Can this ideal be called border thinking? If the borderland becomes global, then there are no borders anymore. Let us return to the difference between Huntington and Gülen. Huntington argues that the West is the only civilized civilization. I would interpret Gülen's global civilization as something that can only be realized in the borderland. It is realized by the golden generation, and their special power comes from the fact that they are brought up in

23 Again we encounter the problem of translation. Is it only the Turkish term *medeniyet* that is translated as civilization? *Medeniyet* is derived from the Arabic *medeniyyet*, and even if the meanings given in dictionaries are rather similar, the Arabic origin unavoidably has different connotations than the very Enlightenment-derived concept of civilization as opposed to barbarism. Instead of the dominating opposition to barbarism and a connection to Roman *civitas*, we have in the Arabic concept a link to the Medina of the Prophet and his companions. They lived a truly civilized life. If that etymology is taken seriously, we might read Gülen's extensive use of *ahadith* as an important part of his concept of the global civilization of love and tolerance.

a borderland.[24] Of course this takes the notion of borderland from its localized setting in the southern United States and transforms it into the broader concept or metaphor of a global borderland hinted at earlier in this paper. Everyone can share the experience of living in borderlands, and in that respect everyone is part of the same global entity. However, the understanding of that entity is always colored by a specific local experience. Even if this is a possible interpretation, it would hardly be endorsed by either Mignolo or Anzaldúa; they would most probably find it too utopian.

One of the important aspects of Turkish Islam highlighted by Gülen is the importance of love and tolerance (Gülen 2000a, 53, 196) that is the Sufi strand. Like mystics in all religions, the Sufis seek the experience of oneness and are less prone to border building and sectarianism (Khuri 2007). Since we are parts of the same whole, we belong to the same creation. Civilizations in the meaning of cultural entities are just different ways of expressing life in this creation. Every civilization has developed some knowledge and understanding, but often failed to see that it was only a partial understanding. From the mystical perspective, however, they are not dichotomous but complementary. We can sing different harmonies in the same song, describe different parts of the same elephant; if we break all the cups, the water will be one. There are countless images to express this belief that the ultimate truth is Unity. "Sufism is the way of being God's friend," Gülen says and makes Sufism a very natural part of Islamic life (Gülen 2000a, 259). There

---

24 Gülen's idea of a golden generation is a powerful inspiring force, especially when it was formulated as a utopian idea to strive to make real. But it is one thing to formulate lofty goals and, as Gülen did, talk about a perfection that is in the making, which belongs to the future. Then the idea of a golden generation is an inspiration, something that all the dedicated students could strive to embody. It is very good to strive for perfection. But can perfection be realized by men? To me it seems extremely difficult to identify oneself as part of the golden generation and still keep the humbleness and modesty of Gülen. He never talks of himself as one who shall put things right. He talks about those that will come. But how shall they identify themselves? How can the movement handle the transformation from a small and dedicated marginal force into a well established and in many ways powerful voice?

is no tension between the exoteric and the esoteric aspects of Islam or religion as such in Gülen's writings (Michel 2007).

Something bordering a conclusion

Mignolo is a Latin American leftist, and he mainly reads and uses other thinkers with a leftist approach. Gülen is a preacher more connected to the political right, and building his message from Islamic sources (Özdalga 2003). However, they are both deeply committed to furthering dialogue and respect between different traditions of knowledge. The fact that they come from perspectives often seen as opposing each other, as maybe the main opponents, is interesting and might shed light on their respective views on dialogue. Are there hidden borders? Can there be dialogue between these perspectives?

I think that the mystical can be a meeting place and a starting point. From a post-modern point of view mysticism can be seen as rational humility towards the complexity of the world. There are things we cannot know, that others might have come closer to by other means than epistemic knowledge. From a religious point of view mysticism opens for a curiosity of how others have experienced and explained the ungraspable mystery. In this paper I have tried to explore the concept of border thinking to better understand Fethullah Gülen and reach that meeting place beyond East and West.

References

Anzaldúa, G. 1999. *Borderlands/La frontera: The New Mestiza*. San Francisco: Aunt Lute Books.

Beck, U. 1992. *Risk Society: Towards a New Modernity*. London: Sage.

Clack, B. R. 1999. *Wittgenstein, Frazer and Religion*. London: Macmillan Press.

Gandhi, L. 1998. *Postcolonial Theory: A Critical Introduction*. Edinburgh University Press: Edinburgh.

Gillman, L. 2007. "Beyond the Shadow: Re-scripting Race in Women's Studies." *Meridians: Feminism, Race, Transnationalism* 7(2).

Göle, N. 2000. "Snapshots of Islamic Modernities." *Daedalus* 129(1).

Gülen, M. F. 2000a. *Advocate of Dialogue*. Fairfax: The Fountain.

———. 2000b. *Questions and Answers about Faith*, Vol. 1. Fairfax: The Fountain.

———. 2001. *Kalbin Zümrüt Tepeleri*. Istanbul: Nil Yayınları.

———. 2004a. *Essays–Perspectives–Opinions*. New Jersey: The Light Inc.

———. 2004b. *Key Concepts in the Practice of Sufism: Emerald Hills of the Heart*, Vol. 1, revised edition. New Jersey: The Light Inc.

———. 2004c. *Toward a Global Civilization of Love and Tolerance*. New Jersey: The Light, Inc.

———. 2005a. *Questions and Answers about Islam*, Vol. 2. New Jersey: The Light, Inc.

———. 2005b. *The Essentials of the Islamic Faith*. New Jersey: The Light, Inc.

Haraway, D. J. 1991. "Situated Knowledges: The Science Question in Feminism and the Privilege of Partial Perspective." *Simians, Cyborgs, and Women: The Reinvention of Nature*. London: Free Association Books.

Huntington, S. P. 1993. "The Clash of Civilizations?" *Foreign Affairs* 3.

International Studies Review. 2000. Special issue – Continuity and Change in the Westphalian Order 2(2).

Jasanoff, S., ed. 1995. *Handbook of Science and Technology Studies* (published in cooperation with the Society for Social Studies of Science). Thousand Oaks: Sage publications.

Khuri, R. K. 2007. "Intersections of Ways towards Tolerance and Coexistence: From Daoism and Sufism to Kant and Gülen." *Peaceful Coexistence: Fethullah Gülen's initiatives in the Contemporary World*, ed. İhsan Yılmaz. Leeds: Leeds Metropolitan University Press.

Kuhn, T. S. 1970. *The Structure of Scientific Revolutions*. Chicago: University of Chicago Press.

Michel, T. 2007. "Fethullah Gülen: Following in the footsteps of Rumi." *Peaceful Coexistence: Fethullah Gülen's Initiatives in the Contemporary World*, ed. İhsan Yılmaz. Leeds: Leeds Metropolitan University Press.

Mignolo, W. D. 1999. *Local Histories/Global Designs: Coloniality, Subaltern Knowledges, and Border Thinking*. Princeton: Princeton University Press.

Mohanty, C. T. 1989–90. "On Race and Voice: Challenges for Liberal Education." *Cultural Critique* 14.

Motturi, A. 2003. *Filosofi vid mörkrets hjärta: Wittgenstein, Frazer och vildarna*. Göteborg: Glänta produktion.

Nursi, B. S. 2004. *The Words: On the Nature and Purposes of Man, Life and All Things*. Istanbul: Sözler Publications.

Özdalga, E. 2003. "Worldly Asceticism in Islamic Casting: Fethullah Gülen's Inspired Piety and Activism." *Critique* 17.

Rosenthal, F., 1970. *Knowledge Triumphant: The Concept of Knowledge in Medieval Islam*, Leiden: E. J. Brill.

Sardar, Z. 1989. *Explorations in Islamic Science.* London: Mansell.

———. 2002. *Introducing Science.* Cambridge: Icon Books.

Sevindi, N. 2008. *Contemporary Islamic Conversations: M. Fethullah Gülen on Turkey, Islam, and the West*. New York: SUNY Press.

Stenberg, L. 1996. *The Islamization of Science: Four Muslim Positions Developing an Islamic Modernity*. Stockholm: Almqvist & Wiksell International.

Suhrawardi, Y. D. 1999. *Hikmat al-Ishraq/Philosophy of Illumination*. Provo: Brigham Young University Press.

Sunnemark, F. 2001. *An Inescapable Network of Mutuality: Discursivity and Ideology in the Rhetoric of Martin Luther King, Jr.* Gothenburg: Acta universitatis Gothoburgensis.

CHAPTER 4

The Limits of Otherness in Fethullah Gülen's Dialogic Methodology for Interfaith Encounters

Irina Vainovski-Mihai

INTRODUCTION

This essay aims to explore Fethullah Gülen's teaching on interfaith encounters, highlighting his dialogic methodology proposed to a globalized world in which models and theories of clashes are still prominent. These theories, concludes Gülen, stem from lack of trust in the religion of the "other" and, rather often than not, from easily passing over the common points. According to Gülen, dialogue is not a superfluous endeavor, but an imperative ("Dialogue is a must") and it should start by "giving precedence to common points." Gülen holds that the tendency toward factionalism exists within human nature. A meaningful and nonetheless necessary goal, he says, should be to make this tendency non-threatening and even beneficial. To fully appreciate the significance of Gülen's accomplishments and the challenges he is facing, one must understand the perspective from which he approaches the subject of interfaith dialogue. Based on his viewpoints about representation constructs mentioned above, the purpose of my paper is to investigate the way in which this renowned Islamic thinker limits the "domain" of "otherness" or dilutes many apparently consolidated boundaries.

My paper starts from the assumption that recognizing the "other" on common grounds is a prerequisite of dialogue. The first section of the essay focuses on conceptual frameworks for defining the "relevant" alterity (Orientalism, Balkanism, Occidentalism) and theories of conflict (models of clashes, competing meta-narratives). The second section looks into identity markers expressed or implied by Sufi thinkers (Al-Ghazzali, Rumi, Nursi). The third section discusses Gülen's awareness of the "other" and consequently (as detailed in the fourth section) his identification of common grounds for dialogue.

To achieve the aim of my study, throughout all four sections, Gülen will be presented in a textual exchange of ideas with other thinkers and authors.

In Search of the Other

The first question of the possibility or impossibility of establishing a dialogue revolves around the issue of "otherness" and the way in which the representation of the "other" is construed. From the mere cognitive category (that generally separates the world into "us" and "them"), to the more intricate pattern of exclusion (in-group, out-group) and to the confrontational mentality (*us*-versus-*them*), the discourse on identities assumes different statuses and has distinctive implications. "For the nation to exist, it is presupposed that there is some other community, some other nation, from which it needs to distinguish itself" (Triandafyllidou 1998, 594). Furthermore, the relevance of the identity is valued in terms of alienation: "The culture of the Other is perceived fundamentally not within its own coherence but as a distance (*écart*) that separates it from our own culture" (Todorov 1989, 342).

For Edward Said (in his book first published in 1978 and then reprinted in 1995 under the title *Orientalism: Western Conceptions of the Orient*), "Orientalism" is a discursive system and a cultural creation through which the West imagined the East as its immature "other." Orientalism, he asserts is "a style of thought based upon an ontological and epistemological distinction made between 'the Orient' and 'the Occident'" (Said 1995, 8). Said's notion of the modes of making if not an entirely conflictual Other, at least a problematic one, is brought further conceptually and extended geographically by Larry Wolff (*Inventing Eastern Europe: The Map of Civilization on the Mind of the Enlightenment*, 1994) and Maria Todorova (*Imagining the Balkans*, 1997). An attempt at a mirror image came in 2004, with Ian Buruma and Avishai Margalit's *Occidentalism: The West in the Eyes of its Enemies*. The representations of the West are equally biased and stereotyping, Buruma and Margalit show, and even more, they formulate the conflicting identities already in the title. It is beyond the scope of this paper to evaluate the terms *Occidentalism* and *West* as set forth by the two authors in a rather unsystematic way. Nonetheless, they offer a counter-reflection to the other imagined identities (Orientalism and Balkanism), a partial one in as much as Buruma and Margalit identify the roots of Occidentalism (hostility to the city, revulsion felt towards materialism, adherence to commercial rather then heroic models, etc.) in both the East and Europe.

All the above-mentioned authors succeed, to paraphrase Fethullah Gülen's words, in summing up an entire book and theory in a title. Literally, Gülen says that "sometimes the sun appears in an atom, a flood in a drop, and a book in a sentence" (Gülen 2005, 108), after he warns that "every flood comes from tiny drops whose existence and size are neglected. Gradually, it reaches a level that cannot be resisted. A society's body is always open to such types of flood" (Gülen 2005, 107). Cultural regions like the Orient, the Occident, the Balkans, Eastern Europe are interrogated by these authors and deconstructed as a process of imagining in the quest for self-identification and self-assertion. Scholarly literature draws substantially from their findings, either acknowledging or denying them, but in both cases broadening the field of research. Moreover, elements of their deconstruction become the tiny drops of possible floods since they are conceptualized, legitimated and put forward as a utility at hand for cross-cultural understanding. In 1994, the professor of international management and business strategy Martin J. Gannon proposed to a globalized world "an innovative method, the *cultural metaphor*, for understanding easily and quickly the cultural mindset of a nation and comparing it to those of other nations" (Gannon 2004, 7). The book was followed by several related volumes (*Cultural Metaphors: Readings, Research Translations, and Commentary*, Sage Publications, 2000; *Working Across Cultures: Applications and Exercises*, Sage Publications, 2000; etc.) and new editions in which the author gradually extends the application of his methodology from seventeen to 23, then to 28 nations and ultimately to 29, in the May 2009 version.

Religion remains a strong cultural signifier embedded with many layers of meaning and a crucial dimension in the representation of the "other" (Vainovski-Mihai 2000, 192). In so far as identity turns out to be meaningful only through distinction from the alterity, the "significant others" (Triandafyllidou 1998, 595) thus conceived, invented, imagined (to use Said's, Wolff's, and Todorova's terms) may shape the construction of the in-group individuality itself (Appollonia 1996, 138) and draw a clear-cut borderline between the in-group of *us* and the out-group of *them*. Nowadays religion is no more a mere marker of otherness in tune with the overtones of travel literature, in which the author's homeland "serves as organizing center for the points of view, the scales of comparison, the approaches and evaluations" (Bakhtin 1981, 103), and neither is it a label for exoticism. "Exoticism presupposes a deliberate opposition of what is alien to what is one's own, the otherness of what is foreign is emphasized, savored, and elaborately depicted against an implied background of one's own ordinary and familiar world" (1981, 101). Narratives of belonging are founded on old discursive practices and a new hegemonic understanding of modernity. The rhetoric and mechanisms of othering formulate religion as a key element of definition, as a crucial factor in assessing the same and the other, the center and the periphery, thus embedding the opposition between modernity and non-modernity.

"Currently much intellectual effort, in academic circles as well as in the larger political and cultural arena, is devoted to probing many of the world's problems in terms of a clash between secular modernity and religious tradition. At the center of this controversy is a critique of Islam, treated as a more or less coherent culture, civilization, or historical tradition. Typically, Islamic 'fundamentalism' is seen as the prototype of religious extremism. And Islamic 'civilization,' according to scholars such as Bernard Lewis and Samuel P. Huntington, has remained 'backward' in comparison with 'the West,' because 'something went wrong' earlier in 'Islamic history'" (Matin-Asgari 2004, 293). In fact, less smoothly than in Matin-Asgari's paraphrase, Huntington (1996, 217) claims in all-encompassing terms that "the underlying problem for the West is not Islamic fundamentalism. It is Islam." Huntington's article "The Clash of Civilizations?" appeared in the Summer 1993 issue of *Foreign Affairs* and then developed into a book published three years later. His theory of clashes stands on the assumption that people define their identity by what they are not and makes, among others, the dichotomy between Western "*homo economicus*" and Eastern "*homo Islamicus*" (Bilici 2006, 16). He puts forth the same belligerent way of thought with regard to Western multicultural communities, within which the viable solution for coexistence is not the respect for differences as part of our nature (Gülen 2004, 249), but assimilation: "Western Culture is challenged by groups within Western societies. One such challenge comes from immigrants from other civilizations who reject assimilation and continue to adhere to and to propagate the values, customs, and cultures of their home societies" (Huntington 1996, 304). For Gülen, the multicultural experience fosters the dialogue between two entities that authenticate each on equal terms while perceiving, accepting and even valuing the differences. The desire for mutual understanding should not mean a desire for the monologue engendered by a process of assimilation.

In his turn, Edward W. Said stands far from denying the theory of global cultural conflict; he only plants it in another ground and labels it as "the Clash of Ignorance":

> In fact, Huntington is an ideologist, someone who wants to make 'civilizations' and 'identities' into what they are not: shut-down, sealed-off entities that have been purged of the myriad currents and countercurrents that animate human history, and that over centuries have made it possible for that history not only to contain wars of religion and imperial conquest but also to be one of exchange, cross-fertilization and sharing. This far less visible history is ignored in the rush to highlight the ludicrously compressed and constricted warfare that 'the clash of civilizations' argues is the reality. (Said 2001, 12)

Thomas Michel too implies that conflicts, tensions, and misunderstandings proceed from ignorance. The visibility of Islam in the last decades is often due to sensational events complemented by a certain disinterest or suspicion towards non-violent forms of Islam and the efforts to find common grounds for dialogue: "Someone whose knowledge of Islam is limited to the headlines of the daily newspapers is likely to believe that the religion teaches terrorism, suicide attacks, oppression of women, and hatred for those outside its community." (Michel 2004, i–ii)

In the same vein, Philip Marfleet argues, "Among the many criticisms of Huntington, one is central: that in order to construct global cultural blocs he has imposed uniformity upon a vast range of people of diverse beliefs and practices. This homogenization of cultures serves to simplify to an extreme degree the complexity of human experience. It denies the fluidity of cultural forms—the complex processes of appropriation and modification of ideas which have taken place for millennia across all manner of borders." (Marfleet 2003, 83)

Among the theories of conflicts, a third one is gaining preeminence, with Stanley Hoffmann's "clash of globalizations" (Hoffmann 2002). His model is not grounded on the conflict between separate civilizations, but between different visions of globalization like secularism, fundamentalism or multiculturalism and the sharing of commonly acceptable values. "How can one make the global house more livable? The answer presupposes a political philosophy that would be both just and acceptable even to those whose values have other foundations" (Hoffmann 2002, 109).

On account of Hoffmann's model, John O. Voll (2003, 247) includes Gülen among the designers of bridges arching over the clashes of globalizations: "In the clashing visions of globalizations, Fethullah Gülen is a force in the development of the Islamic discourse of globalized multicultural pluralism. As the impact of the educational activities of those influenced by him attests, his vision bridges modern and postmodern, global and local, and has a significant influence in the contemporary debates that shape the visions of the future of Muslims and non-Muslims alike."

Meanwhile, Michel regards Gülen's thinking and deeds as an alternative to the theory of the "clash of civilizations":

> The need for dialogue among people of faith has been underscored by the events of the past few years. Interreligious dialogue is seen as an alternative to the much-discussed "clash of civilizations." Those who do not subscribe to the theory that a civilizational clash is inevitable are proposing instead a dialogue of civilizations, an exchange of views aimed at mutual enrichment, a sharing of insights that can lead all to a deeper understanding of the nature of God and God's will for humankind on this planet. (Michel 2004, i)

As for Gülen himself, the clash is a matter of deep awareness and accountability both for the self and the other: "Humanity is a tree, and nations are its branches. Events that appear as heavy winds hurl them against each other and cause them to clash. Of course, the resulting harm is felt by the tree. This is the meaning of 'Whatever we do, we do it to ourselves'" (Gülen 2005, 106). On the other hand, confrontation may result from turning a deaf ear to the seemingly contradictory ideas of the other:

> People who do not think like you might be very sincere and beneficial, so do not oppose every idea that seems contradictory and scare them off. Seek ways to benefit from their opinions, and strike up a dialogue with them. Otherwise, those who are kept at a distance and led to dissatisfaction because they do not think like us will form huge masses that confront and smash us. Even if such dissatisfied people have never achieved anything positive, the number of states they have destroyed is beyond counting. (Gülen 2005, 89)

Gülen makes here a good point in the appeal to dialogue and in showing the possible consequences of the "competing meta-narratives," a phenomenon deemed by Robert A. Hunt to be one of the main problems facing interfaith dialogue in the contemporary world. "It is the problem of Western civilization claiming to provide the paradigm within which it can understand all other civilizations better than they understand themselves. It is the notion that science can understand religion better than religion understands itself. It is the notion that Christianity understands other religions better than they understand themselves, or that Islam understands Christianity and other religions better than they understand themselves. In the face of such meta-narrative claims, all dialogue essentially ceases because from within a meta-narrative there is no need to listen to the other" (Hunt 2006, 6).

Maintaining the dichotomy between Western "*homo economicus*" and Eastern "*homo Islamicus*" reinforces the monistic conception of modernity as a Western product. The substitution for "homo Islamicus" of "Muslim homo economicus," on the other hand, implies a multiplicity of modernities and the existence of commonalities. Emphasis on such commonalities enables interaction and cooperation rather than competition between these two identities (Bilici 2006, 16). Or, as Gülen puts it, "We were in friction with one another. We separated in order to solve the problem, but we didn't attain what we expected to. As a result, we lost our own paradise" (Gülen 2000a, 218).

Sufi Perceptions of the Other

"Although a term comes into popular or academic usage at a certain given historical period, this does not mean that the concept itself is new. The idea may have been discussed in previous ages, but other terms were used to describe it. [Terms like] 'tolerance,' 'engagement with the other,' and 'future of dialogue' are good examples of this," points out Michel (2002, 5) in analyzing Bediüzzaman Said Nursi's views on engagement with the other and taking on the task of identifying Bediüzzaman's ideas couched in the popularly accepted terminology of the day. Michel draws attention to the nine rules of sincerity spelled out in *Risale-i Nur* as a summing up of Nursi's principles of tolerance towards alterity (defined as a "particular outlook"):

i. To act positively, that is, out of love for one's own outlook, avoiding enmity for other outlooks, not criticizing them, interfering in their beliefs and sciences, or in any way concerning oneself with them.
ii. To unite within the fold of Islam, irrespective of particular outlook, remembering those numerous ties of unity that evoke love, brotherhood and concord.
iii. To adopt the just rule of conduct that the follower of any right outlook has the right to say, "My outlook is true, or the best," but not "My outlook alone is true," or "My outlook alone is good," thus implying the falsity or repugnance of all other outlooks.
iv. To consider that union with the people of truth is a cause of Divine succor and the high dignity of religion.
v. To realize the individual resistance against the attacks of the people of misguidance and falsehood, which arise from

their solidarity, and through the union of the people of truth, to create a joint and collective force also, in order to preserve justice and right in the face of that fearsome collective force of misguidance.

vi. To preserve truth from the assaults of falsehood,
vii. To abandon the self and its egoism,
viii. And give up the mistaken concept of self-pride,
ix. And desist from all insignificant feelings aroused by rivalry. (Nursi 2000, 203)

Moreover, Nursi ranks the designation of the relevant other in terms of moral values and ethics when he speaks about "the collective personality of Europe":

> It should not be misunderstood; Europe is two. One follows the sciences which serve justice and right and the industries beneficial for the life of society through the inspiration it has received from true Christianity; this first Europe I am not addressing. I am rather addressing the second corrupt Europe which, through the darkness of the philosophy of Naturalism, supposing the evils of civilization to be its virtues, has driven mankind to vice and misguidance. As follows: On my journey of the spirit at that time I said to Europe's collective personality, which apart from beneficial science and the virtues of civilization, holds in its hand meaningless, harmful philosophy and noxious, dissolute civilization. (Nursi 2000, 160)

J. B. Schlubach (2005) steps further back along the Sufi tradition in quest of the representation of the other. Although, when he is evaluating al-Ghazzali's and Jalaluddin Rumi's thinking, he is not setting up his textual methodology like Michel, he is ultimately finding the perception of the other standing implicitly in the discourse of tolerance. He concludes that identity markers entirely melt away and "tolerance does more than just hinder hostilities. In this sense of tolerance, the boundaries between Other and One become indistinct and lose focus" (Schlubach 2005, 6).

Gülen engaged in Nursi's call for dialogue taking up equally an entire rich and generous Sufi heritage. "Gülen must be located and understood squarely within that Sufi tradition indicated by al-Ghazzali and Rumi. Both the latter insist on non-belligerence in love and do not prescribe strategies for foreign affairs. Both move toward the ultimate end of dimming distinctions between Self and Other, not of prescriptions for peaceably protecting borders. Both lean away from the possibility of defining each other as 'other.' Both look on the world of humankind as oriented to eternity, not hegemony. Both define Gülen" (Schlubach 2005, 17).

Gülen's Constructs of Otherness

In a broad overview of Gülen's and the Gülen Movement's national-security identity, Hasan Kösebalaban (Kösebalaban 2003) distinguishes three perceptions of the other defined by varying degrees of separation: (1) a strong degree of common identification with the Turkic world (a Kantian other in which the distinction between the self and other is weak, where the self perceives the other as part of its own group), (2) a lack of common identification with the West but a desire to integrate with Western institutions (an approximate of the Lockean other, where the self perceives the other as a peaceful rival), (3) a strong lack of common identification with Iran (an identity shaped in terms of a Hobbesian culture of anarchy in which not only the distinction between self and other is clear, but also the self perceives the other as a security threat) (Kösebalaban 2003,172–173).

Although Kösebalaban applies his research primarily to national-security identity, further on he reformulates Gülen's Lockean other with a view to religion and leaves aside the expression of antagonism: "For him [Gülen], 'it cannot be imagined that a devout person would be against the West,' as the West became supreme following universally applicable rules and principles" (Kösebalaban 2003, 177). Thus, we come upon the irenism characteristic to Gülen's deeds and words, like the following: "To devotees, the value of their ideals transcends that of the earthly ones to such an extent that it is almost impossible to divert them from what they seek—God's gratuitous consent—and lead them to any other ideal. In fact, stripped entirely of finite and transient things, devotees undergo such a transformation in their hearts to turn to God that they are changed because they recognize no goal other than their ideal. Since they devote themselves completely to making people love God and to being loved by God, dedicating their lives to enlightening others, and, once again, because they have managed to orient their goal in this unified direction, which in a sense contributes to the value of this ideal, they avoid divisive and antagonist thoughts, such as "they" and "we," "others" and "ours" (Gülen 2004, 100).

Deliberation as social learning is meant to develop an understanding of various ideational worlds. "Once participants acknowledge that they are interacting with representatives of other traditions, the purpose of deliberation becomes one of appropriation and evaluation of other perspectives by mastering the skills of putting oneself into others' shoes" (Kanra 2005, 516). The awareness of the other, the dialogical approach may transform the experience of the other into an experience of the self. "Different positions mean different understandings. Once you accept that, you can benefit from others' thoughts and ideas" (Gülen 2000a, 206). The hermeneutic exercise of accepting the difference, as a prerequisite to communication, broadens one's ideational scope, without sweeping away the original perspective. "In the fusion of horizons, nobody is fully detached from his/her subjective views, yet [he/she] arrives at a new juncture..." (Kanra 2005, 517).

In today's global village, differences (beliefs, races, customs, traditions) increase in visibility and interact more and more. The desire to level the differences means wishing for the impossible, points out Gülen, because each individual is like a unique realm unto himself/herself; therefore, peaceful coexistence "lies in respecting all these differences, considering these differences to be part of our nature and in ensuring that people appreciate these differences. Otherwise, it is unavoidable that the world will devour itself in a web of conflicts, disputes, fights, and the bloodiest of wars, thus preparing the way for its own end" (Gülen 2004, 250). The respect for the other is equated by Gülen to respect for the self: "When interacting with others, always regard whatever pleases and displeases yourself as the measure. Desire for others what your own ego desires, and do not forget that whatever conduct displeases you will displease others. If you do this, you will be safe not only from misconduct and bad behavior, but also from hurting others" (Gülen 2005, 59). Frustrations might be a result of somebody's own (mis)conduct, because "Deserving what we expect is very important" (Gülen 2004, 34).

Common Points and Shared Responsibilities

> I believe and hope that the world of the new millennium will be a happier, more just, and more compassionate place, contrary to the fears of some people. Islam, Christianity, and Judaism all stem from the same root; all have essentially the same basic beliefs, and are nourished from the same source. Although they have lived as rival religions for centuries, the common points between them and their shared responsibility to build a happy world for all of the creatures of God make interfaith dialogue among them necessary. (Gülen 2004:231)

Gülen rejects conflicting attitudes, prejudice and half-truths and entirely understands the growing interdependencies of today. Establishing and maintaining dialogue should be rooted in giving precedence to the common points and in avoiding divisive issues. Completely aware that "globalization is rapidly making dialogue between holders of meta-narrative claims a near existential necessity" (Hunt 2006, 6), Gülen invites to emotional coexistence through dialogue across differences and on the basis of joint ethical criteria. A famous verse of the Qur'an calls the People of the Book to a common ground with Muslims: "Say: O People of the Book! Come to an agreement between us that we will not worship other than God, and that we shall ascribe no partner unto him, and that none of us shall take others for lords beside God" (Qur'an, 3:64).

All the great universal religions share the same ethical values. "Regardless of how their adherents implement their faith in their daily lives, such generally accepted values as love, respect, tolerance, forgiveness, mercy, human rights, peace, brotherhood, and freedom are all values exalted by religion. Most of these values are accorded the highest precedence in the messages brought by Moses, Jesus, and Muhammad, upon them be peace, as well as in the messages of Buddha and even Zarathustra, Lao-Tzu, Confucius, and the Hindu prophets" (Gülen 2000b, 4). Thus, Gülen limits the distance between the self and the other and defines dialogue as "an activity that has human beings at its axis" (Gülen 2004, 50) forming a bond between people. Meanwhile, he rejects confrontational models of dialogue as detrimental. In support of this approach he quotes Bediüzzaman Said Nursi: "'Those who are happy about their opponent's defeat in debate have no mercy.' He explains the reason for this: 'You gain nothing by defeating someone. If you are defeated and the other person is victorious, then you would have corrected one of your mistakes'" (Gülen 2004, 74).

As Hunt aptly remarks, the Muslim Sufi tradition offers Gülen a generous resource for overcoming the problem of competing meta-narratives, and "it allows him, and it can allow those inspired by him, to come to fellow humans not just as bearers of truth, but as seekers of truth" (Hunt 2006, 9). Through him, Muslim practice and traditions are preserved and brought into consonance with the timely need for interfaith encounters meant to draw understanding and sharing of interpretations.

Conclusion

This paper has shown that the images built on the *us–them* disparity tend to create a perceptual gap much larger than the real one, stimulating divergence. Discourses on imagined entities like "Islam," "the Orient," "Europe," "the West" threaten to become a significant obstacle to setting up a dialogic methodology. Our findings in this paper highlight the fact that the drawbacks of such conflicting or competing images and meta-narratives are felt equally by both entities. "Whatever we do, we do it to ourselves." Or, to use the terminology of post-colonial studies, one is simultaneously both the subject and the object.

This study pinpoints Fethullah Gülen's methodology fundamentals for interfaith encounters, in a hermeneutical approach. Gülen's concrete interaction with the *other* deserves a further study on its own.

Gülen condenses his notion of dialogue and sets out its main pillars as follows: "I believe that interfaith dialogue is a must today, and that the first step in establishing it is forgetting the past, ignoring polemical arguments, and giving precedence to common points, which far outnumber polemical ones" (Gülen 2000b, 6). He examines the boundaries that separate *us* from *them* and shows that they are always volatile even if they are sketched in terms of objectivity or impartiality. In reality, they only lay down the contour of a divide and define the span of distance. Gülen is not denying the existence of the other, neither does he overlook its importance, but he warns of the implications of instituting boundaries or of maintaining the apparently consolidated ones. With this in mind, he reformulates the definition of the other as a reverse projection of the self into one that assesses the other as an autonomous entity outside the self and puts forward a dialogic methodology which relocates the landmarks for the domain of alterity and at the same time dilutes the frontiers between an *us* and a *them*.

References

Appollonia, A. C. d'. 1996. "Les morales de l'autre: les identités nationales." B. Badie, ed. *L'Autre: études réunies par Alfred Grosser*. Paris: Presses de Sciences Politiques, 137–150.

Bakhtin, M. M. 1981. "Forms of Time and the Chronotope in the Novel." *The Dialogic Imagination. Four Essays,* M. M. Bakhtin, M. Holquist, C. Emerson. Austin: University of Texas, 84–258.

Bilici, M. 2006. "The Fethullah Gülen Movement and Its Politics of Representation in Turkey." *The Muslim World*, 96:1–20.

Gannon, M. J. 2004, 3rd edition. *Understanding Global Cultures: Metaphorical Journeys through 28 Nations, Clusters of Nations, and Continents*. Thousand Oaks, California: Sage Publications.

Gülen, M. F. 2000a. "Dialogue." *Advocate of Dialogue: Fethullah Gülen* comp. A. Ünal and A. Williams. Fairfax, Virginia: The Fountain, 193–217.

———. 2000b. "The Necessity of Interfaith Dialogue: A Muslim Perspective." Fairfax, Virginia: *The Fountain* magazine, 3: 4–9.

———. 2004. *Toward a Global Civilization of Love and Tolerance*. New Jersey: The Light, Inc.

———. 2005. *Pearls of Wisdom*. New Jersey: The Light, Inc.

Hoffmann, S. 2002. "Clash of Globalizations." *Foreign Affairs,* 81:104–109.

Hunt, R. A. 2006. Introduction. *Muslim Citizens of the Globalized World: Contributions of the Gülen Movement,* ed. R. A. Hunt, Y. A. Aslandoğan. New Jersey: The Light, Inc., 1–10.

Huntington, S. P. 1996. *The Clash of Civilizations and the Remaking of the Modern World*. New York: Simon & Schuster.

Kanra, B. 2005. "Democracy, Islam and Dialogue: The Case of Turkey." *Government and Opposition* 40:515–539.

Kösebalaban, H. 2003. "The Making of Enemy and Friend: Fethullah Gülen's National-Security Identity." *Turkish Islam and the Secular State*, ed. H. Yavuz & J. L. Esposito. New York: Syracuse University Press, 170–183.

Marfleet, P. 2003. "The 'Clash' thesis: War and Ethnic Boundaries in Europe." *Arabic Studies Quarterly* 25:71–88.

Matin-Asgari, A. 2004. "Islamic Studies and the Spirit of Max Weber: A Critique of Cultural Essentialism." *Critique: Critical Middle Eastern Studies* 13:293–312.

Michel, T. 2002. "Four Frontrunners in Peace: People Who Have Devoted Their Lives to Peace." *Said Nursi's Views On Muslim-Christian Understanding*. Istanbul: Söz Yayınları, 64–70.

———. 2004. Foreword. *Toward a Global Civilization of Love and Tolerance,* M. F. Gülen. New Jersey: The Light, Inc., i–iii.

Nursi, S. 2000. *The Flashes*. Trans. Şükran Vahide. Istanbul: Sözler Publications.

Said, E. W. 1995. *Orientalism: Western Conceptions of the Orient*. London: Penguin Books.

———. 2001. "The Clash of Ignorance." *The Nation*. October 22:11–12.

Schlubach, J. B. 2005. "Tolerance Is Love: Gülen, Ghazzali, and Rumi." Paper presented at "Islam in the Contemporary World: The Fethullah Gülen Movement in Thought and Practice" conference at Rice University, Houston, Texas.

Todorov, T. 1989. *Nous et les autres. La réflexion française sur la diversité humaine*. Paris: Editions du Seuil.

Triandafyllidou, A. 1998. "National Identity and the 'Other.'" *Ethnic and Racial Studies* 21:593–612.

Vainovski-Mihai, I. 2000. "'A food of their kind.' The gastronomic image of the eastern other in a time of a tensioned self-identification." *Annals of the Sergiu Al-George Institute for Oriental Studies* IX–X:191–200.

Voll, J. O. 2003. "Fethullah Gülen Transcending Modernity in the New Islamic Discourse." *Turkish Islam and the Secular State*, ed. H. Yavuz & J. L. Esposito. New York: Syracuse University Press, 238–247.

CHAPTER 5

Dialogue as a Source of Peaceful Coexistence

Karina Korostelina

INTRODUCTION

In his speeches and writings, Fethullah Gülen stresses the role of democracy, peace, dialogue, and tolerance in the development of peaceful coexistence between Muslim and non-Muslim populations. Some Western concepts of national identity connect tolerance with submission to the values of a majority. However, as Gülen (2004a) explains, "Tolerance does not mean being influenced by others or joining them; it means accepting others as they are and knowing how to get along with them." As Gülen repeatedly stresses, to overcome violence and hate, people of different religions and faiths must develop an atmosphere of mutual respect and peaceful coexistence and engage in dialogue. He stresses that dialogue decreases our disagreements with one another.

This paper analyzes Fethullah Gülen's approach to dialogue and tolerance and uses it as a framework for the development of a dialogue considering the formation of a common secular identity (national or regional). The paper argues that it is possible to negotiate different identities and shows how to employ dialogue as a tool for reconciling identity differences. The aim of a dialogue like this is the development of a peaceful coexistence between Muslim and non-Muslim groups within a secular context. Such a dialogue leads to the development of a new dual identity with one component connected to religious identity and another component that reflects membership in a secular nation. The paper concludes with a summary of the role of interfaith dialogue in the promotion of national and international tolerance, peace, and mutual understanding.

Gülen's Approach to Dialogue

Since the early 1980s, Gülen has developed an approach to interreligious understanding and has formulated a framework for an Islamic approach to interfaith dialogue. "Gülen has championed dialogue as a necessary commitment and activity in the contemporary world" (Carroll 2007, 12). Through his "dialogue" with other thinkers and writers with different perspectives, Gülen showed the importance of dialogue in the process of revision of knowledge by focusing profoundly on the issues of peace and human life. Gülen formulated his conception of dialogue within the framework of the religio-philosophical worldview of Islam, which protects humanity and categorically forbids any disrespect for it. "Gülen... has a clear vision of human greatness, of the traits that define great human beings, those who actualize in themselves the highest and best of human potential" (Carroll 2007, 38).

Even though Gülen acknowledges the differences between the West and Muslim countries, he sees no innate incongruity between Islam and democracy in general. He shows that both approaches have a basic commitment to human beings and their essential rights. Thus, dialogue between people of different cultures and faiths could bring mutual understanding, respect, and dedication to justice. "Dialogue means the coming together of two or more people to discuss certain issues, and thus the forming of a bond between these people. In that respect, we can call dialogue an activity that has human beings at its axis" (Gülen 2004b). Dialogue about identities does not require the acceptance of another group's way of life or values, nor does it provoke assimilation. It offers an opportunity to understand the beliefs, ideas, and positions of others, as well as the basis of their identity. "Accepting all people as they are, regardless of who they are, does not mean putting believers and unbelievers on the same side of the scales. According to our way of thinking, the position of believers and unbelievers has its own specific value… even though I have such strong feelings and thoughts about [the Prophet] this does not prevent me from entering into dialogue with someone who does not think or believe the same" (Gülen 2004a).

The conflicts between European governments and Muslim minorities in the past several years have made clear the necessity of dialogue about vital issues of tolerance, identity and religion in society. As Carroll (2007, 11) stresses, "We may isolate ourselves and craft the arc of our lives into familiar orbits of people who look, think, speak, believe, and pray like us, but such isolation or minimizing of difference is not workable over time. In today's world of global connectedness, we must develop the capacity to dialogue and create relatedness with people vastly different from us. Part of that project involves finding ideas, beliefs, purposes, projects, and so forth, on which we can achieve resonance with each other." In his article (2004a) "Tolerance in the Life of the Individual and Society," Fethullah Gülen points out that "today, more than anything else, our society is in need of tolerance… our citizens in European countries can only live in harmony in those countries by means of a vast atmosphere of tolerance." For Gülen, dialogue, tolerance, and trust reinforce each other: tolerance is the acceptance of differences that arise from dialogue in order to pursue the larger goal of cooperation:

> Hostility is unacceptable. Relationships must be based on belief, love, mutual respect, assistance, and understanding instead of conflict and realization of personal interest. Social education encourages people to pursue lofty ideals and to strive for perfection, not just to run after their own desires. Right calls for unity,

> virtues bring mutual support and solidarity, and belief secures brotherhood and sisterhood. Encouraging the soul to attain perfection brings happiness in both worlds. (Gülen 2002a)

Gülen has not only helped develop the conception of interfaith dialogue, but has actively contributed to the development of concrete action across the globe. He personally brought about several initiatives that strengthened connections among people and cultures involved in conflict. "Our ongoing activities are for the good of all humanity. They should not be considered limited to our own country, Turkey" (Gülen 1993). Thus, in the late 1980s, Gülen initiated dialogue between Greeks and Turks in Turkey in order to discuss discrimination and prejudice against the Greeks. He established good relations with the Greek Orthodox Patriarch Bartholomew. This dialogue brought hope and positive change for Greeks in Turkey.

Negotiating Identities

People sharing the same identity believe they have similar fates and interests and, in some cases, share a mutual experience of deprivation and aggravation due to another group. Identity groups like these establish the common goals of improving their social situation and of reinforcing in-group loyalty and support in order to achieve their aims. Radical religious identity leads to the clear recognition of intergroup differences and can even reinforce the willingness of group members to perceive others as enemies, encouraging them to fight for power and resources. The negotiation of a national identity aims at bringing together previously incompatible identities within a larger, common group concept that would be mutually acceptable to everyone and would connect all groups and parties. As Kelman (1997b, 2001) stresses, the possibility of negotiating and changing identity rests on two facts: (1) identities are not zero-sum concepts like territory and resources; and (2) as social constructs, they can be reconstructed and redefined. "In fact, the reconstruction of identity is a regular, ongoing process in the life of any national group. Identities are commonly reconstructed, sometimes gradually and sometimes radically, as historical circumstances change, crises emerge, opportunities present themselves, or new elites come to the fore" (Kelman 1997b, 338).

Undoubtedly, national identities contain some core elements that cannot be negotiated: a sense of peoplehood, attachment to the land, confidence in history, and commitment to culture and religion (Kelman 2001). In order to protect the essential components of identity, only a few central elements can be reconsidered and redefined. To reduce intergroup tensions and develop a common understanding, these elements can be discussed and negotiated during specially organized workshops.

One of the basic assumptions of the theory of protracted identity-based conflict is that basic needs are not negotiable and that people need universal justice. In reality, basic needs and conceptions of justice are also identity-based concepts, and their meaning depends on the meaning and structure of particular in-group identities. Security, freedom, and community have different meanings and are perceived in various ways among people with different social identities. Even for the same person, a basic human need can have a different meaning depending on which social identity is most salient for that individual at that moment.

Conceptions of justice also differ among groups. For some, justice means revenge and prosecution of perpetrators; for others, it suggests reimbursement in terms of money, contributions, or labor. In other cases, people can be satisfied with truth and reconciliation committees where people who have committed violence confess and admit their crimes, and some communities are ready to forgive the perpetrators if they show their commitment to peace. The study conducted in Uganda (Pham et al. 2005) has showed that four groups within the country (the Gulu, Kitgum, Lira, and Soroti regions) have different perceptions of justice. Over half of the respondents perceived "reconciliation" as "forgiveness" (52%). Thirty-one percent defined justice as trials; however, the respondents in Soroti showed only 15 percent agreement with this statement. For one-third (35%) of people in that region, justice meant reconciliation, while only 12 percent and 3 percent of Gulu and Kitgum, respectively, agreed that justice was reconciliation. Eleven percent of all respondents associated justice with "truth and fairness," while 22 percent of the respondents in Kitgum saw this association.

Understanding of the different meanings associated with concepts like justice, reconciliation and basic human needs can help to reconcile different identities, even conflictual ones. An identity negotiation workshop includes a dialogue which considers differences in the meaning of these basic concepts, and which develops ways for their accommodation. Because of variations in the perception of basic human needs and justice among different groups, it is possible to negotiate these concepts among groups in order to develop new common perceptions and a new identity which reconciles existing identities.

The process of identity negotiation in a workshop setting has been described by Kelman (1982, 1997b, 2001, 2004) as an informal, unofficial progression of give-and-take among groups whose ideas of their respective national identities conflict with one another. In this paper I describe negotiation processes that are designed to create a new common identity or reconcile conflictual identities. Such a practice can be organized into different forms, ranging from mediation between ethnic groups in the self-determination process of creating a new nation, to the redefinition of identity through reconsidering history, and from negotiations among political leaders to discussion workshops in communities. Kelman (2001) describes negotiation of national identity within the context of the Israeli–Palestinian conflict. He stresses that each group perceives its own relationship to land and history, the defining element of identity, as its exclusive right, rejecting the claims of the opposing group as illegitimate. To overcome this, the parties have to "accept the possibility that certain elements of identity may be shared with the other, acknowledging that the other also has a profound attachment to the land, anchored in authentic historical ties to it" (Kelman 2001:193). Sharing the land requires developing common elements of identity as well as an understanding that land can belong to two groups simultaneously. As Kelman describes in his work, the Israelis and Palestinians began to accept a shared concept of land but failed to perceive Jerusalem as a mutual element of their identities.

The example of Morocco shows that, in a Muslim country, national identity can be negotiated in two ways: through an exchange among the new nationalist elites, and by stressing characteristics and traditions common for all religious groups. A vision of a national Moroccan identity was developed during a negotiation led by the king as a compromise among various visions of the elite (for a more in-depth analysis, see Mezran 2001).

One of the most important problems for newly independent Morocco was a confrontation between the mainly urban Arab Istiqlal Party and the Berber tribes of the interior. King Mohammed realized the importance of creating a common concept of Morocco's national identity and decided to act as a mediator in order to facilitate agreement around the various competing concepts of identity. The concept of national Moroccan identity had various meanings among different parties, including the Arabist party, the Islamist conservative portion of the Istiqlal Party, the Democratic Party, the Berber socialist Popular Movement, and secular republican Marxist groups. Instead of acting as a party in this conflict over identity, Mohammed V declared himself a national leader and symbol of national unity. He aimed to develop a shared national identity and to unite fragmented elites under the monarchy. To make the negotiation process more compelling, the king himself intervened as the mediator at the center of numerous competing visions and interests.

The basic concept of national identity which emerged included three main components: Islam, Arabism, and Moroccanism. Moroccan Islam became the central component of the uniting national identity. Mohammed V stressed the strong connection between Islamic and democratic principles, the "innovative" role of

Islam in society, and its function as a basis for national identity. To mediate differences between the Arabist Istiqlal and the Berberist Popular Movement, the king developed the idea of Moroccan Arabism, stressing that the vast majority of Moroccans are not pure Arabs but rather Arabized Berbers. As a basis for territorial nationalism that would unite different elites, Mohammed V developed the conception of Moroccanism (*Marocaineté*). This national territorial idea became the main content of a new Moroccan national identity that encompassed, but never denied, local Arab and Berber as well as tribal and urban identities.

Using these three concepts, King Mohammed developed agreement among all the rival groups. He conducted his negotiations on the basis of an "issue" framework, approaching the development of a common identity by discussing single issues. As Mezran (2001, 156) describes, the King "acted in such a way as to appease each party within this framework while asking concessions of others." Thus, he convinced the left wing of the Istiqlal Party to support the formation of a National Consultative Assembly by offering a wide agrarian reform. He combined recognition of the Berbers' political party, the Popular Movement, with the implementation of a wide campaign of Arabization.

In addition to being an integral part of nation building, the negotiation of identities is also essential in the process of developing peaceful coexistence between former adversaries. Conflictual identities have to be reconfigured to accommodate a new type of intergroup relations and to accept multiple meanings of events. This step-by-step process of re-creating identity demands the cooperation of both parties.

Identity Dialogue

Identity dialogue aims to transform dominant identities into multiple identities with polymodal meanings. The structure of narratives that are based on the perception of them as an enemy and that reflect negative attitudes, feelings, and stereotypes, can be replaced by a new structure rooted in a nonviolent self-image. This type of dialogue has to involve participants in a discussion of the values, needs, and traditions of each religious group and the possibilities for the creation of a common identity concept that would satisfy and respect the values and needs of all religious groups. This new common identity resolves contradictions between religion and the secular state, expands people's conceptions of membership from exclusive groups in conflict to a single more inclusive group, and makes attitudes toward other religious groups more positive, even in spite of a long history of mutual offences. On the basis of a positive balance between religious and secular values as well as differences and similarities, all members of the new group develop positive attitudes and stereotypes of each other.

The first step for identity reconstruction involves increasing awareness of the role of identity in conflicts, of we–they perceptions, and of collective axiology which leads to violence. Stories of different conflicts and violent actions, analyzed through the prism of identity, provide insights about the salience and dominance of identity, alterations of perception, misbalanced and projective axiologies, and accepted or expected aggressive behaviors. It is important that the cases of conflict discussed at this stage of the workshop be dissimilar to the conflict in which the participants are themselves involved. Similar events and situations will provoke comparisons and strengthen negative attitudes and emotions. The more distinct the cases are from the participants' experience, the lower the resistance to understanding the possibility of misperceptions. Thus, in Crimea, where conflict developed between Muslim Crimean Tartars and Orthodox Russians, the discussion of conflict in Bosnia exacerbates strong negative feelings and aggravates aggressive attitudes toward other ethnic groups. On the other hand, the discussion of conflicts perceived as very different from the Crimean situation, such as discriminatory practices in the Dominican Republic or violence in Sudan and Rwanda, allows for more objective analysis which increases understanding of the roots of vicious actions and which facilitates changes in perceptions, leading to the recognition of aggressive behaviors of one's own group.

The recognition of the violent actions of one's ingroup, as well as the human rights of outgroups, poses a threat to ingroup identity, which rests on the idea of "positive *we*–negative *they*." As Gülen (2002) has stressed, "Many Muslims, even educated and conscious ones, believe the West seeks to undermine Islam with ever more subtle and sophisticated methods... Western colonialism is remembered. The Ottoman State collapsed due to European attacks. Foreign invasions of Muslim lands were followed with great interest in Turkey." Gülen sees this problem in the framework of the global problem of increasing negativity in the perceptions of others. He stresses that "communities and diverse groups within communities live with apparently endless anger, hatred, and detestation, pursuing plans of murder and complete destruction that would never previously have been held possible. Nations and all segments within nations wish to get rid of the people or groups that they see as *other*" (Gülen 2008a).

Gülen points out that the ways in which people perceive each other are influenced by hate and disgust: "It seems that we have forgotten how to act like human beings... We are overcome with rancor and hatred, flushed with fury, and regard one another with feelings of vengeance. Our breasts are drained of love, a haze of loathing obscures our feelings, and for so many years now the magical aura of love is alien to our perceptions. We constantly produce evil in our thoughts" (Gülen 2008b). Another source of negative perceptions between Muslims and non-Muslims is the prevalence of emotion over rational vision. Gülen shows that people who are possessed by anger and hate cannot think or perceive the world rationally: "He or she is paralyzed in terms of faculties, disabled in terms of reasoning, and so lost that she or he can neither think healthily nor can behave normally. Nor is he or she consistent. Bursting into anger, they sometimes destroy and reduce everything around them to ashes, and sometimes they are even in unrelenting rage and fury to the point that they eat out their own heart" (Gülen 2008a). In his article "Longing for Love" Gülen further develops this idea: "So many of us act upon our emotions and abandon rational thinking. We trample and silence those who do not think the same as us; this, indeed, is our most distinct character. We plunge forward, headstrong, on our own way, without considering for even a moment that there may be other solutions to different problems; thus, we lead the way to destruction in many cases where we could have been a means for constructive solutions" (Gülen 2008b).

The gradual "transformation" of Islam into an ideology of conflict or into a political ideology by "Islamists" has also made people suspicious of Islam and Muslims. Inter-religious perceptions impact the personalities of people: "While a person keeps looking at things or events from the perspective of certain considerations, their character and temperament will gradually take shape in line with that way of thinking" (Gülen 2008c). Negative views foster negative traits of character. Gülen shows that negative thoughts about others, called "ill-opinion" (*sui dhan*) are connected with suspicion, jealousy, and rancor. In addition, they lead to self-pride and vanity. People became prisoners and victims of their own negative perceptions: "They never become tired of rancor and cannot get over their anger. Never even attempting to manage their anger, they incessantly run after wickedness, one evil deed after the other, under the influence of these evil thoughts, and they try to make the wrong seem right" (Gülen 2008a).

These images of others as evil and non-human also influence people's behavior. As Gülen (2008c) notes, "People's way of thinking shapes their behavior." The results of negative perceptions filled with hate are violent actions, bombings and murders: "One party carves out the eye of another or murders them; the other responds by running into crowds as suicide bombers or driving a car filled with explosives through them. Violence is everywhere, as savage as, or perhaps even more atrocious than that caused by any barbarian"

(Gülen 2008b). Dialogue also can change the negative perception of Muslims: "This negative image has been fed to the world and now we must once more communicate the essential facet of Islam to those who are presumed to be civilized, using the principle of 'gentle persuasion'" (Gülen 2004b).

Emphasis on people's good will and good nature is one of the major themes of Gülen's teaching: "This is not constructing something from zero point, but revealing things which were about to be declared 'extinct' despite their existence, and became alien to us due to their inactiveness as reemerging waters in useless holes. We say, 'Human beings are not animals… They are human beings…' Therefore, our behavior should be on a different line and should include different criteria. Our relations with human beings should be based on being human" (Gülen 2006b). Thus, the humanity of people can serve as an important basis for overcoming negativity in relations and perceptions.

The values, needs, and traditions of each religious group has to be perceived not as contradictory to each other, but in the framework of the respect for religion that would satisfy and respect the values and needs of all religious groups. Gülen (2004c) stresses "the necessity of increasing the interests we have in common with other people. In fact, even if the people we talk with are Jews and Christians, this approach still should be adopted and issues that can separate us should be avoided altogether." He also emphasizes that "for interfaith dialogue to succeed, we must forget the past, ignore polemics, and focus on common points" (Gülen 2002b*)*. This approach can also help resolve contradictions between religion and the secular state, change people's conceptions of a membership from different groups in conflict to much more inclusive group, and make attitudes toward other religious groups more positive, even if they have a long history of mutual offence.

As discussed above, one of the ways of transforming negative perceptions into positive ones involves redefinition of us and acceptance of in-group negative deeds. As Gülen (2008c) has stressed, "when an individual is performing self-criticism—given that they do not give in to hopelessness—they should be harsh." Describing people of good heart, he also stresses that it is important to analyze and fight one's own negative intentions and thinking: "People of heart are too busy fighting their selves and their misdemeanors to be interested in the misdeeds of others. In contrast, they set an example to others of what a good person should be, leading others to attain higher horizons" (Gülen 2006a).

The acknowledgment of negative in-group actions requires reviewing and reconceptualization of in-group identity that always invokes strong resistance. In-group members have a strong aspiration to defend their positive self-image and refuse to accept negative information that can destroy it. Stressing other important components of the meaning of identity, such as cultural heritage, deep traditions, history of peaceful coexistence with other groups, and so on, can help preserve a high level of self-esteem and in-group pride.

Such narrative intervention has to emphasize the positive features in the self-description of an in-group, such as "peaceful people," "values of tolerance," "open-mindedness and understanding," and "pleasure of forgiveness." These images always exist in the self-portrayal of all people and serve as powerful sources of self-esteem and pride. As Gülen (2004c) points out, "I can and do say that peace, love, forgiveness, and tolerance are fundamental to Islam." He continues, "Indeed, peace is of the utmost importance to Islam; fighting and war are only secondary occurrences which are bound to specific reasons and conditions. In that respect, we can say that if an environment of peace where all can live in peace and security cannot be achieved in this land, then it would be impossible for us to do any good service for society or for humanity" (Gülen 2004b).

The next step is to change the negative perception between Muslims and non-Muslims. Gülen (2008c) emphasizes that people do not have the right to judge others and blame them for their mistakes and deeds: "A person should not see all other people as superior to themselves, nor should they project the weakness or ugliness that is in their own person on others through suspicion or make the mistake of criticizing certain attitudes and acts of others without knowing the underlying reasons… There is no such ethical rule that requires us to investigate the faults of others, to divulge them, or to embarrass these people. On the contrary, searching out faults and mistakes, divulging sins, and humiliating others are considered to be immoral in Islam."

The emphasis on peaceful images of the in-group and out-group can provoke supporting narratives that describe the in-group's peaceful history and glory and positive situations in inter-ethnic relations. Such storytelling by different people will reinforce them through complementary ideas and constructive character. The positive emotions produced during this process will strengthen the formation of peaceful self-concepts and positive perceptions of others, with an emphasis on tolerance, reconciliation, and goodwill. Gülen shows the importance of positive acceptance of the other, avoidance of competition and judgment. "People of heart ... open their hearts to everyone, welcoming them affectionately, and appearing as an angel of preservation in society. Regarding their deeds and attitudes, they try to be compatible with everybody, they try to avoid vicious competition with others, and they avoid resentment…Furthermore, they give generously to other people in pursuit of positive activities and they try to show as much respect as possible to the philosophy and ideas that other people adopt" (Gülen 2006a). Moreover, Gülen calls for perception of others without criticism. Describing people of heart, he says that "they turn a blind eye to what other people may do wrong. Responding with a smile to those who have displayed negative attitudes, such people nullify bad behavior with kindness, not thinking to hurt anybody, even when they have been hurt over and over again" (Gülen 2006a).

By stressing peaceful images of the in-group and the out-group simultaneously, dialogue can provoke supporting narratives that describe the in-group's peaceful history and glory as well as positive situations in interethnic relations. Such storytelling by different constituents of each group will reinforce these narratives through complementary ideas. The positive emotions produced during the dialogue workshops will strengthen the formation of peaceful self-concepts, with an emphasis on tolerance, reconciliation, and goodwill.

To turn such models into positive attitudes and actions, the intervener has to take the next step: form a common, overarching identity that can lead to the de-escalation of conflict. Common or shared identities can reduce intergroup hostility by minimizing attention to ethnic/racial/religious differences and instead creating the sense that all involved are "one unit." Sources for an overarching identity can be found in a common geographic location, common national ideas, shared community problems, and so forth. For example, Gülen (2002a) shows the similarities of democracy and Islam: "In democratic societies, people govern themselves as opposed to being ruled by someone above. The individual has priority over the community in this type of political system, being free to determine how to live his or her own life. Individualism is not absolute, though. People achieve a better existence by living within a society and this requires that they adjust and limit their freedom according to the criteria of social life... As Islam holds individuals and societies responsible for their own fate, people must be responsible for governing themselves."

By asking questions about positive present and future developments and the possibilities of collaboration with others, the intervener can reinforce the formation of a common identity. The intervener's task is to facilitate the creation of narratives of productive partnership, which are based on peaceful concepts of the in-group and which emphasize possible positive images of out groups.

The formation of a new common identity is possible only if in-group members do not perceive that the new overarching identity being created poses any danger or threat to their primary identity (ethnic/racial/religious). If values, core ideas, or new identity needs contradict the possible (perceived) values and ideas of the existing identity, a new circle of violence can begin as a response to this sense of threat. The intervener has to construct the concept and perception of the new common identity very carefully, using narratives of existing collaboration and situations of successful teamwork. By asking such questions as, "What can we do together to make our future better?" and "What can we do for our children?" practitioners can shift the emphasis of narratives from past opposition to mutual understanding, mutual responsibilities, and the mutual defense of human rights among former enemies. In this case, the concepts of a peaceful in-group and of a new "*we*-ness" will be developed simultaneously and will reinforce each other.

Conclusion

In his teaching and writing, Gülen constantly stresses the necessity of dialogue as the way to overcome differences and bring about peace to society. "People with different ideas and thoughts are either going to seek ways of getting along by means of reconciliation or they will constantly fight with one another.... In fact, our nation should have this dynamic today and should give it priority; it should represent tolerance to the world because our glorious ancestors captured the hearts of people by means of tolerance and became the protectors of the general peace. The longest period of peace in the Balkans and the Middle East, which have always been volatile areas, was realized with the enduring tolerance of our ancestors. From the moment that tolerance and those great representatives left history, this region became void of peace and contentment...At the same time, our citizens in European countries can only live in harmony in those countries by means of a vast atmosphere of tolerance" (Gülen 2004a).

The formation of a peaceful common identity requires a set of actions that includes increasing identity awareness, re-conceptualizing salient identities, negotiating a common identity concept, and forming a civic and multicultural meaning of national identity. The construction and understanding of national identity can be created by the facilitation and mediation of an *ongoing dialogue* among representatives of ethnic and religious groups. Gülen points out essential components of the process of dialogue, including the recognition of the in-group's violent actions and the human rights of the out-group, and focusing on common points. He also stresses the importance of emphasizing the positive features in the self-description of an in-group, such as "peaceful people," "value of tolerance," "open-mindedness and understanding," and "pleasure of forgiveness." Gülen argues that no interfaith dialogue will be successful without increasing interest in the values and ideas that people have in common and without an understanding of the similarities between democracy and Islam.

Gülen stresses that dialogue may be possible only if people will change their aggressive blaming perceptions and behavior. To alter their negative perceptions, people have to recognize and accept their own good nature: "We are far removed from representing our unique status among all of existence. Despite all the qualities we possess which the angels envy, we engage in acts that even evil spirits would be embarrassed by... We are all humans; this means our genes all come from those of Prophet Adam and our essence is from the Truth of Ahmad. Then, come! Let us rise up against all the evil motives and cry out to all the worlds that we are vicegerents on the earth and that we are racing for the heavens! Let us make angels appreciate the eminence of being human!" (Gülen, 2008b). Thus, the structure of narratives, based on the perception of *they* as an enemy and reflecting negative attitudes, feeling, and stereotypes, can be replaced by a structure rooted in a nonviolent self-image.

Dialogue about the meaning and content of a common national identity also includes discussion of and planning for specific actions in specific regions that must be achieved in order for the successful formation of this identity to take place. The formation of a national identity with an emphasis on multicultural and civic meanings will help to construct a society with (1) equal rights for all ethnic groups and adequate resources to maintain their ethnic culture and (2) a distinctive non-ethnic civic culture with peaceful coexistence and civic responsibility among all citizens. A new common identity would include elements of the particular ethnic and religious identities and common goals, values, and aims. It would be based on the reconciliation of past grievances, with an emphasis on future mutual development and peaceful coexistence within the state. As Gülen (2004b) stresses, "we can say that if an environment of peace where all can live in peace and security cannot be achieved in this land, then it would be impossible for us to do any good service for society or for humanity." His teaching is a roadmap that can be used for establishing sustainable dialogue between Muslim and non-Muslim groups and civilizations.

References

Byman, D. 1997. "Explaining Ethnic Peace in Morocco." *Harvard Middle Eastern and Islamic Review*, 4, 1–29.

Carroll, B. J. 2007. *A Dialogue of Civilizations*. The Light, Inc.

Gülen, M. F. 1993. *Günler Baharı Soluklarken*. Izmir: Nil Yayınları.

———. 2002a. "A Comparative Approach to Islam and Democracy." Retrieved September 23, 2007, from http://en.fgulen.com/content/view/1027/49/.

———. 2002b. "The Necessity of Interfaith Dialogue." Retrieved September 25, 2007, from http://en.fgulen.com/content/view/1053/49/.

———. 2004a. "Tolerance in the Life of the Individual and Society." Retrieved September 25, 2007, from http://en.fgulen.com/content/view/1800/33/.

———. 2004b. "The Two Roses of the Emerald Hills: Tolerance and Dialogue." Retrieved September 24, 2007, from http://en.fgulen.com/content/view/1806/33/.

———. 2004c. "Dialogue in the Muhammadan Spirit and Meaning." Retrieved September 25, 2007, from http://en.fgulen.com/content/view/1811/33/.

———. 2006a. "The Portrait of People of Heart." Retrieved September 25, 2007, http://www.fethullahgulen.org/recent-articles/2234-the-portrait-of-people-of-heart.html.

———. 2006b. "An Analysis of the Tolerance Process." Retrieved September 23, 2007, http://www.fethullahgulen.org/recent-articles/1942-an-analysis-of-the-tolerance-process.html.

———. 2008a. "Compassion." The Fountain, 63.

———. 2008b. "Longing for Love." The Fountain, 64.

———. 2008c. "We Should Think Well of Others." The Fountain, 64.

Kelman, H. C. 1982. "Creating the Conditions for Israeli–Palestinian Negotiations." *Journal of Conflict Resolution* 1, 39–76.

———. 1997a. "Nationalism, Patriotism, and National Identity: Social-psychological dimensions." *Patriotism in the Lives of Individuals and Nations*, ed. D. Bar-Tal and E. Staub. Chicago: Nelson-Hall, 165–189.

———. 1997b. "Negotiating National Identity and Self-determination in Ethnic Conflicts: The Choice between Pluralism and Ethnic Cleansing." *Negotiation Journal* 13, 327–340.

———. 2001. "The Role of National Identity in Conflict Resolution." *Social Identity, Intergroup Conflict, and Conflict Reduction*, ed. R. D. Ashmore, L. Jussim, and D. Wilder. Oxford and New York: Oxford University Press, 187–212.

———. 2002. "Interactive Problem Solving: Informal Mediation by the Scholar-practitioner." *Studies in International Mediation: Essays in Honor of Jeffrey Z. Rubin*, ed. J. Bercovitch. New York: Palgrave Macmillan, 167–193.

———. 2004. "Reconciliation as Identity Change: A Social-psychological Perspective." *From Conflict Resolution to Reconciliation*, ed. Y. Bar-Siman-Tov. Oxford, England: Oxford University Press, 111–124.

Mezran, K. 2001. "Negotiating National Identity in North Africa." *International Negotiation* 2, 141–173.

Pham, P., Vinck, P., Wierda, M., Stover, E., and di Giovanni, A. 2005. *Forgotten Voices: A Population-based Survey of Attitudes about Peace and Justice in Northern Uganda.* Retrieved September 25, 2007, from http://www.ictj.net/downloads/ForgottenVoices.pdf.

Rosoux, V. B. 2001. "National Identity in France and Germany: From Mutual Exclusion to Negotiation." *International Negotiation* 2, 175–198.

Chapter 6

Gülen on Healing the Rift between Islam and the West

Richard Penaskovic

Introduction

Ever since 9/11 the Western world has been gripped by Islamophobia. The first part of the word refers to Islam, the religion, rather than to Muslims. The second part of the word, phobia, denotes an unreasonable and irrational fear. Islamophobia has been fanned in large part by some media outlets. One has only to listen to the anti-Muslim bigotry spewed by some commentators to get a glimpse of the extent of the problem. The media speaks of Islam in terms of violent terrorists, veiled women, super-rich sheikhs, and bearded mullahs. One wonders whether a negative image of Islam is often unconsciously compared with an idealized image of Christianity. Should we not strive to understand Islam as Muslims understand it?

Many people in the Western world associate Muslims with terrorism as if they were the first group to use terror as a tactic. Actually, several groups in the 1970s used terror as a tactic, including the Japanese Red Army, the Irish Republican Army, the Weathermen in the United States, and the Baader-Meinhof Gang in Germany. Also, suicide bombing was first used not by Muslims but by the Tamil Tigers of Hindu heritage.

At times the labels "terrorist" and "freedom fighter" are interchangeable. When the Afghan Mujahiddin conducted terror operations against the USSR, many observers, including US President Ronald Reagan, called them "freedom fighters." In fact, some evangelicals made support for the Afghan Mujahiddin part of a biblical checklist for members of Congress (Cole 2007, 4). The adage, "One person's terrorist is another person's freedom fighter," contains more than a morsel of truth.

Whether one uses the terrorist label to describe violent acts depends to a large extent whether one considers the acts to be morally legitimate or not. To call another a terrorist is a subjective judgment about the moral correctness of specific violent acts, as well as a descriptive statement about them (Juergensmeyer 2001, 9). The Islamic world resents the infiltration of foreign products, such as movies, ideas, and music from the West. In the West, on the other hand, we see a resurgence of flag-waving nationalism along with an increasingly strong suspicion of immigrants and foreigners.

Gülen on Globalization

The term *globalization* has become part of our global consciousness, that is, an aspect of the proliferation of words centered on and connected with the word *global*. As a concept globalization refers both to the compression of the world and the intensification of consciousness of the world as a whole (Robertson 1992, 8; Fletcher 2008, 395). How, precisely, does Gülen see globalization? Gülen argues that we live in a global world, one tremendously different from the past. Today what happens in one part of the world is known throughout the world almost instantaneously because of the Internet and the cell phone.

Technology has caused our world to shrink (Ameli 2004, 324). Those who think that any radical changes in a particular nation will be determined by that nation alone are in for a rude awakening. We exist in a totally interdependent world, a global village (Gülen 2002,

28; Stiglitz 2002, 9; Kellner 2007, 54). Today we see quite clearly that because of globalization the international system operates as a single economy. For example, the 2009 financial crisis in the United States over sub-prime loans and the bailout of banks and mortgage holding companies such as Fannie Mae and Fannie Mac had repercussions in stock markets in London, Tokyo, and Moscow.

Moreover, the events of 9/11 show that the world has become one place. The attacks on the United States shook the world on a global scale. For example, within two hours of the terrorist attacks on the World Trade Center towers, almost 80 percent of Sweden knew about it. In fact, both national radio and television in Sweden changed their programming in order to cover the story (Larsson 2005, 34).

Gülen (2000a, 240) notes that today's world has a plethora of problems that can only be solved by many nations working together in unison. Some examples of these transnational problems are global warming, the regulation of outer space, over-fishing of the seas and oceans, water pollution, and dealing with international terror, to name but a few. Like the word *spirituality*, globalization has no one specific meaning but is an ambiguous term. Globalization means different things in various cultures and geographical regions.

The West often views globalization in economic terms, namely as the free and untrammeled movement of capital, goods, labor, and services across borders. In other words, globalization refers to the integration of technologies, nations, and markets to an unprecedented degree. However, globalization has taken on a different meaning in the Middle East and North Africa (MENA) region. There globalization is perceived in mainly ideological terms and hence attacked as a new brand of imperialism, although some like King 'Abdullah of Jordan view globalization in positive terms. In the MENA region many people see globalization as a threat to their cultural, economic, or political independence. This is the case despite the fact that the MENA region, *in toto*, remains one of the least globalized areas in the world (Looney 2007, 342).

Gülen thinks of globalization in more than economic and ideological terms. For him, globalization is a more encompassing term and as such refers to connectivity and interdependence in all areas of life: cultural, ecological, economic, political, religious, social, and technological. Gülen would be comfortable in saying that globalization is the process by which the experience of everyday living is becoming standardized around the world (Penaskovic 2007, 194).

How precisely has the world become a global village according to Gülen? Gülen (2004, 230) attributes globalization to advances in communication, science, and technology. He points out that thanks to advances in technology, more specifically electronic technology, both the acquisition and exchange of information is gradually growing. The Internet would be a good example of globalization. Through the Internet people all over the world can be linked together. At the same time, though, those without computer access are left in the dark and ignored. Sometimes entire regions are cut off from the Internet and telephone, for example, in parts of South America where the Amazon River flows in areas inaccessible to roads.

Gülen points out that we should appreciate the wonders of civilization such as technology and scientific research. However, he argues that science and technology and the speed and globalization they bring in their train ought to serve a higher purpose. He asks whether space (which is being compressed more and more on a daily basis until the world is no larger than a village) and time (which people are trying to shrink to zero) simply serve a small minority of individuals or whether they serve a transcendent purpose. (Gülen 2004, 235)

Gülen does not believe that science and technology are ends in themselves. Rather, they are completely at the service of human needs and desires, respect for individual privacy, and human values. It is extremely important to ask who controls science and technology and what purposes they serve. In the hands of an irresponsible minority, science and technology can turn our lives into a living hell. In the hands of angels, however, no one will suffer. Science and technology are worthy of respect only to the extent that they direct us toward humane goals, bring about happiness and peace, and serve the general harmony of the world.

Gülen came upon the notion of globalization by reflecting on the nature of the universe. For him, the universe is clearly and unmistakably an inseparable whole. Every being on every level is interrelated to every other being. Quantum physics points toward this unity or unbroken wholeness of the universe, including human beings (Gülen 2000b, 4). Since there exists an interdependence of all beings in the universe, whatever causes a flower to exist must be responsible for a tree, notes Gülen; and whatever causes a tree to exist must be responsible for the forest. Such interrelatedness and interconnectedness mean that all beings in the universe help each other.

Gülen finds the order, organization, and harmony in the world completely fascinating. He does not believe that this order and harmony derive from matter or come about randomly through chance. Rather, in his view, everything that happens in the universe takes place according to certain laws. The most trifling event cannot occur without putting into the equation one who has an absolutely perfect knowledge of the universe and who possesses absolute power. That one is God the Creator. Gülen (2000b, 13) argues that God reveals himself in the book of nature which, addressed to humanity as a whole, makes known its Author.

Islam and the West: Friends or Foes?

In the last century a number of factors have escalated the confrontation between Islam and the West. Population growth in the Muslim world has increased unemployment. Hence, we have increasing numbers of Muslim youth who migrate to the West or join Islamist causes. The Islamic resurgence has restored Muslim pride in their own identity and cultural values vis-à-vis the West. The efforts of the West to make universal its institutions and values, to maintain its economic and military superiority, and to intervene in conflicts within the Muslim world continue to generate strong resentment among Muslims. As long as both Islam and the West refuse to change, the conflict will continue in the future as it has for the past fourteen centuries (Huntington 1996, 212).

In speaking about Islam and the West several important distinctions must be made. First, one must distinguish between Islam as a religion and Islamism as a political ideology. This distinction is implicit in Gülen's writings, for example, in his essay, "True Muslims Cannot Be Terrorists" (2002, 95–98). As a religion Islam insists very strongly on peace, love, and tolerance. For Gülen, love binds existence. Gülen notes that Muhammad, a man of affection, was given the title, "Habibullah," which comes from the word, *habib*, meaning "he who loves God and is loved by God." Gülen narrates several stories (*hadith*) from the Prophet Muhammad that make the point that there is no room for hatred in Islam or in the multicolored world of its ambassador, Muhammad, the Prophet, may his name be blessed. For Gülen (2002, 99), the entire Qur'an has tolerance and forgiveness as its foundation.

Second, when Gülen speaks of Islam is he thinking of *customary* Islam characterized by the combination of regional practices and those shared by most Muslims around the globe who desire to surrender themselves to the will of Allah as revealed in the Qur'an or of *revivalist* Islam? Note, though, that this customary tradition is not a unitary one, since each region of the Islamic world has made its own version of customary practices. For example, the customary tradition in Morocco includes reverence for saintly figures that some Muslims argue have no basis in the Qur'an. Does Gülen have in mind *revivalist* Islam, the most common alternative to customary Islam? The revivalist tradition, also known as fundamentalism or Wahhabism, argues against local deviations and practices. Instead, it stands for a renewed stress on Arabic as the language of revelation, the illegitimacy of local political institutions, (since they usurp the sovereignty of Allah), the revival of practices from the early period of Islam, and, lastly, the authority of the revivalists like

Muhammad ibn 'Abd al-Wahhab as the sole qualified interpreters of Islam. I would argue that Gülen speaks of Islam in the former sense, that is, of *customary* Islam (Kurzman 1998, 6).

Gülen thinks that Islam has become a way of life or a culture for some Muslims who do not adhere to Islam as a faith. These Muslims have restructured Islam in accordance with their own thoughts. Gülen sums up his feelings on this matter by asserting that an Islamic world does not exist. What does this imply? Gülen means that some Muslims live Islam as it suits their own purposes so that a Muslim culture is dominant rather than an Islamic one (Gülen 2004, 186).

Many so-called Muslim intellectuals, rejecting their societies' traditional modes of thinking and acting, blindly import and imitate the modern Western worldview, which they see as based entirely on materialism that excludes the metaphysical and spiritual dimensions of life. Instead, they restrict their thinking to what they can perceive and experience through their senses, thus excluding the spiritual, metaphysical dimensions of life. These Muslim intellectuals discard metaphysics and spirituality in the name of certain notions such as *civilization*, *enlightenment*, *modernity*, *progress*, and *Westernization* (Gülen 2000a, 355).

Gülen sees this as a huge mistake. He points out that Western scientific thought, although materialistic, has not always been separate from metaphysics and spirituality. He notes that it is difficult to find an atheistic scientist and philosopher in the West before the nineteenth century. He also notes that modern Western civilization has its foundation in three entities: Greek thought, Roman law, and Western Christianity, the last of which contributes a spiritual dimension to Western thought. For Gülen there exists only one way to fully understand and value life, viz., to experience existence through the prism of metaphysical thinking and spirit (Gülen 2000a, 356).

If the term *Islam* can be problematical, so too does the term *the West* have its ambiguities. First, the latter term can be understood geographically. As such, it refers to those countries in which most of the inhabitants are Christian and where pluralistic political systems and free-market economies thrive. Historically, this would include Canada and the United States, Europe west of the former East Germany, plus Australia and New Zealand, along with South Africa and possibly Israel since the majority of Israelis are Jewish and not Christian.

Today, however, one could argue that past geographical boundaries defining the West no longer hold and are porous. In the post–Cold War era the West incorporates Russia, the urbanized, moneyed elites in Latin America, and an advanced capitalist, democratic Japan as well as Taiwan, and the power-brokers in the oil-rich Gulf States like Dubai (Abramsky 2007).

Second, the term *the West* can be understood culturally either as part of the world that shares a Judaeo-Christian heritage or as synonymous with secular humanism and the mind-set of the Enlightenment. The question, then, boils down to this: Does *the West* refer to a state of mind or to a particular plot of land? There exists no doubt where Gülen comes down on this question. Gülen understands the West mainly in cultural and religious terms. For him Western civilization has been based on the hard sciences, such as physics and mathematics. In his estimation a gigantic conflict has arisen in the West between the hard sciences and religion, a conflict that need not exist. Gülen sees the West as succumbing to materialism and secularization.

The East, on the contrary, has emphasized moral, religious, and spiritual values, while at the same time, giving short shrift to the hard sciences and technology. Gülen (2002, 27) notes that the estrangement between Islam and the West began with the Crusades, followed by the Mongol invasion of the Muslim world. The Crusades were crucial in setting a pattern for the long history of mistrust and conflict between Islam and the West (Lewis 2004, 47). Although Jesus in the gospels taught love of neighbor, the Crusaders apparently never learned the meaning of love of neighbor.

The Crusades have made Muslims wary of entering into dialogue with Christians, but many other factors also play a role. For example, Gülen (2002, 33) points out that in the twentieth century far more Muslims were killed by Christians than all Christians killed by Muslims throughout the march of history. Attacks by Europeans collapsed the Ottoman Empire, while Christendom's portrayal of Islam as a crude, distorted version of Judaism and Christianity upsets many Muslims to this very day.

Gülen notes that Islam and the West existed apart from one another. This separate existence was a gigantic mistake. Islam downplayed science and the intellect, whereas the West lost sight of metaphysics, spirituality, and eternal values and verities. As a result, the last centuries have seen colonialism, destructive wars, racial discrimination, immense massacres and holocausts, and social injustice (Gülen 2002, 28). In hopes of building a better future, Gülen insists on interfaith dialogue as the key to overcoming the historical conflict between Islam and the West. Gülen says, in effect, "Let the healing begin." We now turn to this extremely important matter of dialogue.

The Absolute Necessity of Dialogue

Just as there has been a re-thinking of Islam by Christians in the last two decades, so too there has been a reassessment of the West and of Christianity by Muslims in recent years. Despite the tension and struggles between Muslims and Christians for almost fourteen centuries, Gülen calls interfaith dialogue a necessity. Throughout his writings Gülen (2002, 34) insists that for interfaith dialogue to succeed, we must forget the past, ignore polemics, and focus on the points both religions have in common. He notes that all revealed religions are based on peace, security, and world harmony. Like Jesus' call to "turn the other cheek," Gülen (2000a, 192) exhorts us to return good for evil and overlook discourteous treatment.

Gülen calls dialogue and tolerance the two roses of the emerald hills. What exactly does Gülen mean by dialogue? Gülen understands dialogue as the encounter between two or more individuals in order to discuss specific issues. What does dialogue bring about? Dialogue helps form strong bonds between the dialogue partners. Gülen calls dialogue an activity that has the human person as its axis. In dialogue the discussants share their thoughts and their feelings. Knowledge alone does not suffice. In dialogue we open our minds and hearts to others in a compassionate and loving way. Dialogue is not something we achieve on our own. Only with the help of God can we concentrate on matters of dialogue and toleration, says Gülen (2004, 55).

Does it make sense for Muslims, Christians, and Jews to engage in dialogue if all the discussants know ahead of time that unity of faith will not come about? I would answer this question with a resounding yes. An outsider's perspective may shed light on how I see my own religion. The questions and challenges of others may force me to think more deeply about my own beliefs. Also, what comes out of the dialogue cannot be known ahead of time.

What is the goal or purpose of dialogue? Is it to convert others? Is it to drive one's dialogue partner into the ground using tools of superior logic and insight? Not at all, retorts Gülen. Dialogue exists so that the truth emerges from the dialogue more clearly. One enters into dialogue neither to best one's dialogue partner nor to satisfy one's ego. Rather, the goal is to know one's dialogue partner better and to understand why others believe as they do. It is to be hoped that the truth will emerge out of the conversation. In dialogue we seek to find God's truth in other men and women who are also God's creatures. I would also note that in a dialogue one must be willing to be convinced by the arguments of one's dialogue partners. Gülen (2000a, 259) would say that in dialogue with others, particularly in interfaith dialogue, one must not neglect such important items as mutual understanding, dedication to justice, and, above all, respect for one's dialogue partner.

In short, Gülen sees dialogue as a give and take between two or more parties involving respect, honesty, and compassionate love. In dialogue one must retain one's own integrity while encountering the other as a true other, who is neither falsely similar, nor too alien from oneself. Not only is interfaith dialogue critical to peace in today's world, there must also be a dialogue of cultures, and of civilizations, that is, a dialogue between Islam and the West, one that transcends the dialogue between Islam and Christianity.

The Awesome Power of Love

Gülen speaks of love in conjunction with compassion, forgiveness, and tolerance. For him these are the pillars of dialogue and basic human values. Love has the ability to overcome every force and to elevate every soul that absorbs it. It also prepares the soul for the journey to eternity. Love is, then, our human way of making contact with eternity. Gülen speaks eloquently of love as the greatest power, the most radiant light, and the chain that binds humans one to another. On the individual level, love is the sultan that reigns on the throne of the human heart. On the social level, there is nothing more lasting or more real than love in any nation or society. For Gülen, it is axiomatic that love should be as vast as the oceans. Love calls us to take every soul to our bosom.

Those who have the greatest share in this love are the greatest heroes on earth. Such heroes live on even after death. These lofty souls light a new torch of love in their hearts on a daily basis. In turn, they are loved by others. What makes these heroes of love so special? They transcend the generality of others by their ability to uproot from their hearts any personal feelings of animosity toward others (Gülen 2000a, 253).

Imagine what the world would look like if more people possessed true, spiritual love. What a difference this would make if leaders of nations possessed such a deep, dynamic, and transforming love. If they did, they could solve an entire mountain of problems and there would be no clash of civilizations. This is Gülen's message to today's broken, fractured world of egoism, individualism, and greed.

The Future Looks Hopeful

In light of the preceding section on love, it is not surprising that Gülen has an upbeat, optimistic view of the future. Most assuredly, Gülen does not subscribe to the clash of civilizations thesis advanced by Samuel P. Huntington. Whereas Huntington looks upon the world as a political scientist, Gülen views the same world through the lens of his Islamic faith. This faith of Gülen may be compared to a glass of water: without color, without odor, without taste, yet when held up to the light of day, it is a prism that reflects and captures all the beauty, mystery, and wonder in the entire cosmos. Reality remains the same; however, the Islamic faith gives Gülen new eyes to see reality in an entirely different way than does Huntington (Penaskovic 2007, 415). By focusing on such qualities as dialogue, peace, and love, Gülen has high hopes that Islam and the West can resolve their differences amicably through dialogue. By focusing on dialogue, tolerance, peace, and love, the future of the relationship between Islam and the West looks rather rosy.

In sharp contrast to the naysayers and pessimists, Muslim radicals and extremists, Gülen, a moderate and modulating voice within Islam, argues that the world of the coming millennium will be a happier and more compassionate place than it now is. He reminds us that the Abrahamic religions have basically the same set of beliefs and that their nourishment derives from the same source. Despite the fact that the Abrahamic religions have been in competition with each other over the centuries, Gülen prefers to stress the commonalities among them.

He also observes that the Abrahamic religions have a shared responsibility to construct a better world in the future. It is Gülen's fondest hope that the Abrahamic religions will see the need for interfaith dialogue and that this dialogue will develop as a necessary process in the course of time. In this way the followers of all religions will come closer together and assist one another in times of troubled water (Gülen 2004b, 231).

In the past, science and religion were at loggerheads with one another. This conflict accounted for the rise of materialism and atheism. Gülen believes that the conflict between science and religion is misplaced. Science attempts to understand nature and humanity, each of which manifests God's attributes of will and power. Religion, on the other hand, has its font or source in the divine attribute of speech, which was manifested in the course of history as the sacred scriptures. Thanks to the combined efforts of Muslim and Christian scientists and theologians, the science–religion conflict will come to an end, observes Gülen (2004b, 231).

Gülen notes that before its demise our old world will experience an amazing second spring, in which the gap between rich and poor will narrow, the riches of the world will be distributed in a just and fair manner, discrimination on the basis of race, color, language, and worldview will vanish, and basic human rights will be protected. In this new springtime people will come to see that the current level of science and technology resembles the stage of life when a baby learns to crawl. Trips into space will be organized as if they were simply traveling to another foreign country. Pilgrims and travelers on the journey to God will carry the inspirations within their hearts to another spiritual world. This new or second spring will commence on the foundations of compassionate love, dialogue, acceptance of others, mutual respect, and justice. During this period of time humans will discover their true essence, that of goodness, kindness, virtue, and righteousness. The world will come to this path ineluctably. Nothing can stop it. God will effect a peaceful and beneficent future for the human race (Gülen 2004, 232).

How Does Gülen Come to This Optimistic and Hopeful View of the Future?

Gülen's belief in the resurrection and last judgment helps him look at life in a qualitatively different way than the secular humanist and others who believe that life ends with the grave. For Gülen, life on earth prepares us for an eternal life with God in heaven. Gülen views this present life as a test for the human race. We are to brace ourselves, so to speak, for the future by caring for others and by putting on such qualities as love, gentleness, and inner peace. Those who live their lives on the plane of eternity can forgive others their trespasses and overlook their shortcomings. In short, Gülen remains convinced that human life on earth is absurd and meaningless without a strong belief in the resurrection of the dead (Gülen 2000b, iii).

Gülen argues that if we look at life through the windows of God, then it follows that hope is the dynamic of action that does not falter. We are all children of hope. When we lose hope, we lose our *raison d'être*, although our physical existence may continue on for years. Gülen notes that hope is directly proportional to our faith. Just as winter constitutes merely one-fourth of a year, so too are the winters in our lives of short duration. Every New Year arrives with hope for a new spring (Gülen 2002, 22).

Hope may be regarded as the life-giving nourishment of those souls who live for others, rather than looking out for number one. Gülen calls hope a source of energy which never diminishes for souls that are other-centered. Finally, Gülen's reflections on hope are epitomized in these poetic words: "I am keeping my hope alive for the world and humanity, fresh as evergreen leaves, and I keep on looking upon tomorrow with a smile" (Gülen 2004, 234).

Summary

Taken together, Muslims and Christians constitute about one-half the population of the entire world. The relationship between the two represents the most important factor contributing to a meaningful peace on earth. Yet today's world seems to be hopelessly split into two halves at each other's throats, Islam versus the West. In Islam one notices the rise of radical fundamentalism, whether of the Sunni or Shiite variety, while in the West one observes a recurrence of xenophobia in countries with a Christian tradition. Some Muslims feel that the problem lies in the negative image of Islam in the consciousness of the West and in the continuous efforts to destabilize the Muslim world as a means to guarantee the security of Israel (Sammak 2002, 2). On the other hand, some in the West are wondering if there are any moderate Muslims around willing to speak out against al-Qaeda and other radical Islamic groups that espouse terrorism.

This essay has attempted to summarize the views of M. Fethullah Gülen and his ideas on healing the rift between Islam and the West. It begins by reflecting on the nature of globalization according to Gülen. We live in a global world so that what happens in one part of the world reverberates in the rest of the world instantaneously. For Gülen globalization means connectivity and interdependence in all areas of life: cultural, ecological, economic, political, religious, social, and technological. Gülen sees globalization in positive terms noting that science and technology are not ends in themselves but should serve a higher, transcendent purpose.

Science and technology should be respected to the extent that they direct us toward humane goals and values, that is, to the extent they serve the greater good of humanity. Gülen hits upon the notion of globalization by reflecting on the nature of the cosmos. For him the universe is a seamless whole, since there exists an interdependence of all beings in the universe. Everything that happens does so for a purpose in accordance with certain laws. The most trifling event occurs because God the creator allows it to happen. Nothing escapes this divine providence.

In commenting on the relationship between Islam and the West, Gülen makes several important distinctions. For example, he distinguishes between Islam as a religion and Islamism as a political ideology. Islam the religion stands for peace, love, and tolerance. The entire Qur'an, for example, has tolerance and forgiveness as its very foundation. Although suffused by apocalyptic language and draped in religious imagery, Islamism as an ideology is similar to secular ideologies of terror such as Maoism, the Baader-Meinhof

Gang, and Leninism. As such, Islamism as an ideology ought to be judged as harshly as the above-mentioned ideologies and condemned (Desai 2007, 122).

Gülen observes that the estrangement between Islam and the West began with the Crusades, followed by the Mongol invasion of the Islamic world. The Crusades set the stage for a long pattern of mistrust between Islam and the West, one which Gülen decries. In order to get beyond the rancor and finger pointing of the past between Islam and the West, Gülen insists on a dialogue between East and West. Gülen understands dialogue to be a give and take between two or more parties involving honesty, mutual respect, and compassionate love.

Gülen would have us remember that love is one of the main pillars of dialogue. If the leaders of nations possess a deep and transforming love, they could solve an entire ocean of difficulties and avert a culture war between Islam and the West. Moreover, Gülen has a very optimistic take on the world's future in contradistinction to the naysayers and pessimists both in the Muslim world and in the West. Gülen argues that the three Abrahamic religions, Islam, Judaism, and Christianity have the responsibility to construct a better world in the future.

Gülen, the visionary, feels that the world of the future will experience a second spring in which the gap between rich and poor will narrow, discrimination of all stripes will disappear, and basic human rights will be protected. This new spring will commence on the basis of compassionate love, dialogue, social justice, and acceptance of others. The world will come to this path ineluctably. In point of fact, nothing can stop it. How so? God will bring this about.

Concluding Observations

1. The question of migration/immigration is another factor that should be considered in speaking about the relationship between Islam and the West. Immigration has transformed the cultural and

religious landscape of the West. In order to tackle discrimination against Muslims, the West needs to consider the issue of migration or immigration on both the national and international levels. Migration has become a structural element of many societies in today's world, modifying their cultural and religious makeup. For example, there are about 3.5 million Muslims living in Germany today, of whom 75 percent are from Turkey or of Turkish descent. In the 1960s Germany imported "guest workers" from Morocco, Tunisia, and Turkey. Another 180,000 refugees came to Germany fleeing the war in Bosnia, most of whom were Muslims and another 125,000 Muslims came to Germany after the Islamic Revolution in Iran in 1979 (*Christen und Muslime in Deutschland* 2003, 12).

The dismantling of the Berlin Wall in 1989 redrew not only the geographical map but altered the mental landscape of Europe. For example, Muslims presently constitute 20 percent of the population in Brussels and by 2050 about 30 percent of Europe's population will be Muslim. We now have an open Europe, one divided between the rich and the poor. One notices a marked increase of xenophobia and racism in Europe along with more crime and drug abuse among both immigrants and non-immigrants (Siddiqi 2000, 67).

Muslims in Europe have a deep sense of being uprooted from their culture, their history, their language, their religion, and their jurisprudence. Some Western Europeans look on Muslims as a threat to their jobs and their way of life, demanding that they integrate themselves better into the dominant society. For their part many Muslims fear assimilation because it would mean that they would have to give up their own culture, religion, and even their own identity. What we need is greater cooperation between migrants and the wider community that receives them. The basic freedoms and human rights of all must be respected (Celata 2007, 227).

This also holds true, *mutatis mutandis*, for the United States where immigration has increased dramatically since the Hart-Celler Act of 1965. This Act abolished restrictive quotas on immigration from countries other than Europe so that a high number of Africans, Asians, and Latin Americans have come to the United States, making it the most religiously diverse nation in the world (Phan 2004, xix).

2. In the past we have created many dots of dialogue between Islam and the West but not enough lines. Hence a clear picture of dialogue between Islam and the West or between Islam and Christianity has not yet emerged. I would argue that dialogue presupposes a positive orientation and openness to diversity and plurality. Both Islam and Christianity recognize plurality in principle but this does not always filter down to the level of praxis. As Azyurmadi Azra (2008, 145) notes, the search for authenticity among some Muslims has led to a literal understanding of religion and to radicalism. Some Muslims believe in a monolithic Islam, that is, that there exists only one Islam. They argue passionately that differing interpretations of Islam corrupt Islam and weaken Muslims vis-à-vis the West. On the other hand, Christian fundamentalists believe that their interpretation of Christianity trumps all other interpretations, which are then thought to be false.

To Muslims I would point out that the Qur'an itself is the source of differing and divergent interpretations among Muslim scholars. In other words the text of the holy Qur'an itself justifies differing opinions and perspectives, according to Qur'an 49:13. I believe that contemporary Muslim scholars should work on freeing the Qur'anic perspective from its medieval interpretations. In this way, Muslims of all stripes will be encouraged to work for the creation of a pluralistic, global society, intent on bringing about social justice.

I would also note that for the dialogue between the three Abrahamic religions to succeed, the dialogue partners must be linguistically competent, self-critical, credible, and knowledgeable. At times the dialogue falters because the participants lack some of the abovementioned qualities. Some imams in Western Europe, for example, have had a difficult time participating in the Muslim–Christian dialogue because they do not know the language well enough to understand the nuances of meaning on the part of their dialogue partners. Christian scholars participating in the dialogue with Muslims want a dialogue on the theological level, whereas their Muslim counterparts want more than a verbal dialogue. The latter want action, that is, to do things together, such as find jobs for the unemployed and thus help the poor. (Koerner 2008, 542; Schmid 2008, 472).

3. When my wife and I visited Turkey in 2005 we were greatly impressed by the hospitality shown us by Gülen Movement participants. Could not hospitality be an appropriate model for interreligious encounter between and among Muslims, Jews, and Christians? The hospitality we experienced in Turkey was simply the outward expression of an inner attitude of welcome which arises from a profound conviction of faith. My wife and I were given many gifts such as a handmade rug, pottery, and some paintings. These material gifts symbolized a deeper, interior sharing. Although we were strangers, our hosts saw in us a sign of God's presence. We hope our hosts received something from us since hospitality is always a two-way street. Because of the hospitality we received from our hosts, our admiration for the Gülen Movement only increased. We said to ourselves that there must be something to M. Fethullah Gülen if his readers are so hospitable to strangers. As the dialogue between Muslims and Christians intensifies, perhaps all parties need to reflect on the deeper meaning of hospitality.

References

Abramsky, S. 2007. Defining the indefinable West. *The Chronicle of Higher Education* 53: B6–B8.

Ameli, S. R. 2004. Glocal spaces: Globalization and the power of religion. In *Catholics and Shi'a in Dialogue: Studies in Theology and Spirituality*, ed. A. O'Mahony, W. Peterburs, and M.A. Shomali. London: Melisende, 321–353.

Anon. 2003. *Christen und Muslime in Deutschland*. Bonn: Sekretariat der Deutschen Bischofskonferenz.

Azra, A. 2008. Religioeser Pluralismus und innergesellschaftliche Konflikte: Die indonesische Erfahrung auf dem mittleren Weg. *Interkulterelle Theologie* 34, 144–164.

Celata, Archbishop P. L. 2007. Intolerance and discrimination against Muslims: Old prejudices and new targets. *Pro Dialogo* 126, 225–229.

Cole, J. 2007. Islamophobia as a social problem. *Middle East Studies Association Bulletin* 41, 3–7.

Desai, M. 2007. *Rethinking Islamism: The Ideology of the New Terror*. London/New York: I.B. Tauris.

Fletcher, J. H. 2008. Religious pluralism in an era of globalization: The making of modern religious identity. *Theological Studies* 69, 394–411.

Gülen, M. F. 2000a. *Advocate of Dialogue*. Compiled by A. Ünal and A. Williams. Fairfax, Virginia: The Fountain.

———. 2000b. *The Resurrection and the Afterlife*. Compiled by A. Ünal. Fairfax, Virginia: The Fountain.

———. 2002. *Essays, Perspectives, Opinions*. Rutherford, New Jersey: The Fountain.

———. 2004. *Toward a Global Civilization of Love and Tolerance*. Somerset, New Jersey: The Light, Inc.

Huntington, S. P. 1996. *The Clash of Civilizations and the Remaking of World Order*. New York: Simon and Schuster.

Juergensmeyer, M. 2001. *Terror in the Mind of God: The Global Rise of Religious Violence*. Berkeley, CA: University of California Press.

Kellner, D. 2007. Globalization, terrorism, and democracy: 9/11 and its aftermath. In *Contesting Empire, Globalizing Dissent: Cultural Studies after 9/11*, ed. N.K. Denzin and M.D. Giardina. Boulder/London: Paradigm Publishers, 53–77.

Koerner, F. 2008. Reizwort Dialog: Wo das christlich-muslimische Gespraeche schaerfer werden muss. *Stimmen der Zeit* 190, 535–546.

Kurzman, C. ed. 1998. *Liberal Islam: A Sourcebook*. New York/Oxford: Oxford University Press.

Larsson, G. 2005. The impact of global conflicts on local contexts: Muslims in Sweden after 9/11—the rise of Islamophobia or new possibilities. *Islam and Christian–Muslim Relations* 16, 29–42.

Lewis, B. 2004. *The Crisis of Islam: Holy War and Unholy Terror*. New York: Random House Trade Paperbacks.

Looney, R. 2007. The Arab world: Uncomfortable experience with globalization. *Middle East Journal* 61, 341–345.

Penaskovic, R. 2007. M. Fethullah Gülen's response to the 'Clash of Civilizations' thesis. In *Muslim World in Transition: Contributions of the Gülen Movement*, ed. I. Yilmaz et al. London: Leeds Metropolitan University Press, 407–418.

———. 2007. M. Fethullah Gülen: A bridge between Islam and the West. In *Peaceful Coexistence: Fethullah Gülen's Initiatives for Peace in the Contemporary World,* ed. I. Yilmaz et al. London: Leeds Metropolitan University Press, 193–201.

Phan, P. 2004. *Being Religious Interreligiously: Asian Perspectives on Interfaith Dialogue*. Maryknoll, New York: Orbis Books.

Robertson, R. 1992. *Globalization: Social Theory and Global Culture*. London: Sage.

Sammak, M. 2002. The Arab-Muslim world after September 11th. *Islamochristiana* 28: 1–11.

Schmid, H. 2008. Dialog konkret: Worueber Muslime mit Christen in Deutschland sprechen. *Herder Korrespondenz* 62, 470–475.

Siddiqi, A. 2000. Fifty years of Christian–Muslim relations: Exploring and engaging in a new relationship. *Islamochristiana* 26, 51–77.

Stiglitz, J. E. 2002. *Globalization and Its Discontents*. New York/London: W.W. Norton & Company.

Yılmaz, İ. et al. 2007a. *Muslim World in Transition*: *Contributions of the Gülen Movement*, London: Leeds Metropolitan University Press.

———. 2007b. *Peaceful Coexistence: Fethullah Gülen's Initiatives for Peace in the Contemporary World,* London: Leeds Metropolitan University Press.

PART 3

Theology of Dialogue in Comparative Perspective

Chapter 7

Preachers of Dialogue: International Relations and Interfaith Theology

Turan Kayaoglu

Introduction

Globalization disperses people and ideas throughout the world; it brings families and individuals with different beliefs into close contact. Today, more than at any period in history, religious diversity characterizes daily life in many communities. The proponents of interfaith dialogue claim that in an increasingly global world interfaith dialogue can facilitate mutual understanding, respect for other religions, and thus the peaceful coexistence of people of different faiths. In particular, foundations, charities, and schools affiliated with the Gülen Movement are increasingly engaging with peace building, most significantly through their interfaith activities (Sahin 2008). One key factor for the Gülen Movement's success in the interfaith dialogue is Fethullah Gülen's ability to provide an inclusive interfaith dialogue. Gülen is not alone on this path: I argue that prominent leaders of the Abrahamic religions (Judaism, Christianity, and Islam) are already offering separate but overlapping theologies to legitimize interfaith dialogue.

A balanced analysis of multi-faith interactions is overdue in political science. The discipline characterizes religious interactions solely from the perspective of schism and exclusion. The literature asserts that interactions among believers of different faiths will breed conflict, including terrorism, civil wars, interstate wars, and global wars. According to this conventional depiction, interfaith cooperation is especially challenging to Judaism, Christianity, and Islam due to their monotheism; each claims it is "the one true path." The so-called "monotheistic exclusion" refers to an all-or-nothing theological view: you are a believer or you are an infidel. Judaism identifies the chosen people, while outsiders are gentiles; Christians believe that no salvation is possible outside of Jesus; some Muslims call for a perennial *jihad* against non-Muslims. Each faith would claim the "religious other" is a stranger to God. Political "*us* versus *them*" thinking evolves from this "believer versus infidel" worldview. This mindset in turn initiates the blaming, dehumanizing, and demonization of the believers of other religious traditions. Eventually, it leads to inter-religious violence and conflict.

Disputing this grim characterization of religious interactions, the scholars of religion offer a tripartite typology of religious attitudes towards the religious *other*: exclusivism, inclusivism, and pluralism. Exclusivism suggests a binary opposition of religious claims: one is truth, the other is falsehood. In this dichotomy, salvation requires affirmation of the truths of one's particular religion. Inclusivism integrates other religious traditions with one's own. In this integration, one's own religion represents the complete and pure, while other religions represent the incomplete, the corrupted, or both. Pluralism accepts that no religious tradition has a privileged access to religious truth, and all religions are potentially equally valid paths (Race 1983; Eck 1993; Aslan 1998).

This chapter examines the theology of interfaith dialogue (or interfaith theology) in the Abrahamic religions by means of analyzing the works of three religious leaders. First, Jonathan Sacks, the Chief Rabbi of the United Hebrew Congregations of Britain and the Commonwealth, offers a framework for the dialogue of civilizations in his book *Dignity of Difference: How to Avoid the Clash of Civilizations*. Rather than mere tolerance and multiculturalism, he advocates an active engagement to respect and value cultural and religious differences. Second, Pope John Paul II's *Crossing the Threshold of Hope* argues that holiness and truth might exist in other religions because the Holy Spirit works beyond the formal boundaries of the Church. Third, Fethullah Gülen's *Advocate of Dialogue* describes a Muslim approach to interfaith dialogue based on the Muslim belief in prophecy and revelation.

I analyze the interfaith theologies of these religious leaders in five sections: First, I explore variations on the definition of "interfaith dialogue" in their works. Second, I examine the structural and strategic reasons for the emergence and development of these interfaith theologies. Third, I respond to four common doubts about the possibility and utility of interfaith dialogue and theologies. Fourth, I use John Rawls' overlapping consensus approach to develop a framework with which to analyze religious leaders' support for interfaith dialogue. Fifth, I discuss the religious rationales of each religious leader as it relates to interfaith dialogue.

Interfaith Dialogue

These three leaders have been initiators and supporters of interfaith dialogue. More importantly, they articulate religious foundations for interfaith dialogue. While they emphasize the deliberative, formal, and theological nature of interfaith dialogue, distinguishing it from everyday religious encounters and conversations, their notions of dialogue vary. For example, Gülen (2004) defines dialogue procedurally and consequentially: as coming together, discussing, and forming a bond among participants. Privileging the practice (Kantian "practical reason") over the speculative (Kantian "pure reason") in religious epistemology is common in Gülen's teaching. Gülen's minimalist approach aims to facilitate interfaith dialogue both in order to search for the commonalities between different faiths and to stimulate development of an interfaith framework out of interfaith practices.

The Catholic Church's notion of dialogue has a stronger theological connotation; it stresses religious "witnessing." It is more than a verbal act; it is the co-witnessing of each other's faith for mutual growth and enrichment. Witnessing connotes a deeper engagement involving a more spiritual experience than intellectual communication. Furthermore, unlike in Judaism and Islam, ecumenical dialogue has become a significant part of the Catholic Church's approach to dialogue in addition to interfaith dialogue. The Second Vatican Council's *Unitatis Redintegratio* (Restoring Christian Unity) attempts to accommodate and integrate non-Catholic Christian churches into Catholic theology. *Nostra Aetate* (the Declaration on the Relationship of the Church to Non-Christian Religions) emphasizes shared belief and practices between the Catholic Church and non-Christians (Cassidy 2005).

Last, according to Sacks, interfaith dialogue is not about winning an argument or changing one's own beliefs, but a deliberation for an inclusive identity formation with the "other." This is very similar to Gülen's idea that through dialogue participants can establish a new bond transcending the "us" and "other" division. Sacks argues that in this identity formation process, dialogue participants engage in reasoning to explain their views and genuinely listen to others, not to "change one's beliefs but make space for another deeply held belief" (Sacks 2002, 83). This facilitates respect for differences and makes globalization humane. To this end, Sacks envisions two simultaneous dialogues with complementary functions: an interfaith dialogue and a faith-globalization dialogue.

Globalization seems the most important catalyst behind the growing appeal of interfaith dialogue. The theme of globalization, either as cause of increasing inequalities (particularly in Sacks), or as an inevitable process (particularly in Gülen), permeates religious discourse on interfaith dialogue. The Catholic Church's *Nostra Aetate* (literally, "in our age") starts with a statement that links interfaith dialogue to globalization: "In our age, when the human race is being daily brought closer together and contacts between the various nations are becoming more frequent ..." (Flannery 1996).

Globalization prompts these leaders, including Gülen, to see the whole world—a common humanity and a shared physical environment—as visible support for the existence of a single creator. However, globalization creates two challenges for faith communities. First, people of different faiths are meeting each other. Continuing religious diversity undermines the naïve religious expectation that if a person is exposed to the message of Jesus or the Qur'an, she or he will embrace the truth. Furthermore, religious diversity may incite a reflexive fear on the part of some religious leaders and followers that if people are exposed to the teachings of other religions, they will turn toward that religion. Worse, the global unification of markets and the homogenizing consumer culture has created a backlash among some religious leaders who have embraced exclusivist, identity-based claims (Barber 1996, Huntington 1996). Dialogue-oriented religious leaders share a view that globalization is an unstoppable process that shrinks the world and makes isolation impossible. This leaves dialogue or conflict as the only two options. Interfaith dialogue is then a peaceful alternative to solve the problems of a common humanity made manifest by globalization.

Second, globalization intensifies economic inequalities and environmental degradation. Increasingly, similar problems force faith communities to connect in order to moderate the pervasive influences of globalization. The three religious leaders I examine share a belief in the importance of interfaith dialogue and its ability to add a moral dimension to globalization. For example, Sacks argues that although the dialogue of civilizations has always been laudable, new political and economic developments such as economic inequality, environmental destruction and climate change, the spread of information technology, and the increasing power of civil society make this dialogue indispensable for future peace and human welfare.

Facing these huge international challenges, the religious leaders I study seem to believe that economic and political solutions are not enough. These religious leaders are skeptical of such solutions because they feel that economic and political approaches empower the rich and powerful at the expense of the poor and weak, leading to the erosion of human dignity. Among the religious leaders, Rabbi Jonathan Sacks offers the most refined analysis of globalization and its religious implications. According to Rabbi Sacks, lacking a moral dimension, globalization is doomed to remain fragile. Furthermore, the injustices associated with globalization can create anger and resentment among the poor and weak.

However, conflict between the losers and winners in globalization can be avoided. The religious leaders I examine claim that there is a religious authority and responsibility to add a moral dimension to globalization by voicing what Rabbi Sacks describes as "the silent cry of those who today suffer from want, hunger, disease, powerlessness and lack of freedom" (Sacks 2002, 11, also Sacks 2005). For Rabbi Sacks, while interfaith dialogue should focus on finding religious justifications for the dignity of difference, the faith and globalization dialogue should offer ways to enhance economic justice for a more equitable sharing of world resources. Religious communities' participation is imperative in this process because religious individuals feel a particular moral responsibility to alleviate the suffering of the poor and the oppressed.

More than Rabbi Sacks and Pope John Paul II, Gülen underlines the need for interfaith dialogue to combat the materialism that, Gülen (2000, 241) believes, is the root of all evils including wars, conflicts, environmental problems, poverty, and the loss of morality. He claims that the materialist assault on religion damages all religions, particularly Christianity. Under this materialist attack, Christianity can fend off materialism only by allying with Islam (2000, 242). According to Gülen, their similar and powerful teachings can balance a hunger for material gains with service, love, and peace making. If the two faiths united to advocate for this on the world stage, this cooperation would create a strong foundation for a just and compassionate globalization, rather than one of unequal distribution and unsustainable consumption.

While the structural factors of globalization and materialism contribute to the religious leaders' commitment to interfaith dialogue, urgent political incidents also cause these leaders to call for dialogue. These religious leaders maintain that religion is integral to global politics. According to Rabbi Sacks (2002, 11), belying the Enlightenment predictions that religion would become "mute, marginal, and mild," a resurgence in the practice of religion is sweeping across the globe. But religious leaders also realize that the increasing global practice of religion does not necessarily contribute to an ever-increasing peace due to the politicized and potentially violent nature of some forms of religious resurgence. To contribute to peace, religions should engage in interfaith dialogue to find ways to "acknowledge the integrity of those who are not of our faith" and to "hear the voice of God in a language, a sensibility, [and] a culture not our own" (Sacks 2002, 83).

Specific historical events become catalysts for interfaith activities by symbolizing the consequences of a lack of dialogue and the necessity to remove misconceptions about other religions. For example, the Holocaust and the following Nuremberg trials forced the Catholic Church to take steps to change its anti-Semitic teachings. Thus, the Holocaust became a catalyst for Jewish–Catholic Church dialogue (Barnes 2002).

Similarly, post–Cold War developments, concerns about Islam as a new threat, predictions about a clash of civilizations, the terrorist attacks of Al-Qaeda and similar radical groups, and the rise of Islamophobia in Western Europe and the United States increase religious groups' desire to engage in interfaith activities. The subtitle of Rabbi Jonathan Sacks' *The Dignity of Difference: How to Avoid the Clash of Civilizations* reflects a concern shared by religious leaders. For the proponents of interfaith dialogue, such dialogue can create a unified interfaith stand against the alleged clash of civilizations. Rabbi Sacks (2002, 59) stresses that for a unified stand religious leaders should cultivate their ability to "see the presence of God in the face of a stranger," like the Good Samaritan in Christian teaching. Rabbi Sacks warns that if religious leaders fail to accommodate other religions, with the increasing salience of religion in international politics, religions will continue to be a source of discord, not harmony. Rabbi Sacks (2002, 9) is firm in his beliefs about integrating faith into the solutions of global problems: "If faith is enlisted in the cause of war, there must be an equal and opposite counter-voice in the name of peace. If religion is not part of a solution, it will certainly be part of the problem." Proponents of interfaith dialogue suggest that their goal is to re-cast religion in the name of peace.

Critique of Interfaith Dialogue and Theologies

Structural (globalization) and strategic (international politics) factors explain religious leaders' interest in and support for interfaith dialogue. These reasons are external to religion. If external reasons alone explain religious support for interfaith dialogue, a change in these conditions may decrease the support of the religious leaders. In other words, religious leaders' endorsement of interfaith dialogue may reflect individual or group interests consistent with the current political environment rather than a moral commitment to the principle of dialogue.

There are four questions skeptics can raise against the possibility, sustainability, and benefit of interfaith dialogue. First, have these religious leaders deviated from their religious teachings for the sake of providing an interfaith theology? Rabbi Sacks, the late Pope John Paul II, and Gülen have been important Jewish, Catholic, and Muslim leaders. Their commitment to their respective religions and their influence on their co-religionists would prevent them from compromising their religious doctrines. Their explanations rely on religious doctrines and authoritative interpretations of their scriptures. These explanations, rather than significant re-interpretation, identify and magnify what is already in their tradition. Their justifications are anchored in their respective religious traditions and the earlier interpretations of leaders from their religion as opposed to fundamental, marginal, and controversial reinterpretations of their Scriptures.

Second, is the interfaith dialogue just rhetoric to hide the ugly face of religion and religious violence? These religious leaders are not developing theology for the sake of subterfuge, but are actively practicing what they preach. Jonathan Sacks, Pope John Paul II, and Fethullah Gülen have been initiators and supporters of interfaith dialogue. No pope before Pope John Paul II ever visited a mosque or synagogue; he visited both. Fethullah Gülen's activities have brought religious leaders, starting in Turkey and now with a global reach and influence, together on countless occasions.

Third, is this a monotheist conspiracy against non-monotheists? While the interfaith theologies of Rabbi Sacks, Pope John Paul II, and Gülen accommodate Abrahamic religions more easily, their interfaith theologies can be generalized to other religions. In Rabbi Sacks' argument, all religions are particular languages God spoke to different communities. The Christian Holy Spirit can work in non-monotheistic as well as monotheistic faiths. In Gülen's case, prophecy and prophets existed in all communities of belief.

Fourth, is interfaith dialogue a faith-based coalition to undermine secularism? Are supporters of interfaith dialogue in search of an interfaith theocracy? While concerned about the pervasive influence of politics on religion and vice versa, the religious leaders I examine do not engage with political issues directly. Each is avowedly apolitical. They share an apolitical religious position and express a common concern about the danger of the politicization of religion. Gülen (2000, 243–244) is especially critical of the manipulation of Islam for political, national, or personal interests.

A Religious Overlapping Consensus on Interfaith Dialogue

In addition to the problems with each critique by the skeptics, there is a further reason to be hopeful about the possibility, sustainability, and benefit of interfaith dialogue: religious leaders are offering overlapping religious rationales accommodating the "religious other" to substantiate such a dialogue. These internal (religious) rationales are more consequential than external (globalization and international politics) factors because these leaders' justifications are tied to the religious doctrines that mainstream Jews, Christians, and Muslims already believe. Interfaith theologies reflect these religious leaders' commitment to interfaith dialogue as religious value, and not as self or group interest.

John Rawls' concept of overlapping consensus provides a plausible framework with which to analyze religious leaders' interfaith theologies. Rawls develops the concept of overlapping consensus within political liberalism to explain how "there can be a stable and just society whose free and equal citizens are deeply divided by conflicting and even incommensurable religious, philosophical, and moral doctrines" (1996, 133). An overlapping consensus means that groups with incommensurable comprehensive doctrines can agree to a set of principles (in Rawls' case this principle is what he calls "Justice as Fairness") and can support those principles on moral grounds through their respective comprehensive doctrines. An overlapping consensus materializes when what Rawls (1996, 133–134) considers "stability for the right reasons" emerges to "establish and preserve unity and stability" of a plural society without compromising its plural character. Stability for the right reasons in a society exists when its citizens can agree to some principles of justice for moral, not practical or self- or group-centered, reasons (1996, 142–143). Rawls expects that a reasonable plurality of conflicting and incommensurable doctrines will emerge through practical reason over time under enduring free institutions.

Although John Rawls develops his overlapping consensus approach for the domestic politics of constitutionally liberal states, his argument has significant implications for religious interactions in domestic as well as international society. For example, scholars of international relations try to explain how justice and stability can be achieved in a plural society with conflicting and incommensurable (religious) doctrines. While Rawls uses his overlapping consensus concept to explain the possibility of consensus on a political concept (Justice as Fairness), there is no inherent reason to limit its application. Applying the lens of overlapping consensus is particularly useful in explaining religious consensus because it does not impose any value judgment about respective religious truths.

An overlapping religious consensus on interfaith dialogue is emerging as Jewish, Christian, and Muslim leaders develop different underlying reasons, consistent with their religious doctrines, to accommodate the religious other and support interfaith dialogue. The separate interfaith theologies of Rabbi Sacks, Gülen and the late Pope John Paul II aim to accommodate Jewish, Catholic, and Muslim belief in the unity of God with the reality of religious diversity. In his own way, each religious leader leads, inspires, and encourages his co-religionists to join in interfaith dialogue. While these three leaders agree on the importance of this dialogue, they offer different religious justifications for it, reflecting the differences of their religious doctrines. In other words, they develop an overlapping consensus that accommodates "the religious other" from their own religious doctrines to substantiate their support of interfaith dialogue.

Rabbi Sacks' Theology of Difference

Partially due to their Diaspora and minority experience, Jewish philosophers and scholars have been active in developing an interfaith theology. For example, the most important Medieval Jewish philosopher, Moses Maimonides, offers an inclusivist Jewish theology. In his theology of religions, Islam and Christianity are imperfect but important faiths nonetheless. Maimonides links Christianity to Judaism through the Christian acceptance of the Jewish Scripture as authentic and intact. Maimonides notes that Christians, unlike Muslims, misinterpret monotheism through trinity. He links Judaism and Islam through their rejection of idolatry, but acknowledges that, unlike Christians, Muslims do not accept Jewish Scripture as authentic or intact. Despite these imperfections, Maimonides stresses that Christians and Muslims are important for the fulfillment of the universal reign of the Messiah and the triumph of monotheism (Novak 1989).

While drawing on the Jewish tradition to develop his interfaith approach, Rabbi Sacks' interfaith theology differs from Maimonides' as Sacks' argument is not teleological in that it does not envision an end of history with the commencement of Messianic reign. In fact, quite contrary to Maimonides' vision for the convergence of faiths under the Messianic reign, Rabbi Sacks contends that a diversity of faiths is the Divine Will. Rabbi Sacks suggests that monotheism is compatible with the diversity of religions. One God has created natural and religious diversity. In this way, by emphasizing distinctiveness of Judaism—its rejection of religious uniformity—he acknowledges the religious foundation from which other religions can be constructively engaged.

Rabbi Sacks identifies Western universalist cultures that propagated the idea of the existence of one universal truth: ancient Greece and Rome, medieval Christianity and Islam, and the Enlightenment. In addition to these five universalizing cultures, the world is going through a sixth—global capitalism. These attempts to unify the world under one truth are not compatible with the Divine Will that has been revealed by the diversity and complexity of the natural and social world (2002, 50). Accepting diversity of faiths does not lead him to moral relativism; in fact, he believes that some universal moral truths exist. One important set of universal truths is the Biblical "covenant with Noah." The Noahide covenant includes seven commandments: avoid idolatry, blasphemy, sexual immorality, bloodshed, theft, and animal cruelty, and obey the rule of law (Solomon 2005). Rabbi Sacks argues that the Noahide covenant creates a theological space within Judaism to accommodate people of other faiths as well as secular political doctrines because essentially the Noahide covenant sanctions the modern understanding of human rights. Beyond the moral universality of human rights, the diversity of faiths is the Divine Will of one God.

According to Rabbi Sacks, Judaism represents the best example of a monotheistic accommodation of religious pluralism. In contrast to the universalistic monotheisms of Christianity and Islam, Judaism is a particularistic monotheism as it posits that the God of Abraham is the God of all mankind, but the faith of Abraham is not the faith of all mankind. The universality of God and particularity of religions are complementary, not conflicting. One God shows majesty and mercy though diversity in faiths.

Sacks' pluralist approach to religions finds its most complete form in his treatment of Abrahamic religions as he calls them religions of revelation and places them on *equal theological* grounds (2002, 55). Rabbi Sacks has an implicit theology of revelation, but he fails to clarify and substantiate it within Judaism. Lacking a clear theology of revelation as a foundational theology for God's speaking to different communities with different religions, Rabbi Sacks' claim for God's complex creativity in nature and religion remains tenuous and vulnerable to exclusivist Jewish criticisms. These criticisms led him to rephrase and remove statements of Abrahamic equality. For example, in the subsequent editions of his book, Rabbi Sacks removed this statement included in the first edition: "Judaism, Christianity, and Islam are religions of revelation—faiths in which God speaks and we attempt to listen." He also revised the statement "God has spoken to mankind in many languages: through Judaism to Jews, Christianity to Christians, Islam to Muslims" to read "As Jews we believe that God has made a covenant with the singular people, but does not exclude the possibility of other peoples, cultures and faith finding their own relationship with God within the shared frame of the Noahide laws" (Harries 2004). These omissions and revisions indicate interfaith dialogue may require an *intra*-faith dialogue in order to clarify interfaith relevant concepts such as revelation and prophecy.

The Pope's Hope through the Holy Spirit

Compared to Judaism's traditional quest to develop interfaith theologies, the Catholic Church's attempts are rather recent. The recent attempts are mostly related to Church efforts to respond to charges of anti-Semitism at the Second Vatican Council (1962–1965) following the Holocaust. The political concerns of bishops working in Muslim states prevented a Catholic attempt to prepare a document solely on the relationship between the Church and Judaism (Barnes 2002). The result was *Nostra Aetate*: an authoritative and comprehensive interfaith document. The Catholic Church's formal, hierarchical structure facilitates the preparation of authoritative, statements binding on its members. Lacking a formal hierarchy, Jewish and Muslim leaders attempt to offer authoritative statements based on scholarly and sectarian credentials.

Nostra Aetate shaped the late Pope John Paul II's understanding of the purpose, conduct, and goal of interfaith dialogue. A turning point for the Church's relations with non-Christians,[25] the document stresses shared beliefs and practices with the aim of interfaith dialogue and cooperation, rather than an emphasis on the differences for the condemnation of the other. *Nostra Aetate* consists of five articles. The first article explains the rationale for fostering unity and charity in an increasingly global community by stressing shared principles among religions. The second article refers to Hinduism and Buddhism, and proclaims "the Catholic Church rejects nothing

25 Race (1983, 45) suggests, "As official statements by the Roman Catholic Church the documents of Vatican II do not submit a detailed theory of the relation between Christianity and the other faiths. Their role in the catholic theology has been to a signal a change from exclusivism to inclusivism in the approach to other faiths at a fundamental theological level." For the text, see Flannery (1996).

that is true and holy in these religions." Following this statement, the declaration then encourages the members of the Church that "through dialogue and collaboration with the followers of other religions, carried out with prudence and love and in witness to the Christian faith and life, [the followers will] recognize, preserve and promote the good things, spiritual and moral, as well as socio-cultural values found among men." The third article identifies shared beliefs (monotheism, the virgin birth, and the judgment day) and practices (prayer and fasting) with Muslims without commenting on the authenticity of the Qur'an or the prophecy of Muhammad. The fourth article extols Judaism, as Christianity and Judaism share a common spiritual heritage. It also condemns anti-Semitism. The fifth article makes a general plea for religious tolerance.

Following *Nostra Aetate* (and unlike Rabbi Sacks, but similar to Gülen), the late Pope John Paul II (1994) emphasizes similarities between religious traditions. He (1994, 77) argues that diversity of religions should not hide the commonalities that unite these religious traditions. Most importantly, they all try to answer humankind's question about eternity and ultimate destiny. In this perennial endeavor, the late pope (1994, 80) reiterated the statement of *Nostra Aetate* and acknowledged the possibility of the existence of truth and the holy in other religions. However, he fails to elaborate the theological underpinnings of accommodating the existence of the divine in other religions.

Rabbi Sacks implicitly, and Gülen explicitly, link the faith traditions through the notion of revelation—God's speaking to different communities through a variety of prophets. Yet, the Christian notion of Incarnation dominates the concept of revelation. Reducing revelation to God's self-revelation in Jesus (a particular time- and space-bound self-revelation) limits revelation as a tool to link the religious traditions.[26] One way that John Paul II and *Nostra*

26 John Paul II (1994, 92). Among other factors, the problem of revelation makes it difficult for the Catholic Church to accept Muhammad as a prophet and the Qur'an

Aetate circumvent this limitation and link religious traditions is to rely on the notion of the Holy Spirit. Revelation in the form of Jesus does not "travel" across time and space, but the Holy Spirit works "effectively even outside the visible structure of the Church." The Holy Spirit places truth and holiness in other religions, bringing them to Jesus Christ—whether members of these religions are aware or not (anonymous Christians). By linking other religions to Jesus Christ through the Holy Spirit, the Catholic Church creates an inclusive interfaith theology. In John Paul II's terms, "The Church is guided by the faith that God the Creator wants to save all humankind in Jesus Christ, the only mediator between God and man, inasmuch as He is the Redeemer of all humankind" (1994, 81). Furthermore, "Christ came into the word for all these peoples. He redeemed them all and has His own ways of reaching each of them in the present eschatological phase of salvation history. In fact, in those regions, many accept Him and many more have an implicit faith in Him" (1994, 83).

Gülen's Interfaith Theology through Revelation and Prophecy

Unlike Rabbi Sacks and John Paul II, Fethullah Gülen does not have any official status; his authority is based solely on his religious and scholarly credentials. Gülen bases his interfaith approach on Turkish Islamic tradition, such as the work of the Sufi poet and theologian Rumi (1207–1273) and the Ottoman Empire's religious tolerance (such as the Empire's community self-governance or *millet* system). Growing out of this tradition, Gülen's interfaith approach has three religious bases: a history of revelation and prophecy, the commonalities among faiths, and the Qur'an's explicit sanction of interfaith dialogue.

---

as revelation. John Paul II (1994, 94) refers to fundamentalism and the persecution of Christians in Muslim states as an obstacle to dialogue with Muslims.

First, Gülen's unequivocal commitment to interfaith dialogue derives its rationale from his singular and inclusive approach to religion. According to Gülen (2000, 243), Judaism, Christianity, and Islam, and even Hinduism and other world religions accept the same theistic source for themselves, and including Buddhism, pursue the same goal. This accommodating approach to other faiths is rooted in Gülen's understanding of a spiral history of religion. Embedded in an Islamic understanding of religion and history, this spiral history suggests that God sends prophets and revelations to re-establish the universal principle of the existence of God. The spiral history of religion offers an inclusive understanding of religion. The divine revelation and prophecy establish both an axis for religious unity and a framework for religious diversity. Following the Qur'an's declaration (40:78) that God sent many messengers, the number of whom the hadith tradition puts at as many as 124,000, allows Gülen (2002, 243) to argue that to a varying degree any religion reflects the universality of religion. Using this Islamic singular and inclusive conceptualization of religion, Gülen also relates all major religions to each other via the same divine revelation.

Second, Gülen suggest that the similarity of religious teachings supports his inclusive approach to religion and his interfaith theology: "Regardless of how their adherents implement their faith in their daily lives, such generally accepted values as love, respect, tolerance, forgiveness, mercy, human rights, peace, brotherhood, and freedom are exalted by religion. Most of them are accorded the highest precedence in the messages brought by Moses, Jesus, and Muhammad, as well as in the messages of Buddha, and even Zarathustra, Lao-Tzu, Confucius, and the Hindu scholars" (Gülen 2000, 242). The fundamental universal values of love, compassion, tolerance, and forgiveness are the basis of all religions (2000, 253). According to Gülen, the similar teachings of these religious leaders, but not necessarily the practices of their followers, indicate the divine presence in other religions. Gülen emphasizes these common denominators across religions to establish the foundations of an

Islamic interfaith theology and to offer a rationale for interfaith dialogue for common goals of humanity such as peace and justice.

Third, according to Gülen (2000, 249), the Qur'an is a universal call for dialogue. The call primarily—but not exclusively—targets Abrahamic religions: the dialogue between Judaism, Christianity, and Islam is the first pillar of interfaith dialogue. The Qur'an provides scriptural support for a Muslim dialogue with the People of the Book (Jews and Christians), saying, "'O People of the Book! Come to common terms as between us and you that we worship none but God; that we associate no partners with Him; that we take not, from among ourselves lords and patrons other than God.' If then they turn back, say you: 'Bear witness that we are Muslims (surrendered to God's Will)'" (Qur'an 3:64). The Qur'an's twenty-four references to Jews and Christians as "People of the Book" sanctions the Islamic accommodation of them (Saritoprak and Griffith, 2005).

Fethullah Gülen stresses the verse (2:3–4) which states that Muslims are required to believe "in what is sent to you and what was sent before you." From this particular verse, Gülen argues that, in the beginning, the Qur'an calls Muslims to accept "the former Prophets and their Books." By establishing a belief in former prophets and revelations, Islam establishes the foundation of interfaith dialogue. Believing in early prophets is supported by procedural encouragement given to Muslims in the Qur'an (29–46): "And discuss you not with the People of the Book, except with means better (than mere disputation)." Gülen (2000, 251) suggests that the Qur'an establishes that dialogue that should concentrate on finding common points rather than refuting others' religious beliefs. Gülen's approach does not address to what extent and how to legitimize religious differences. In part Gülen's reluctance to delineate legitimate religious difference is due to the minimalism of the Qur'an (3:64) in its invitation to people of Abrahamic faiths to come to the common word (the oneness of God). Also, in an important way, this reluctance is because of Gülen's emphasis on the practical reason of interfaith dialogue. He trusts in the transformative quality of interfaith dialogue to facilitate the creative frameworks religiously sensitive people can construct within dialogue rather than putting conditions and boundaries prior to interfaith engagement.

The unity of the chain of prophecy, revelation, and commonalities of the religious traditions do not necessarily translate into dialogue, particularly between Muslims and Christians. Gülen (2002, 243–244) gives four reasons for Muslim difficulties in this situation: Western assaults on Muslims since the crusades; domestic political repression of Muslims; politicization of Islam; and the misrepresentation of Islam in the West. These mostly political factors are compatible with the general skepticism Gülen has about politics. Politics, with its focus on the allocation of (mostly material) resources, divides people, while religion unites them. These difficulties should not discourage the faithful from participating in dialogue, but rather motivate them to advocate for it more strongly.

In conclusion, the Muslim scholar, Fethullah Gülen, develops an interfaith theology using resources within the Islamic tradition. Gülen's interfaith theology establishes a theology of revelation and prophecy as an axis to link faith traditions. The existence of this axis is supported by shared beliefs and practices across faiths. He also relies on the Qur'an, particularly the Qur'an's positive references to the "Peoples of the Book," to support his inclusive interfaith theology. Gülen emphasizes the shared beliefs and practices among religions to substantiate both of his claims: the divine origins of all major religions and the possibility of interfaith cooperation.

Conclusion

There are three caveats to my argument for the growing presence, possibility, and promise of interfaith theologies. First, interfaith dialogue presents the glass of religious diversity as half full rather than half empty. There are preachers of hate as well as preachers of dialogue. This paper explicitly focuses on the latter. While showing inclusive interpretations of Abrahamic religions, I have ignored the exclusivist interpretations of these religious traditions. An intra-religious dialogue between proponents of exclusivist and inclusivist interpretations of religions can be more daunting than interfaith dialogue. Second, overlapping consensus is not the combination or homogenization of religions. Each of these religious leaders takes a separate route, anchoring their rationales within their own faith doctrines. The better justified one's interfaith theology is within its broader religious doctrine, the more it will appeal to the believers, and the greater its chances of success will be. Third, these religious leaders reject exclusivist (all-or-nothing) interpretations but they do not support pluralist (all-equally-valid) interpretations. While they are not preachers of exclusion and hate, they are not prophets of cosmopolitan ethics either. They emphasize the superiority of their traditions. Second, they establish minimum universal standards for what counts as divine truth. What they develop is a theologically acceptable (reasonable) religious pluralism.

These reservations about interfaith dialogue do not invalidate its vitality, possibility, or promise of a peaceful global coexistence. Interfaith activists claim that religion can and does bring people together and fosters shared values rather than creating inevitable division and fear. The works of such prominent Jewish, Christian, and Muslim religious leaders as Rabbi Jonathan Sacks, the late Pope John Paul II, and Fethullah Gülen indicate that interfaith dialogue is not a spiritual whim but has a rigorous theological framework and value. Their theological leadership thus validates, accommodates, and humanizes the "other" in order to open up religious space for interfaith activities and to establish religious grounds to complement humanity's quest for peace, tolerance, and care for God's creation.

This volume attests to the wide-ranging initiatives that foundations, charities, and schools that the members of the Gülen Movement establish as evidence both of the genuine commitment of the movement to peaceful coexistence and of the intensive work these organizations do for peace building. There are yet stronger links between the movement and peace-building activities: Gülen's teaching and interfaith theology. His teachings have become an important motivating factor for movement participants in their efforts to engage in interfaith dialogue and peace activities. More importantly, his interfaith theology has deeper implications; he articulates a theological rationale for interfaith dialogue. Anchored in mainstream Islamic sources and interpretations, in particular the theology of revelation and prophecy, it offers a religiously secure framework to accommodate, value, and dignify the religious other. While Gülen's interfaith theology may not solve all conflicts in international society, the religious recognition his Islamic interfaith theology creates for the religious other may mitigate and even remove the deep-seated religious anxieties and tensions, and thus contribute toward long-term support for peaceful coexistence in the world.

I thank Jessie Dye, Ahmet Kuru, Kate Marshall, Rainier Jose Reyes, Mike Strausz, and Jennifer Welsh for their comments on earlier drafts of this paper.

References

Aslan, A. 1998. *Religious Pluralism in Christian and Islamic Philosophy*. Surrey: Curzon Press.

Barber, B. 1996. *Jihad vs. McWorld*. New York: Ballantine Books.

Barnes, M. 2002. *Theology and the Dialogue of Religions*. Cambridge: Cambridge University Press.

Carroll, B. J. 2007. *A Dialogue of Civilizations: Gülen's Islamic Ideals and Humanistic Discourse*. New Jersey: The Light Inc.

Cassidy, E. I. 2005. *Ecumenism and Interreligious Dialogue*. New York: Paulist Press.

Eck, D. 1993. *Encountering Gold: A Spiritual Journey from Bozeman to Banaras.* Boston: Beacon Press.

Flannery, A., ed. 1996. *Vatican Council II: Constitutions, Decrees, declarations*. Northport, NY: Costello Publishing.

Gülen, M. F. 2000. *Advocate of Dialogue*. Compiled by A. Ünal and A. Williams. Fairfax, VA. The Fountain Press.

———. 2004. *Toward a Global Civilization of Love and Tolerance*. New Jersey: The Light, Inc.

Harries, R. 2004. "Jonathan Sacks's *The Dignity of Difference*." *Scottish Journal of Theology*. 57(1): 109–115.

Huntington, S. P. 1996. *The Clash of Civilizations and the Remaking of World Order*. New York: Simon & Schuster.

John Paul II. 1994. *Crossing the Threshold of Hope*. London: Jonathan Cape.

Novak, D. 1989. *Jewish-Christian Dialogue: A Jewish Justification*. Oxford: Oxford University Press.

Race, A. 1983. *Christians and Religious Pluralism: Patterns in the Christian Theology of Religions*. London: SCM Press.

Rawls, J. 1996. *Political Liberalism*. New York: Columbia University Press.

Sacks, J. 2002. *The Dignity of Difference: How to Avoid the Clash of Civilizations*. London: Continuum.

———. 2005. *To Heal a Fractured Word: The Ethics of Responsibility*. New York: Schocken.

Sahin, Z. 2008. "Interfaith Dialogue Organizations as Actors of Peace Building: The Case of the Rumi Forum." Presented at Fethullah Gülen and Peace Building Conference. Washington, DC.

Sarıtoprak, Z. and Griffith, S. 2005. "Fethullah Gülen and the 'People of the Book': A Voice from Turkey for Interfaith Dialogue." *The Muslim World* 95(3): 329–341.

Solomon, N. 2005. "Towards a Jewish Theology of Trilateral Dialogue." *Islam and Global Dialogue: Religious Pluralism and the Pursuit of Peace*, ed. R. Boase. Burlington, VA: Ashgate.

Chapter 8

Fethullah Gülen's Theology of Peacebuilding

Zeki Sarıtoprak

O Lord, You are peace and peace comes from You.
Give us, our Lord, a life full of peace.
Prophet Muhammad (peace and blessings be upon him)

Introduction

Our world has become a global village where people are more interconnected than ever. Technological progress continues at an amazing speed. The emergence of human beings' awareness of their place in the universe increases their sharing in one another's happiness and sorrow; this consciousness is unique to our time and carries risks as well as benefits. No nation or ethnicity in the world can claim complete isolation, even the most simple of societies. As a result of increased interaction and access to faster channels of communication, human beings have greater need than ever for the maturity of mind and spirit to coexist peacefully. However, in contrast to the high speed of technological development, the building of human relationships appears to be slower than ever. Where greater communication should foster real relationships between members of the human family, today's world instead faces conditions in which two-thirds of the world's population suffers from interpersonal violence and war. In this paper, I will examine a sampling of Fethullah Gülen's theological views on peace and peacebuilding, and the roots of these views in the Qur'an. This does not claim to be an exhaustive study of Gülen's writings on peace; rather, it is a theological study of the Qur'anic foundations of his thought.

Peace in the Qur'an

Building peace among human beings is the most important task, though one of the most difficult of all, required of the human family. Peace is one of the names of God (*al-Salam*). Many Muslims name their children Abd al-Salam (the Servant of Peace) after this divine name. It is a responsibility of human beings to live peacefully in order to make the entire world a reflection of the divine name, Peace.

The Qur'an makes many references to peace. Muslim scholars have cited many of these Qur'anic verses in their writings on peacebuilding. The Arabic root word for peace is *s-l-m*, which carries connotations of both "peace" and "submission." The words "Islam," "Muslim," "Muslimun" (plural), and "Salam" all come from this same root. The word "Salam" is used many times in the Qur'an, for example, when describing the quality of the servants of God, who are defined by their peaceful response to insult: "The servants of God are those who walk on the earth modestly, and when certain foolish people address them, their answer is 'salam'" (25:63). That is to say, even if they are insulted they do not respond to evil with evil. This principle is also emphasized in the following Qur'anic verse: "When the servants of God pass near negative behavior, they pass by with dignity and kindness" (25:72).

Considering the violence in today's world, and the proliferation of weapons capable of rendering the human family extinct several times over, it is urgent that both Muslims and adherents of other religions follow the instructions of the Qur'anic verse for human relationships: "Peace is better" (4:128). Even in the midst of war, on the battlefield, if there is an opportunity for peace, the Qur'anic injunction is "if the enemy inclines towards peace, you should incline towards it too" (8:61).

Peacebuilding and the Beginning of Islam

The very beginning of Islam was marked by successful peaceful resolutions to ongoing conflicts. The Prophet was known for his nonviolent response to violence and persecution in Mecca. His peacebuilding skills became so well known that he and his followers were invited by the leaders of the city of Medina to build peace among rival tribes that had been fighting for centuries. Under his leadership, a peaceful society was successfully established in Medina, and later, even in Mecca.

One example of the Prophet's peacebuilding is the famous story of the black stone, in which he solved a dispute among several Arab tribal leaders in such a way that all were able to equitably share in the same moment of honor. On another occasion, the reconciliation of two individuals took precedence over even the Prophet's prescribed daily prayer. This occasion is recorded in certain Islamic references which indicate that Abu Bakr led the prayer in the Prophet's absence.

The importance of peacemaking in early Islamic tradition can be deduced from the presence of an entire book on the Prophet's sayings about peacebuilding in *Sahih al-Bukhari*, the most authentic collection of the sayings of the Prophet. One, for example, tells the story of the Prophet making peace between two individuals fighting over a debt owed:

> Once, Allah's Apostle heard the loud voices of some opponents quarreling at the door. One of them was appealing to the other to deduct his debt and asking him to be lenient but the other was saying, 'By Allah I will not do so.' Allah's Apostle went out to them and said, 'Who is the one who was swearing by Allah that he would not do a favor?' That man said, 'I am that person,

O Allah's Apostle! I will give my opponent whatever he wishes.' (Al-Bukhari 1953, Hadith 868)

Human Society and Islamic Values

Scholars of peacebuilding have developed principles that are considered critical to coexistence and mutual cooperation, which are also referred to directly or indirectly in some Qur'anic verses. These are: recognition of human dignity, understanding of the common origins of all human beings, the consideration of diversity as positive, the acknowledgment of other religions, the awareness that judgment belongs to God alone (which occurs on the Day of Judgment), and finally the need for Muslims to practice good deeds. They should deal justly and equitably in their interactions with others (Fahmi 1993 cited in Abu-Nimer 2003, 73).

The Islamic view of human society is based on the principles of harmony, knowledge, justice and peace: wars and violent actions, while part of the history of every major world religion, have no place in the essence of Islam. The Islamic understanding of Paradise is based on peace; in fact, Paradise is called *Dar al-Salam* (the Abode of Peace). Peace is such a central notion to Islam that the very greeting among the people of paradise is Peace, or *Salam* (10:10). The righteous will be told, "Enter paradise peacefully and safely forever" (15:46). Muslims in their daily greetings use the same language: *as-salamu alaikum,* or "peace be with you." Muslims are exhorted to try to make this world as similar as possible to the ideal life of Paradise.

Despite this ideal goal, the Qur'an acknowledges the reality of human nature and the possible conflicts that may arise between peoples. However, it constantly encourages believers to incline towards peace in any situation of dispute. First of all, all human beings should assume the responsibility to make peace, in accordance with the divine principle "Fear God and make peace among yourselves" (8:1). A similar Qur'anic verse speaks of the responsibility of political authorities to make peace and stop violence if it occurs: when fighting occurs between two rival groups, it is incumbent upon the Islamic authority to make peace between the two. The Qur'anic verse says, "If two groups of believers fight against each other, make peace between them. If one party does wrong to the other, you fight that which does wrong until it returns to the ordinance of God. If it returns, make peace between them justly, and act equitably; God loves the just" (49:9). The verse clearly suggests that it is a compulsory duty for adherents of the Qur'an to prevent any aggression if they are able, a duty that requires the intervention of a third-party as mediator to resolve conflict. The verse has been cited by some scholars to justify the use of violence in Islam and thus to refute the pacifist hypothesis. However, other scholars argue that "the passage clearly supports the concept of mediation and fair and just third-party intervention" (Abu-Nimer 2003, 62).

Since God has placed no limitations on the devastating capacity of human anger, building peace is one of the most difficult tasks for human beings. It requires steadfastness, resolve and patience, which are considered prized values in Islam and essential elements for peacebuilding strategies. "Control of emotions and listening to the way of rational thinking are considered essentials to peacebuilding" (Abu-Nimer 2003, 65). It is a long process, and it may take generations to build worldwide peace. The Qur'an encourages peace-builders in this struggle by reminding them of the eternal rewards they will receive. Even if they are not fully successful, still they will be rewarded for their works, and therefore they should not lose hope while working for peace; even the angels in paradise will greet such peacemakers with joy. "Peace be with you," they will say, "because of your patience in the life of the world" (13:24).

Two main principles upon which Islamic civilization is founded are mutual cooperation and the loving interrelatedness of creation. The first principle is one that scholars of peacebuilding refer to as "collaborative action" and "solidarity." According to this principle, the planet depends on the mutual cooperation of all creatures helping one another: rain helps grass to grow; grass helps animals to grow; and animals help human beings to grow. This provides an example for human beings. That is to say, "All human beings have a common origin in God, who created them all equal. Therefore, they should assist one another and not neglect one another's needs" (Abu-Nimer 2003, 73). This principle finds its root in the Qur'anic verse, "[...] Help one another in what is good and pious, not in what is wicked and sinful" (5:2). The second principle insists that all members of creation be considered brothers and sisters. This principle requires all human beings to reject anything that does damage to this essential relationship; therefore, in Islam all forms of chauvinism (including racism and nationalism) are unacceptable. Therefore, communal solidarity is one of the goals that Islam puts forward as a principle.

Some scholars suggest that the five pillars of Islam have a direct relationship to the work of peacebuilding and non-violent action. *Shahadah* indicates obedience to God and the Prophet; the five daily prayers teach discipline; *zakat* provides social solidarity through compulsory charity; fasting trains people to be patient and selfless in times of difficulty and suffering; and the *hajj* creates unity and friendship between members of the community through pilgrimage. These pillars of Islam provide the necessary elements through which one is prepared to make peace and to accept peace (Abu-Nimer 2003, 45; see also Satha-Anand 1993).

Religious Peacebuilding in the Global Context

Nowadays, as mentioned above, the majority of the world's population suffers the effects of global conflicts and wars. The victims are mainly the vulnerable: children, women and the elderly. The world experienced history's most devastating war just decades ago, and there is fear that history may repeat itself. The major European cities were in the midst of intense bombing. According to one account, as many as 35 million people were killed during World

War II. Enlightenment and civilization did not help to prevent the leaders of the "civilized" world from engaging in such destruction.

When reflecting upon the world wars, the global community agrees, "never again." However, the current trend of our world is unfortunately not peace-oriented; indications are that we are headed for worse destruction than our world has ever seen. Therefore, Muslims, Christians, Jews, Hindus, Buddhists, and adherents of all other religions should make every effort for the dominion of peace.

Peacebuilding in Gülen's Thought

In the Islamic world one can see important efforts in this direction. Fethullah Gülen was named the world's most influential intellectual in 2008 in a survey by *Foreign Policy* magazine. As elaborating on Gülen's biography is beyond the scope of this paper, suffice it to say that Gülen's passionate pursuit of a theology of peace began at a young age, in an era when anarchy and chaos were dominating Turkish society. Marxist and nationalist groups were in armed conflict with one another. More than 10,000 people in Turkey were killed in two decades during these clashes. Even families were not immune to this violence and tragedy; members of the same family could be found fighting on opposite sides of the conflicts. Gülen made great efforts to extinguish the fire of conflict amidst this chaos, and his faith-based efforts had a significant impact on building peace between rival groups. Gülen, in an interview with Safa Kaplan in Istanbul's *Hürriyet,* 21 April 2004, says the following concerning his continuing theology of peace:

> When anarchy was everywhere in our country, I called for calmness and controlling of anger. I had received death threats, yet I called upon... to continue working for peace, "If I am assassinated, despite all your anger, I ask you to bury my body and seek order, peace and love in our society." Regardless of what happens, we believers should be representatives of love and security. I continue saying the same today.

While Gülen did not directly intervene to stop the armed conflict, his educational efforts have equipped millions of young people with religious and moral values that have prevented them from engaging in such conflicts. Gülen believes that the new generation should be equipped with qualities such as wisdom, compassion, faith and knowledge.

It is a tradition among Turkish intellectuals to work for the creation of an "ideal generation." For example, Mehmet Akif Ersoy, the writer of the Turkish National Anthem, chose the name Asım as the proper name for the ideal generation: the "Generation of Asım" (*Asım'ın Nesli*). Bediüzzaman Said Nursi spoke of the "New Generation" (*Nasl-i Jadeed*: *Nesl-i Cedid*, in Turkish). Necip Fazıl Kısakürek, another prominent Turkish poet and author, idealized his generation as the "Faithful Youth Generation" (*Imanlı Genclik*).

Gülen, having read the work of his predecessors, examined his own generation and found the lack of proper education to be the essence of the problems the young people faced. Through his writings and encouraging the founding of educational institutions, he has attempted to help develop such a generation, for which he has coined the term "the Golden Generation" (*Altın Nesil*). The aim of the Golden Generation idea is to provide a perfect education for a perfect generation in order to obtain a perfect society. The Golden Generation also requires the young people of the community to show a great respect for religious and national values. Gülen hopes that a lasting peace can be achieved through the work of a generation which is peaceful, made up of individuals who are living examples of peace, who will build bridges of dialogue and mutual understanding to make peace among people. To Gülen, the Golden Generation has certain specific qualities: knowledge, faith, love, idealism, altruism, and action (Agai 2002, 27–47, see also Agai 2003). In the last decade, when some political scientists spoke of a "clash of civilizations," Gülen ardently urged the building of "breakwaters" in order to prevent such a clash.

It is not an exaggeration to assert that Gülen's theology through such endeavors has, and will continue to have, a global impact on building peace. Gülen's philosophy of peace and his efforts are not isolated instances in Islam; in fact, as briefly mentioned above, the entire heritage of Islam is the foundation of Gülen's understanding of peace. He counts among his role models, certainly, mystics such as Hasan al-Basri and Abu-Talib al-Makki; scholars and mystics such as Abu Hamid al-Ghazzali, Jalaluddin Rumi, Ahmad Sirhindi, and Bediüzzaman Said Nursi; and most importantly the companions of the Prophet. One can argue that if any of these Muslim personalities had lived in our time, they would be involved in the same work as Gülen.

Education as Peacebuilding

Contemporary scholars of peacebuilding have elaborated on certain elements that are essential for making peace in any part of the world. Two of these elements are education and knowledge. There is no doubt that Gülen's greatest efforts and contributions are related to these two fields. Bediüzzaman Said Nursi, in the beginning of the twentieth century, stated that "there are three major enemies of Muslims: ignorance, poverty, and internal division (Nursi 1996, 1921). If we take a closer look at our modern world, we can easily understand the importance of education, particularly for Muslims, who constitute 22 percent of the world's population. Population growth is faster among Muslims than any other population, while literacy rates remain significantly low (Ahmed 2005). Gülen considers lack of education to be a disease requiring a cure; his efforts are an attempt to cure the disease.

Today in Turkey, Central Asia, and many other parts of the world, the educational institutions that were established by Gülen Movement participants have continued to contribute greatly to the education of people of different religions and ethnicities. In fact, his Golden Generation has already contributed, through educational endeavors, to the building of peace in many areas of conflict, including the Balkans, northern Iraq, Northern Ireland, and the Philippines.

Thomas Michel, in an article about Gülen, describes his own visit to a school established by Gülen Movement participants on the Philippine island of Mindanao. Michel visited an area of the island where kidnapping, guerrilla warfare, and armed conflict were constant between Moro separatists and the Philippine state. Michel states, "The school [the Philippine-Turkish School of Tolerance] offers Muslim and Christian Filipino children an excellent education and a more positive way of living and relating to each other" (Michel 2003). Michel (2003) found in the school students from all backgrounds and described it as a "haven of peace" in this region of conflict.

My own experience echoes that of Michel's. I visited Skopje, Macedonia in the summer of 2004, where I had the opportunity to visit a school established by some Turkish businessmen who were supporters of the Gülen Movement. I was told that when civil war was going on in the region, members of many different ethnic groups were sending their children to this school. Their parents were fighting one another, but the children were living peacefully under the roof of the same school. This same situation is true also in educational institutions established in other areas of conflict, such as Iraq and East Africa.

Ibn Khaldun and Gülen

In order to contextualize Gülen's peacebuilding theology, I would like to draw upon the famous fourteenth-century Muslim sociologist Ibn Khaldun's understanding of peacebuilding. In Ibn Khaldun's philosophy, individual efforts and sacrifices remain essential for building peace. He suggests that peace in society is possible through the willingness of an individual to subordinate himself or herself to the group. Without this, peace and social development are not possible (Ibn Khaldun 1958).

Ibn Khaldun addresses the development of urban society in the term *asabiyya*, or "group solidarity," in a way which empties the term of its original connotations of racism and nationalism, both of which are prohibited in Islam. I would like to borrow this term from Ibn Khaldun to indicate solidarity around a value or an idea that is shared by members of society. Gülen's "Golden Generation" exemplifies Ibn Khaldun's idea of the establishment of peace in society. Gülen considers peacebuilding as a sacred task. One can compare people who contribute to the activities of this movement to those who go to Friday prayer. Just as people perform their prayer as a sacred duty without being asked to do so, people are also coming together to build peace. In other words, people think that the activities of the movement positively affect society and their spiritual life. Therefore, many want to be part of these activities. This togetherness between people is not based on emotion; rather, it is based on shared values. Following this theology people come together around a particular ideal; therefore, the effectiveness of the movement is not solely attached to the charismatic leadership of one person. Gülen, for example, insists that the movement should never be dependent upon his personality. This approach will guarantee that the movement will continue beyond the death of its founder.

Gülen's theology of peace is based on the integrity of the individual; his approach to social restoration and peacebuilding, therefore, is one of "bottom-up" social change. It should be noted that Ibn Khaldun's concept of *Asabiyya* carries its own risks of an excessive group loyalty, which can be dangerous for a harmonious society. Gülen, by emphasizing the quality of individuals, believes that the Golden Generation should be able to practice and spread justice and compassion in their societies. Therefore, his ideal Golden Generation is based not on ethnicity, but on moral and ethical dimensions. There is no doubt that compassion and justice are two important components of peacebuilding. Compassion requires justice. In

Islam, a person is always encouraged to forgive even when his or her rights are violated. Therefore, while the individual's right to seek retributive justice is retained, restorative justice is the preferred response. Gülen in his theology of peace describes his ideal generation as a "selfless people, sincerely thinking of others rather than themselves." He says:

> Who knows? Maybe in the near future some selfless people, who sacrifice themselves to make others live, will unite hearts and minds through their efforts. Conscience and logic will become two different, deeply rooted dimensions of their lives that will complete each other. Physics and metaphysics will abandon the fight between themselves: in order to give the opportunity for the beauty of everything to express itself in its own language, each will return to its own field. These selfless people will discover the interconnectedness of the divine command and the laws of nature. People will repent of their previous meaningless fights with one another. An atmosphere of serenity will be built and be felt in homes and in schools. No dignity will be stepped on. Hearts will be full of respect to the extent that no one will trespass on the property or the dignity of others. The powerful will act justly so that the weak and the poor will have a chance to live humanely. No one will be arrested just because of an assumption. No one's house or business will be attacked. No innocent's blood will be shed. No oppressed person will cry out. Everyone will love human beings as a duty towards God. It is exactly this time when the world, which is a corridor to Paradise, will become a paradise-like place that will always be enjoyed (Gülen 2006a, 110).

He strongly advocates selflessness and living for others as the most essential qualities of the builders of peace. He calls them "devoted souls" (*adanmış ruhlar*). Selflessness has enormous potential in the building of a sustainable peace. Selflessness helps those who dedicate themselves to peace better understand the situation and sufferings of victims. This eventually brings about a collective approach, which "allow[s] victims of injustice to exert influence and power over the other side" (Abu-Nimer 2003, 75). By living for others, Gülen believes that the ideal individual should always prefer the advantages of others over his or her own. This is in fact a description of the believers in early Islam, the companions of the Prophet. The Qur'an says of them that "they prefer others over themselves even if they are in need" (59:9). Without a generation with similar qualities, Gülen, like Ibn Khaldun, argues that peace would not be possible. This is why he constantly emphasizes the need for faithful and selfless individuals to dedicate themselves to the establishment of peace. In Gülen's theology, educational institutions should serve to bring up such individuals from the realm of imagination to the realm of realization. It can be argued that all of Gülen's educational efforts work towards this goal.

Hope and Love

Despite the overwhelmingly negative and violent state of the world, Gülen remains hopeful about the future of humanity. He believes that the efforts to build peace in the world and attempts to create a harmonious society will bear fruit. This great hope is exemplified in the following statement:

> Once, despite obstacles, through the teaching of the Qur'an, an enduring love, respect, and dialogue were achieved. These days, I have full faith that through the efforts of these *holy people* a new atmosphere, new understandings and dialogue will be achieved. Even now, through the *migrants* who carry this idea around the world, the rivers of love have started to flow. Now they are heard in every corner of the planet. The breezes of tranquility and happiness have started to be felt. And in every corner of the world, they are creating *islands of peace* for stability and harmony (Gülen 2006a, 111).[27]

According to Gülen, his ideal Golden Generation will always think of positive steps to build peace. His Golden Generation will not be distracted by historical mistakes. He would say, despite some negative historical experiences like the Crusades and colonization, "We

---

27 My emphasis.

are resolved not to remember those events and not to give an opportunity for the rebirth of animosity. We strongly encourage the confining of historical mistakes within the limits of the history books so as not to resurrect feelings of animosity between people" (Gülen 2006b, 158).

Describing his ideal generation further, Gülen says, "Everyone in their capacity is like an apostle of revivalism carrying in their hands the flowers of friendship, on their lips the songs of brotherhood. Their tongue, which takes its essence from the eloquence of the Qur'an, is stronger than any sword. Their words are afterlife-oriented. These words shatter darkness without harming anyone" (Gülen 2006a, 112).

In Gülen's ideal world "there is no bullying, no greed, no quarrelling, no distrust, no lies, no oppression, and no deception. On the contrary, there is chivalry, tenderness, the efforts of revival, the love for life, kindness and dialogue, respect for truth, trust, acknowledgement of kindness and generosity, the spirit of righteousness, justice, and the following of the straight path" (Gülen 2006c, 88–92). In Gülen's theology such an ideal generation can be an important instrument for establishing such a world of peace where "people love love and hate hatred" (Nursi 1996, 1930). Gülen compares hatred to a destructive flood which destroys trust among segments of society. This hatred brings baseless accusations against the people who strive for peace. Through hatred, words can be taken out of their context and even the most innocent statement can be used against an individual (Gülen 2006a, 75).

"Lighting Candles" through the Media

One must acknowledge that building global peace is not an easy task. It requires patience, an important Islamic virtue that is repeatedly mentioned in the Qur'an.[28] It also requires the sacrifice of indi-

28 For example, see 2:45, 2:153, 2:177, 2:250, 3:200, 8:46, 11:11, 16:126, 14:12, 31:17, 40:55, 42:43, and 46:35.

viduals. Gülen suggests that individuals who dedicate themselves to working for humanity and building peace have to be patient and uninfluenced by the trend of hasty and sloganeering politics.

Gülen's own experience indicates some of the political difficulties that peace builders face: in the 1990s, when Gülen promoted dialogue between different ethnicities and adherents of different religious traditions, both some extreme secularists and some extreme Muslims opposed him. Eventually, he left Turkey for the United States, for medical reasons, but also to avoid this conflict.

Gülen compares his opponents in Turkey to the Kharijites of early Islam, saying, "Similar to the logic of Kharijites, this destructive group destroys everything positive; like an anarchist under the control of hatred and revulsion, they attack everything. They run from one wildness to another, destroying the bridges of understanding and making the roads of dialogue impassable, causing despair in the loving spirits and injecting violence and hatred into hearts that beat with love" (Gülen 2006a, 75–82). These thoughts express his deep concern and fear for the future of peace in his own country.

Even in the midst of great fear and concern, Gülen remains hopeful that the efforts to build peace will eventually be successful. His hope grows out of his own experience: at one point, the media and the secular elite of Turkey pronounced him *persona non grata* to the extent that his life was threatened.[29] As a result of this experience, he later worked to develop a media presence that would "light candles" of hope for believers in his community. Gülen was aware that any theology, in order to communicate successfully, must have access to the media. Those who opposed him had this access and were able to communicate their own theological and social ideologies in ways which, Gülen believed, damaged the hope and faith of the people.

It is the duty of the ideal generation, he says, to enlighten people rather than sulk in darkness. For this reason, during the 1980s,

29 For the details of Gülen's feelings, see Gülen 2006a, 75-82.

the Gülen Movement worked towards the establishment of a newspaper and later a television channel. Both projects became highly successful both within and outside Turkey. Through these, as well as through monthly and weekly journals, the Gülen Movement successfully established a powerful media presence, communicating a consistent theology of peacebuilding (Barton 2006). In an era when the media is dominated by conflict, violence and shifting values, Gülen's media presence offers a powerful theological corrective.

Theology of Forgiveness and Compassion

In Gülen's theology of peacebuilding, there is no place for revenge. Despite the hardships that Gülen has faced during a process of legal accusations, spiritual persecution, and exile, he has never sought revenge. "We are going to respect our character," he says. "We will not harm those who persecute us. We will not seek an eye for an eye. We will never curse them. We will not break hearts, and in the manner of Yunus [Emre, the famous fourteenth-century Turkish poet], we will invite everyone to love.... As a believer, I promise that I will never shun any person, and I will not persecute those who have transgressed against me" (Gülen 2006b, 217).

Scholars of peacebuilding consider forgiveness a cherished virtue in Islam and an essential for peacebuilding. Gülen sees forgiveness as one of the indispensable qualities of his Golden Generation. Therefore, according to him, the most important gift for the coming generation is to teach children how to forgive. Gülen states, "Today's generation's greatest gift to their children and to their grandchildren is to teach them how to forgive even the most offensive behavior and nauseating actions" (Gülen 2006d, 77). He calls forgiveness a "heavenly medicine" that can cure the many wounds of society.

For Gülen, another effective element with which to build peace is love. He considers love to be an effective "weapon"; he embraces this weapon of love against all violent actions:

> In a time when people are defeated by their sense of revenge and animosity, when the masses are driven into struggles and wars, when truth is silenced before force, when those who wield power behave as tyrants against those who disagree with them, when dictators and oppressors are applauded and promoted, while the oppressed are treated badly, we once again say: love. I believe that love has the capacity to change the rhythm of our life (Gülen 2006e, 113).[30]

According to Gülen, once one is equipped with love and compassion, there will be no difference between "you," "we" and "others." Gülen considers love an essential element of his theology of peacebuilding. He says, "We need love and compassion more than water and air" (Gülen 2006a, 184). Gülen describes those who love others and live for others as heroes. He says, "Happy are those who make love their guide in their journey. How unfortunate are those who do not perceive the love that is grounded in their spirit and who spend an entire life blind and deaf" (Gülen 1997a, 98).

Fethullah Gülen, who is unmarried and lives simply, has no worldly possessions.[31] Gülen has renounced the material benefits that could come from activities inspired by his teaching. Gülen's tremendous compassion for all people allows him to feel the spiritual benefits of building peace. Such spiritual benefits can be felt by anyone who builds peace through compassion.

In the tradition in which Gülen was raised, his understanding is that no matter how small, every creature praises God in its own tongue (17:44), and therefore deserves its proper respect and compassion. Gülen says:

> Compassion is the beginning of being; without it everything is chaos. Everything has come into existence through compassion and by compassion it continues to exist in harmony.... Everything

30 For further reading on Gülen's understanding of love for human beings, see Gülen 2006b, 34–38.

31 He has made it clear that he never made an intentional vow of celibacy, but just never married because it "never happened." He does not uphold lifelong celibacy as an Islamic value.

> speaks of compassion and promises compassion. Because of this, the universe can be considered a symphony of compassion. All kinds of voices proclaim compassion so that it is impossible not to be aware of it, and impossible not to feel the wide mercy encircling everything. How unfortunate are the souls who don't perceive this.... Human beings have a responsibility to show compassion to all living beings, as a requirement of being human. The more one displays compassion, the more exalted one becomes, while the more one resorts to wrongdoing, oppression and cruelty, the more one is disgraced and humiliated, becoming a shame to humanity (Gülen 1996, 40-42; see also Gülen 1997b, 90-95).

In fact the above statement from Gülen reflects the Qur'anic teaching of compassion which is necessary for solving the contemporary conflicts and bringing peace to our world.

Conclusion

As an ardent student of the Qur'an and Islamic tradition, Gülen has developed his theology of peacemaking based on the Qur'anic principles of peace and the examples of early Islamic history. What gives us hope, after a discussion of Gülen's thought, is that Gülen's influence on public opinion has been significant through his powerful media presence and work in education. His influence is deeply rooted in the best theological traditions of Islam, consistently referring to themes of hope, love, compassion and forgiveness. These are essential elements to any faith-based peacemaking activity. The world is blessed to have such a strong personality as Gülen calling so forcefully for the establishment of peace in a world that is suffering deeply as the result of conflict.

References

Abu-Nimer, M. 2003. *Nonviolence and Peace Building in Islam: Theory and Practice*. Gainesville, Florida: University Press of Florida.

Agai, B. 2002. "Fethullah Gülen and His Movement's Islamic Ethic of Education." *Critique: Critical Middle Eastern Studies* 11, 27–47.

———. 2003. "The Gülen Movement's Islamic Ethic of Education." *Turkish Islam and the Secular State: The Gülen Movement*, eds. M. H. Yavuz and J. L. Esposito. Syracuse: Syracuse University Press, 48–68.

Ahmed, A. 2005. "Islam and the West: Clash or Dialogue of Civilizations?" *Islam and Global Dialogue: Religious Pluralism and the Pursuit of Peace,* ed. R. Boase. London: Ashgate Publishing, 103–118.

———. 2005. "Islam and the West: Clash or Dialogue of Civilizations?" *Islam and Global Dialogue: Religious Pluralism and the Pursuit of Peace*, Roger Boase, ed. London: Ashgate Publishing, 103–118.

Al-Bukhari, Abu Abdillah Muhammad bin Ismail. 1953. *Sahih al-Bukhari.* Cairo: Mustafa al- Bab al-Halabi.

Barton, G. 2006. "Turkey's Gülen *Hizmet* and Indonesia's Neo-Modernist NGOs: Remarkable Examples of Progressive Islamic Thought and Civil Society Activism in the Muslim World." *Political Islam and Human Security,* Fetih Mansouri and Shahram Akbarzadeh, eds. Cambridge: Cambridge Scholars Press, 140–160.

Fahmi, H. 1993. *Al-Islam wa al-demugratiah* (*Islam and Democracy*). Cairo: Cairo Center for Translation and Publication.

Gülen, M. F. 1996. *Towards the Lost Paradise*. London: Truestar.

———. 1997a. *Yitirilmiş Cennete Doğru (Çağ ve Nesil Serisi 3).* Izmir: Nil Yayınları.

———. 1997b. *Fatiha Üzerine Mülahazalar*. Izmir: Nil Yayınları.

———. 2006a. *Örnekleri Kendinden Bir Hareket (Çağ ve Nesil Serisi 8)*. Istanbul: Nil Yayınları.

———. 2006b. *Işığın Göründügü Ufuk* (*Çağ ve Nesil Serisi 7*). Istanbul: Nil Yayınları.

———. 2006c. *Yeşeren Düşünceler* (*Çağ ve Nesil 6)*. Istanbul: Nil Yayınları.

———. 2006d. *Çağ ve Nesil (Çağ ve Nesil Serisi 1)*. Istanbul: Nil Yayınları.

———. 2006e. *Yeşeren Düşünceler* (*Çağ ve Nesil 6*). Istanbul: Nil Yayınları.

Ibn Khaldun, Abu Zayd 'Abdur-Rahman bin Muhammad. 1958. *The Muqqadimah,* Vol. 1. Trans. Franz Rosenthal. New York: Bollingen Foundation.

Michel, T. 2003. "Fethullah Gülen as Educator." *Turkish Islam and the Secular State: The Gülen Movement*, ed. M. H. Yavuz and J. L. Esposito. Syracuse: Syracuse University Press, 69–84.

Nursi, S. 1996. "Divan-i harb-i orfi." *Risale-i Nur.* Istanbul: Nesil.

Satha-Anand, C. 1993. "Core Values for Peacemaking in Islam: The Prophet's Practice as Paradigm." *Building Peace in the Middle East,* ed. E. Boulding. Boulder: Lynne Rienner.

CHAPTER 9

Islamic Prospects for Interreligious Dialogue: The Voice of Fethullah Gülen

Douglas Pratt

INTRODUCTION

We live at a time where "the importance of dialogue among people of faith for the effective pursuit of peace" is without parallel (Michel 2004). The dialogue of civilizations, which is in effect a dialogue between the members of religions, is an imperative which is laid upon us in an unprecedented way. Into this context, as Thomas Michel (2004) has observed, Fethullah Gülen has emerged as one "of the most persuasive and influential voices in the Muslim community" calling for dialogue as a step toward peace. Indeed, he offers "a way to live out Islamic values amidst the complex demands of modern societies and to engage in ongoing dialogue and cooperation with people of other religions." And the faith-based movement inspired by him promotes "truly spiritual values like forgiveness, inner peace, social harmony, honesty, and trust in God" as the basis for inter-communal peace and interreligious dialogue. Fethullah Gülen has had, and continues to have, a considerable impact upon the thinking and sensibilities of Muslims throughout the Turkish Islamic world and beyond. As Paul Weller has observed, Gülen's teaching "has particularly aimed at encouraging the younger generation to aspire to a combination of intellectual engagement and spiritual wisdom, and to give expression to this combination through concrete commitments in the service of humanity" (Weller 2006, 76).

Without doubt "one of the major figures in defining the contemporary global Islamic experience," Fethullah Gülen's work "helps to redefine the nature of Islamic discourse in the contemporary world" (Voll 2003, 238). Poet, philosopher and educator, Gülen has "inspired many people in Turkey to establish educational institutions that combine modern sciences with ethics and spirituality" (Yılmaz 2005b, 175). Indeed, Gülen and the movement that bears his name may be primarily—if not only—known in some quarters in respect to such educational activities (Michel 2003). Yet it is educational priority that has led into interfaith advocacy. Also, "Gülen insists ... the basic Islamic sources advise Muslims to engage in dialogue with other faiths" (Albayrak 2006, 127; Yavuz 2003). In this chapter I seek to address, in a somewhat overview fashion, the matter of Islamic interfaith relations and dialogue and identify and discuss some of the unique perspectives of Fethullah Gülen on interreligious dialogue and the relations of Islam to other faiths. In what way does Gülen signal new perspectives and transitions for contemporary Muslims in a world of manifest religious plurality?

Islam and Interfaith Relations: Context and Perspective

When it comes to Muslim interfaith relations with Peoples of the Book there is a legacy of shared fundamental convictions, as well as a history of divergence. Distinctions are real, and so too are the prospects for peaceful coexistence. There are, of course, deep issues to be addressed and resolved. One starting place, I suggest, is with the underlying paradigms that each side in any relationship holds with respect to the other. Another has to do with the dynamics of Islamic interfaith activity from an historical perspective (Pratt 2005). Jean-Marie Gaudeul (1990) has offered a useful review of the history of the relationship between Islam and Christianity, in which the mutual challenge and response that has engaged the attentions of each may be tracked through broad ages or epochs. These "epochs," which I denote for heuristic and hermeneutical purposes as *expansion, equilibrium, exhortation, enmity, emancipation* and *exploration*, do not just arbitrarily mark out historical eras. Rather they serve to delineate the ebb and flow of a relationship of encounter, particularly that of intellectual engagement. However, as well as indicating the state of play in the relationship between Islam and Christianity at particular times in history, these terms also indicate modes of relationship and interaction *per se*. While each may have dominated a particular historical period, it could be argued that they are always part of the wider picture of interreligious encounter. They certainly persist into the present day so far as the interaction between Islam and Christianity is concerned.

Expansion stands for the expansiveness of self-confidence, embracing self-righteousness on the one hand and magnanimity on the other. Religion in the expansion mode is determined and assertive. This can be seen today in both Islam and Christianity, for instance. However, there is also more than a hint of *equilibrium* that shows through in the hesitancy to be overly self-assertive: an inclination to humility that properly counterpoints self-righteousness; a measure of openness that marks a balanced approach to the religious "other." Mutual *exhortation*, the proclamation and witness which, in its more extreme forms, seeks to declare an exclusive truth and engages with the "other" in order to win, is certainly very much evident in some quarters. In addition, there is evidence aplenty of *enmity*, of dismissive, derogatory and deprecatory prejudice that makes of the religious other an enemy to be fought and vanquished. At the same time, the cultural and socio-political expressions of, and concomitant realities in respect to, the religions of Islam and Christianity, as well as Judaism I would suggest, are ever engaged in the quest for *emancipation*: that seeking self-determination and finding a rightful place in the affairs of the day; finding and asserting meaningful identity as communities and for the individuals who comprise those communities; seeking socio-economic justice; and sustaining unique ways of life and cultural expressions.

Interpretive perspectives on the past notwithstanding, perhaps we might say that the underpinning feature of the early twenty-first century of the Common Era, and the feature that holds all these dynamics together in some sort of creative tension, is the motif of *exploration*. For, despite evidence of resistance and instances of opposition, there seem to be abroad in the world today intimations of a spirit of sincere, tentative, open and honest questing to know the religious other—for Christians, Jews and Muslims to come together in a variety of forums, for instance—and to do so in a climate of mutual recognition of integrity and validity, even as there is recognition of real difference and diversity. However, in order for the exploration to proceed, it is necessary to identify not only the patterns of the past, but also the predominant paradigms that influence the present which, if not properly understood and possibly modified, will predetermine the future of interfaith relations.

Together with an appreciation of the broad historical dynamics of the relationship between Islam and the Peoples of the Book, another dynamic, that of the Muslim paradigms governing interfaith relations, needs to be acknowledged. This is not the place to delve into this in close detail; nonetheless, a cursory overview does help to highlight the specific distinctiveness that marks out the voice of Fethullah Gülen today. In essence, I suggest that what may be called "originating paradigms" emerge from the life and times of Medina and the revelations given in the Holy Qur'an. By contrast, "historico-legal paradigms" emerge around the phenomenon of dhimmitude, the rules and protocols governing the Peoples of the Book, the dhimmi communities. More recently—that is, since around the middle of the twentieth century at least—the dominant contemporary paradigm would seem to be the emergence of an Islamic exclusivism.

The socio-political context in which Islam came to birth was decidedly diverse, but in this context the founding Islamic attitudes toward religious plurality were positive. Significantly, as one Muslim commentator has noted of the situation at Medina, it "was absolutely necessary that the Muslim, the Jew, and the Christian have an equal opportunity in their exercise of religious freedom as well as in their freedom to hold different opinions and to preach their own faiths" (Haykal 1993, 175). However, in the establishment of the new Islamic *ummah* (community), nothing less than a far-reaching socio-political upheaval was required. Arabic personal and societal identities were to undergo an immense upheaval. Nevertheless, it can be said with confidence that at the birth of Islam, in the city of Medina the first intimations of the nascent religious system were positive so far as relations with both Christians and Jews were concerned, but as developments unfolded things tended to change for the worse. As Esposito (2002, 81) has remarked, the resulting confrontation

> became part of the baggage of history and would continue to influence the attitudes of some Muslims in later centuries. Recently, this legacy can be seen in official statements … [that amount to reiterating] … an age-old conflict dating back to the Jews' "rejection and betrayal" of Islam and the Prophet's community at Medina.

If the problem of the relationship between Muslim and a non-Muslim who was yet a theistic believer (as in being a Jew or a Christian, for example) was evident during the lifetime of the Prophet, what are the clues to the Qur'anic solution? A careful reading of the Qur'an, especially in the light of the biography of Muhammad, indicates an early Medinan period in which Judaic and Christian elements and issues loomed large, albeit generally in a favorable light. Arguably, the principal originating Qur'anic paradigm of Muslim interfaith engagement could be said to that of "positively contending with ambiguous otherness," meaning recognizing a need to relate to faith communities with which there is a measure of affinity, but also difference and distinction.

If initially there was a climate of positive predisposition and relationship, historically speaking it would seem this was for the most part eclipsed by a comparatively negative perspective, namely that of regarding interfaith relations with Peoples of the Book in the context of a belief in the divinely-ordained socio-political subservience of these "ambiguous" others. From out of this context there arose regulations of protection, submission, and deference applied to communities of those religions that were also "of the Book," such as Christians and Jews—the *dhimmi* communities. The Qur'anic injunction to honor such co-religionists was tempered by the motif of submission: Muslim superiority to both Jews and Christians, for example, was soon asserted in overt political terms, even as fruitful and enriching cultural interactions more or less continued. Nonetheless, the scene was set for a problematic history of interaction. A lot would depend on local circumstances. Clearly, a paradigmatic line was established: limits to dhimmi autonomy would be determined down the centuries of Islamic rule by Islamic expectations. Non-Muslims would know themselves to be a people submitted to those who themselves live in submission to Allah. If the originating Islamic paradigm of interfaith relations was on the basis of a concept of the "ambiguous other," and the historical paradigm has been largely that of subservient dhimmitude, what appears to be the case at present?

With the dawn of the modern era, and the early penetration of European influence and colonization in Islamic lands of the Middle East, there was a weakening of traditional Islamic norms of society and a concomitant improvement in the lot of dhimmi communities. While political and ideological elements play a part, the underlying paradigmatic driver is, arguably, theological or religious. For example, from a Muslim perspective, "Islam did not supersede Christianity and Judaism, it preceded them. Islam, in fact, was the faith of Abraham, which his descendants twisted for their own purposes" (Feiler 2002, 176). Contemporary attitudes have contemporary referents; but in this case they also have a paradigmatic history. An exclusive and excluding portrayal of Islam is undoubtedly found in many quarters of today's *dar-al Islam*, but is it the only contemporary paradigm? Patterns and paradigms discerned from historical and phenomenological analysis are instructive. We need to be aware of them and to appreciate them in terms of both their historical significance and their contemporary impact, but we are not bound by them: innovative religious thinkers who appreciate the traditions of the past can offer illuminating insight, an interpretation that yields fresh appreciation and even novel application. Thus, a new future can be envisioned. Fethullah Gülen is just such a thinker. It is to his perspectives on Islam and interfaith dialogue (see Gülen 2000a) that we now turn to see what contribution can be made that could complement the past and open up the future.

Fethullah Gülen on Interreligious Dialogue and Islamic Interfaith Relations

Fethullah Gülen is absolutely correct in noting that desire for mutual understanding, a dedication to justice, and a priority on mutual respect are requisite principles for engaging in interreligious dialogue (Gülen 2004f). Gülen is of the view that in today's world the task of "representing faith with its true values has gained an even greater importance than before" (Gülen 2004b). Indeed, he regards interfaith engagement as a function of the "necessity of increasing the interests we have in common with other people." He and the movement seeking to promote his teachings and views within the Islamic world and beyond are firmly committed to the cause of interreligious engagement and dialogue. In the light of my general analysis of the paradigms and dynamics that have pertained to Muslim interfaith relations, what might be the paradigmatic perspective and prospects that are embedded in the thought of Fethullah Gülen? Lester Kurtz (2005, 377), noting that, for Gülen, "spiritual practice and morality are … more important than ritual and dogmatism" speaks of four pillars of dialogue—love, compassion, tolerance, and forgiveness —as descriptive of Gülen's understanding. Indeed, it is this perspective "that opens the way for dialogue with other faith traditions" for Muslims (Kurtz 2005, 378). My own reading of Gülen expands this threefold analysis. I suggest that from Gülen we may derive some seven elements for a possible contemporary Islamic paradigm for interreligious relations and dialogue.

1. Distinction of Values: primary and secondary

Arguably, love is a primary word in Gülen's vocabulary of dialogue (Gülen 2004a; Albayrak 2006). Love, says Gülen (2005a, 21), "exists in everyone as a seed. This seed germinates under favorable circumstances and, growing like a tree, blossoms into a flower, and finally ripens, like a fruit, to unite the beginning with the end." Indeed, it is clear that, for Gülen, primary values such as "peace, love, forgiveness, and tolerance are fundamental to Islam," whereas values such as jihad are regarded as a secondary matter (Gülen 2004b). Keeping these categories of primary and secondary value distinguished and in proper perspective is critical for, as Gülen avers, "failure to establish a proper balance between what is primary and what is secondary leads others to conclude that Islam advocates malice and hatred in the soul, whereas true Muslims are full of love and affection for all creation" (Gülen 2004e).

2. Intentionality: a principal perspective

Intentionality is also an important element of Islamic thought and a key to Gülen's perspective: "In every task undertaken, there should be a certain meaning, sincerity should be sought, and reason and good judgment should be the priority" (Gülen 2004c). Gülen remarks that the "Prophet of God said, 'Deeds are judged by intentions,' and he emphasized that the intention of the believer is more important than the act itself" (Gülen 2004f). Intentionality is applied naturally to the sphere of interfaith engagement. Noting that "the Qur'an calls people to accept the former Prophets and their Books," Gülen avers that "having such a condition at the very beginning of the Qur'an seems very important ... when it comes to starting a dialogue with the followers of other religions" (Gülen 2000d, 251).

3. Tolerance: an inherent element

Gülen argues that "society has to uphold tolerance. If we don't announce jihad for anything else, we should announce it for tolerance" (Gülen 2000c, 206). Tolerance, properly understood, is inherent to dialogue for, as well as "being commanded to take tolerance and to use dialogue as his basis while performing his duties," Muhammad was guided toward things in common with the People of the Book (Jews and Christians), as the Holy Qur'an (Al-Imran 3:64) bears witness: "O People of the Book! Come to common terms as between us and you: that we worship none but God; that we speculate no partners with Him; that we take not some from among ourselves for Lords other than God" (Gülen 2004d). Tolerance—together with forgiveness—is a virtue enjoined throughout the Qur'an such that, in the context of today, Gülen is quite clear: Muslims are to "behave with tolerance and forbearance" in the interfaith arena. In his critique of certain Muslim propensities he asserts that "the method of those who act with enmity and hatred, who view everyone else with anger, and who blacken others as infidels is non-Islamic, for Islam is a religion of love and tolerance" (Gülen 2004e). Yet Gülen is positive overall: "We are rediscovering tolerance, something that is inherent in the spirit of Islam and something that was explained to us in the Qur'an and by Prophet Muhammad" (Gülen 2004g).

Of course, tolerance is not to be equated with attitudes of "passively putting-up with" that which we would prefer to have nothing to do. This is often the default perspective that we find in our societies—what might be better called "mere tolerance." The tolerance to which Gülen alludes, on the other hand, is far more active and intentional, for it has to do with an underlying aim of dialogical engagement: the fostering of that peace and harmony to which the Qur'an refers and for which Islam stands: "peace is better" (Al-Nisa 4:128). Gülen asserts that "Muslims will lose nothing by employing dialogue, love, and tolerance," and that indeed there are many verses in the Qur'an that extol these virtues (Gülen 2004f).

4. Dialogue: an expression of a divinely-inspired love

Fethullah Gülen arguably regards interfaith dialogue as an expression of a divinely-inspired love, for the primary theological verity that binds together all peoples of the Book—Jews, Christians and Muslims especially—is the belief in God as Creator. The act of creation is not an act of arbitrary whim but of intentional love of the Creator for the creature. As Gülen states, "Love is the reason for existence and its essence, and it is the strongest tie that binds creatures together. Everything in the universe is the handiwork of God" (Gülen 2004g). Love issues in practical actions, and at the level of inter-communal and inter-religious relations, love is expressed in terms of dialogical engagement: thus "dialogue is the real remedy for terror, chaos, and intolerance" (Albayrak 2006, 129). Gülen is himself succinct and to the point: "Those who seek to build the happy world of the future on foundations of spiritual and moral values should arrive first at the altar of belief, then ascend to the pulpit of love, and only then preach their message of belief and love to others" (Gülen 2000b, 107).

The complementarity of tolerance and love as being not just human virtues but in reality indicators of primary values with which the Creator imbued the creation underscores an essential oneness of human existence that itself suggests dialogue is the right and proper mode of interaction. "Even though we may not have common grounds on some matters," says Gülen, "we all live in this world and we are passengers on the same ship. In this respect, there are many common points that can be discussed and shared with people from every segment of society" (Gülen 2004h).

5. Reconciliation: the essence of religion

The motif of religion as a force for and of reconciliation is very strong with Fethullah Gülen. Indeed, love, compassion, tolerance, and forgiveness are at the heart of all religions (Gülen 2004m). It is thus of the nature of religion to promote the values and virtues that engender reconciliation. Specifically, for Islam, the Qur'an itself enjoins reconciliation with the wider religious context of the Peoples of the Book, a view that Gülen derives directly from Sura al-Baqara (Gülen 2004a). Allah commands against disputing one with another; instead the reconciling interaction of dialogical debate is encouraged. In particular, Gülen notes that there are "many common points for dialogue among devout Muslims, Christians, and Jews." The imperative to dialogue is therefore strong, and must be conducted in a context of "giving precedence to common points, which far outnumber polemical ones" (Gülen 2004j).

6. Hermeneutical authority for dialogue

Gülen recognizes the need to read the Qur'an carefully and intelligently when it comes, for example, to the issue of specific relations with Jews and Christians. Some expressions in the Qur'an regarding Christians and Jews are indeed very sharp and rather negative, even hostile in some cases. At best there seems to be a measure of revelatory paradox. However, such paradox may be the effect of taking things out of context, or at least not taking context sufficiently into account. Thus, on the one hand "verses condemning and rebuking the Jews and Christians are either about some Jews and Christians who lived in the time of the Prophet Muhammad or their own Prophets," as opposed to all Jews and Christians at all times; or on the other hand they are about "stubborn unbelievers who lived during the Prophet's lifetime and insisted on unbelief" who happened to be Jews or Christians (Gülen 2004r). Such verses cannot be taken to refer to all Jews and Christians since, for it was never Jewish or Christian belief and believing as such which was being criticized, but the presence of unbelief—Jews and Christians ignoring their own heritage wherein they, together with Muslims, are believers in the one God. As Gülen himself remarks, it was not Christianity or Judaism that was the subject of condemnation but rather "the Qur'an goes after wrong behavior, incorrect thought, and resistance to the truth, creation of hostility, and non-commendable characteristics" (Gülen 2004r). Rather than counting against dialogue, a careful and correct contextual reading of the Qur'an would seem to be advocated by Gülen. In this way, a proper interpretive Muslim authority for dialogue may be discerned.

7. Ijtihad: the struggle for dialogue

The final element in a possible Islamic paradigm for interreligious dialogue and relations has to do with the notion of *ijtihad* as meaning a proper intellectual and spiritual struggle. Ihsan Yılmaz (2005b, 175) writes that

> Gülen believes that there is a need for *ijtihad* in our age. He says that he respects the scholars of the past but also believes that *ijtihad* is a necessity: to freeze *ijtihad* means to freeze Islam and to imprison it in a given time and space. He argues that Islam is a dynamic and universal religion that covers all time and space, and renews itself in real life situations; it changes from one context to another, and *ijtihad* is a major tool in enabling this.

The struggle to live a life of true faith, to follow the way of peaceful submission to God, has led Fethullah Gülen into significant arenas of social and educational action, not the least of which is the promotion of interfaith dialogue and interreligious relations. Such dialogue inheres to the agenda of the Gülen Movement because Gülen juxtaposes the struggle to live as a good and true Muslim with the task of engaging with the religious neighbor. This contrasts with forms of *ijtihad* coming from other quarters in the Islamic world that result in advocating jihad against the religious other. Thus Lester Kurtz (2005, 373) can speak of Gülen's "paradoxical fusion…of intense faith commitment with tolerance," for example, thus resulting "in a paradigm of Islamic dialogue." The essence of Gülen's paradigm is nothing less than the application of *ijtihad* to the question and challenge of Muslim interfaith relations. Hence, "tolerance of others and genuine interfaith dialogue [is] not simply a pleasant ideal that will be fulfilled in some future paradise, but ... [is]... at the core of what it is to be Muslim in the here and now" (Kurtz 2005, 375). Indeed, Gülen argues that dialogue is demanded by the very nature of religion as such.

Conclusion

Yılmaz (2005a, 200) notes that "Gülen has found a wide audience for his ideas, which are described as reformative by some scholars," yet the thrust of reformation, interestingly, is that in "exercising *ijtihad* without flagging it as *ijtihad*, Gülen reinterprets Islamic understanding in tune with contemporary times and develops a new Muslim discourse" (Yılmaz 2005a, 200). Today, Fethullah Gülen "continues to practice the theology of dialogue, since he believes that his teachings are well grounded in the principles of Islam" (Sarıtoprak 2005, 424). A relatively cursory reading of some representative works of Gülen yields elements for a paradigmatic perspective that is indicative of new possibilities for Muslim interpretation of and sensibilities toward interfaith relations and dialogue. Where these values, patterns and perspectives on dialogue are not put into place, the outcome is quite dire. Gülen himself avers that "the present, distorted image of Islam that has resulted from its misuse by both Muslims and non-Muslims for their own goals scares both Muslims and non-Muslims" (Gülen 2004r). In reality, at the heart of Islam is the call to dialogue (Gülen 2004k). Peace also lies at this heart with "war and conflict as aberrations to be brought under control" and security and world harmony the underlying divinely desired goal (Gülen 2004l).

It must be remembered that for any faith-based movement there is a dialectical tension in its ongoing relationship to its founder: on the one hand, it always stands open to the criticism of not living up as fully as it might to the standards, demands, or expectations of its founder; on the other hand, neither must it remain bound by the inevitable limitations that any human founder brings. Rather, the trick is to proceed along the path in the direction pointed to by the founder, cognizant of the values and insights supplied, but capable of applying and developing them as new circumstances and contexts arise. This is the stuff of the inherent and internal dialogical dialectic of all faith-based movements. The Gülen Movement is no exception. Paul Weller (2006, 88) has rightly observed that Fethullah Gülen himself affirms

> the existence of a fundamental continuity in the issues faced by human beings in relation to their behavior with one another and their place in the universe. At the same time, he recognizes the specific nature of the challenges of diversity and plurality—challenges which have previously been present in individual historical societies but which, in the twenty-first century, have been elevated onto a global stage. ... Gülen stands against ways of thinking and acting that promote the illusion that the uncomfortable plurality of the contemporary world can simply be abolished.

In respect to the issue of relations between Christians and Muslims or, more broadly speaking, between the West and Islam, and prospects for the ongoing dialogue between those two faiths and their respective cultures, we might agree with Charles Kimball (1991, 48) that

> For many people in both communities the basic theological issues constitute the primary agenda.... Understanding different orientations is an important step, but it does not resolve the seemingly inherent conflicts. Thoughtful, creative, and persevering efforts are required in order to bridge some of the real and perceived differences in foundational theological understandings. ... Although we all carry the cumulative baggage provided by our deep-rooted heritage, developments in the past 150 years have challenged traditional assumptions and prompted the vexing questions confronting people of faith today.

Religious prejudice, expressed in the form of claims to superiority and exclusivity of one over another, is an issue that ever needs to be addressed. Parties to any Muslim interfaith dialogue—be they Jewish, Christian, Muslim or any other "religion of the Book"—need to recognize that indeed, "each religion is an interpretive venture" (Feiler 2002, 202). The "book" is ever a text requiring interpretive understanding and application. Triumphalism must be countered if there is to be any genuine eirenical advance. As Rabbi David Rosen, a leading Jewish figure in the cause of interfaith relations, has commented, "We should indeed keep the differences ... and learn to respect them. Each religion has its *particular* approach to God. But we also have a *universal* dimension to our traditions that we share, and we must emphasize that as well" (cited in Feiler 2002, 204). By pursuing the challenge of dialogue we seek to comprehend better the respective faiths in which we live, and move, and have our being.

In dialogue with Fethullah Gülen Muslim and non-Muslim alike are moved "beyond prejudice, suspicion, and half-truths so that they might arrive at an understanding of what Islam is really about" and see that "tolerance, love, and compassion are genuinely Islamic values that Muslims have a duty to bring to the modern world" (Michel 2004). The call of Islam is a call to dialogue. Fethullah Gülen certainly offers "Muslims a way to live out Islamic values amidst the complex demands of modern societies and to engage in ongoing dialogue and cooperation with people of other religions" (Michel 2004). Dialogue with Gülen and the Gülen Movement is an avenue wherein the non-Muslim can join with Muslims in the greater journey of the dialogical quest.

References

Albayrak, I. 2006. "The Juxtaposition of Islam and Violence. *Muslim Citizens of the Globalized World: Contributions of the Gülen Movement*, ed. R. A. Hunt and Y. A. Aslandoğan. Somerset, NJ: The Light, Inc & IID Press, 119–130.

Esposito, J. 2002. *What Everyone Needs to Know about Islam*. New York: Oxford University Press.

Feiler, B. 2002. *Abraham: A Journey to the Heart of Three Faiths*. New York: William Morrow.

Gaudeul, J. M. 1990. *Encounters and Clashes: Islam and Christianity in History*. Rome: Pontifico Instituto di Studi Arabi e Islamici.

Gülen, F. 2000a. "The Necessity of Interfaith Dialogue." *The Fountain*, 3 (31), (July–September), 4–9.

———. 2000b. "For the Conquest and Dominion of Hearts." *Advocate of Dialogue: Fethullah Gülen*, comp. A. Ünal and A. Williams. Fairfax, Virginia: The Fountain, 105–108.

———. 2000c. "We Must Struggle (Make Jihad) for Tolerance." *Advocate of Dialogue: Fethullah Gülen*, comp. A. Ünal and A. Williams. Fairfax, Virginia: The Fountain, 206–207.

———. 2000d. "The Necessity of Interfaith Dialogue: A Muslim Perspective." *Advocate of Dialogue: Fethullah Gülen*, comp. A. Ünal and A. Williams. Fairfax, Virginia: The Fountain, 241–256.

———. 2005a. *Pearls of Wisdom*. Somerset, NJ: The Light, Inc.

Haykal, M. H. 1993. *The Life of Muhammad*. Kuala Lumpur: Islamic Book Trust).

Hunt, R. A. and Y. A. Aslandoğan. 2006. *Muslim Citizens of the Globalized World: Contributions of the Gülen Movement*. Somerset, NJ: The Light, Inc. & IID Press.

Kimball, C. 1991. *Striving Together: A Way Forward in Christian–Muslim Relations*. Maryknoll, New York: Orbis Books.

Kurtz, L. R. 2005. "Gülen's Paradox: Combining Commitment and Tolerance." *The Muslim World* 95 (July), 373–384.

Michel, T. 2003. "Fethullah Gülen as Educator." *Turkish Islam and the Secular State: The Gülen Movement*, ed. M. H. Yavuz and J. L. Esposito. Syracuse, NY: Syracuse University Press, 69–84.

Pratt, D. 2005. *The Challenge of Islam: Encounters in Interfaith Dialogue*. Aldershot: Ashgate.

Sarıtoprak, Z. 2005. "An Islamic Approach to Peace and Nonviolence: A Turkish experience." *The Muslim World* 95 (July), 413–427.

Voll, J. O. 2003 "Fethullah Gülen: Transcending Modernity in the New Islamic Discourse." *Turkish Islam and the Secular State: The Gülen Movement*, ed. M. H. Yavuz and J. L. Esposito. Syracuse, NY: Syracuse University Press, 238–250.

Weller, P. 2006. "Fethullah Gülen, Religions, Globalization and Dialogue." *Muslim Citizens of the Globalized World: Contributions of the Gülen Move-*

ment, ed. R. A. Hunt and Y. A. Aslandoğan. Somerset, NJ: The Light, Inc & IID Press, 75–88.

Yavuz, M. H. 2003. "The Gülen Movement: The Turkish Puritans." *Turkish Islam and the Secular State: The Gülen Movement*, ed. M. H. Yavuz and J. L. Esposito. Syracuse, NY: Syracuse University Press, 19–47.

Yılmaz, I. 2005a. "Inter-madhhab Surfing, Neo-ijtihad, and Faith-based Movement Leaders. *The Islamic School of Law: Evolution, Devolution and Progress*, ed. P. Bearman, R. Peters and F. E. Vogel. Cambridge, Mass: Harvard University Press, 191–206.

———. 2005b. *Muslim Laws, Politics and Society in Modern Nation States: Dynamic Legal Pluralisms in England, Turkey and Pakistan*. Aldershot: Ashgate.

Internet sources

Gülen, F. 2004a. Dialogue with the People of the Book. http://en.fgulen.com/content/view/1812/33/.

———. 2004b. Dialogue in the Muhammadan Spirit and Meaning. http://en.fgulen.com/content/view/1811/33/.

———. 2004c. Sports and the Process of Dialogue. http://en.fgulen.com/content/view/1813/33/.

———. 2004d. Tolerance and Dialogue in the Qur'an and the Sunna. http://en.fgulen.com/content/view/1810/33/.

———. 2004e. Islam–A religion of tolerance. http://en.fgulen.com/content/view/1808/33/.

———. 2004f. The Two Roses of the Emerald Hills: Tolerance and Dialogue. http://en.fgulen.com/content/view/1806/33/.

———. 2004g. Making the Atmosphere of Tolerance Permanent. http://en.fgulen.com/content/view/1801/33/.

———. 2004h. Tolerance in the Life of the Individual and Society. http://en.fgulen.com/content/view/1800/33/.

———. 2004i. Fethullah Gülen's Speeches and Interviews on Interfaith Dialogue, Introduction. http://en.fgulen.com/content/view/1334/13/.

———. 2004j. Dialogue Is a Must. http://en.fgulen.com/content/view/1336/13/.

———. 2004k. Islam's Ecumenical Call for Dialogue. http://en.fgulen.com/content/view/1337/13/.

———. 2004l. How to Interact with Followers of Other Religions. http://en.fgulen.com/content/view/1338/13/.

———. 2004m. Love, Compassion, Tolerance, and Forgiving: The Pillars of Dialogue. http://en.fgulen.com/content/view/1339/13/.

———. 2004n. Tolerance and Dialogue in the Perspective of the Qur'an and Sunna. http://en.fgulen.com/content/view/1340/13/.

———. 2004p. Dialogue with the People of the Book (Jews and Christians). http://en.fgulen.com/content/view/1341/13/.

———. 2004r. Jews and Christians in the Qur'an. http://en.fgulen.com/content/view/1342/13/.

Michel, T. 2004. "Two Frontrunners for Peace: John Paul II and Fethullah Gülen." Paper presented at the *Front Runners of Peace Symposia*, organized by Cosmicus Foundation, on March 16–18, 2004, in Amsterdam, Holland. http://en.fgulen.com/about-fethullah-gulen/commentaries/1944-two-frontrunners-for-peace-john-paul-ii-and-fethullah-gulen.html, last visited on 03 February 2010.

Chapter 10

Tolerance in the Theology and Thought of A. J. Conyers and Fethullah Gülen

David B. Capes[32]

Introduction

In his book *The Long Truce: How Toleration Made the World Safe for Profit and Power* (2001a) the late A. J. Conyers argues that tolerance, a principal doctrine in western democracies, is not a public virtue; rather he contends that it is a political strategy employed to centralize power and guarantee profits. Tolerance, of course, seemed to be a reasonable response to the religious wars of the sixteenth and seventeenth centuries, but tolerance based upon indifference to all values except political power and materialism has relegated ultimate questions of meaning to private life. Conyers offers another model of tolerance based upon values and resources already resident in pre-Reformation Christianity.

In this paper, we consider aspects of Conyers' case against the modern, secular doctrine of tolerance. We examine his attempt to reclaim the practice of Christian tolerance based upon humility, hospitality and the "powerful fact" of the incarnation. Furthermore,

32 I wish to thank Mr. Phuc Luu for his assistance in researching and writing this paper. Luu was a student of Conyers at George W. Truett Theological Seminary at Baylor University. Likewise, I wish to acknowledge and thank Dr. Alp Aslandoğan for his contributions to my own understanding of Gülen and his writings.

we bring the late Conyers into dialogue with Fethullah Gülen, a Muslim scholar, prolific writer and source of inspiration for a transnational civil movement. We explore how both Conyers and Gülen interpret their scriptures and tradition in order to fashion a theology and political ideology conducive to peaceful coexistence.

In many ways Conyers is a suitable dialogue partner for Gülen on the question of tolerance.[33] Until his untimely death at the age of 60, Conyers had distinguished himself as a gifted Baptist theologian with an ever-increasing audience. He was a consummate "southern gentleman" (in the American sense of the word), kind, welcoming, sincere. As a scholar, he had benefited from a positive relationship with Jürgen Moltmann, whose influence appears consistently, though not uncritically, in his work.[34] As a Baptist, Conyers was a member of a denomination in the United States that is not typically associated with tolerance but with strong convictions, passion and fervency in faith. Still, despite popular perceptions, there is a significant tradition of tolerance and freedom of conscience within the work of many Baptist thinkers beginning with Thomas Helwys. Baptists, of course, were a religious minority at the turn of the seventeenth century, and so they faced hostility from both established churches and government officials. As a result, they advocated for religious liberty initially for themselves but by extension for all. They formulated the doctrine directly from Christian Scripture, reason, and human experience. Essentially, they argued that governments should not meddle in matters of religion and conscience. Had they known it, they would have agreed wholeheartedly with the Qur'anic injunction that there is no compulsion in religion (2:256). Baptist leaders scandalized some by advocating religious liberty for Roman Catholics, Turks, Jews and heretics alike (Helwys 1612, 69). Religious uniformity, they believed, was not necessary to ensure domestic tranquility (McBeth 1987,

33 For a helpful overview of Gülen's life see Ünal and Williams (2000).

34 See, for example, Conyers (1988).

85–86). In the last century this Baptist distinctive is articulated carefully in the work of E.Y. Mullins,[35] and Conyers builds and expands on that tradition in his own unique way. Conyers then represents one of the most recent and articulate advocates for tolerance in American Baptist life. However, Conyers also recognizes that the practice of toleration is "not an exclusively Christian predisposition, for the practice of toleration is often touchingly and effectively expressed in such religious philosophies as one finds associated with Hinduism, Taoism, Confucianism, and among the Sufi mystics of Islam" (Conyers 2001a, 228). This is all the more reason to bring Conyers and Gülen into conversation.

Conyers' Critique

Since the seventeenth century tolerance has often been considered a public virtue. In the last decades of the twentieth century tolerance/toleration became one of the principle virtues, institutionalized in western democracies in a variety of ways.[36] Conyers, however, questions whether tolerance should be considered a virtue at all. Compared with other, classical virtues such as love, courage, and moderation, Conyers argues that tolerance is different because everyone acknowledges that there must be limits regarding tolerance. When John Locke wrote famously regarding tolerance,[37] he argued that it must not be limitless. Some are not to be tolerated including atheists and Roman Catholics, according to Locke. While we might disagree with where the line of toleration is drawn, everyone acknowledges that the line has to be drawn somewhere. In

35 See, for example, Mullins (1978).

36 Marcuse, "Repressive Tolerance," argues that tolerance is an end in itself. Marcuse, who is a Hegelian, sees history as eventually telling the "truth." So the end of this virtue itself is played out in "extralegal means," i.e., violence and revolution. The irony is in how the original purpose of tolerance, namely, to assuage the problems of religious wars in earlier centuries will climax in violence. This is one of the reasons why Conyers sees the twentieth century as being the most violent. See Marcuse (2001).

37 Locke (1950).

Conyers' view, true virtue has no limits and all lesser virtues serve the chief virtue, love (Conyers 2001a, 7–8).

So then, what is tolerance if it is not a virtue? Conyers proffers that tolerance is a modern strategy to establish power and to protect economic prosperity. While it may depend on virtues such as humility, moderation, patience, and so forth, tolerance is in fact a policy to achieve a particular end. That particular end itself is a good. Tolerance aims to ease the tensions rooted in the significant differences facing a shrinking, global world; as such it is not an end but a means to an end, a strategy that seeks harmony and peace within our common life (Conyers 2001a, 7–8). Now Conyers advocates for peaceful coexistence as a good worthy of all our efforts. However, he questions whether the modern strategy of tolerance advocated in secular democracies has a sufficient basis.[38]

With the rise of the nation states the influence of the natural associations, that is, associations based on ethnic, religious, familial, and economic ties, is diminished in favor of more centralized authority. As this transpires, there is a concomitant development: a growing isolation of the individual. In the pre-modern period identity had been constructed in relation to a group. Now, with the authority and the influence of the group eclipsed by the larger, more powerful state, identity is confused. According to Conyers, "the result was a powerful state and a lonely individual, two distinctive features of the modern period" (Conyers 2001a, 6).

While we tend to think of the world today almost exclusively in terms of large, diverse nation states, this rather recent phenomenon brought with it significant changes to social, political and religious life. In the modern nation state the centralization of the government depends largely on the secularization of public life. As Michael Walzer has argued, in order to establish peace differences must be managed (Walzer 1997, 25). Generally, they are managed

38 He bases his argument upon an analysis of key writers on tolerance including Thomas Hobbes, Pierre Bayle, John Locke and others (Conyers 2001a: 66–168).

by a single, dominant group that organizes public life in such a way as to reflect and maintain its own culture. Unmanaged differences will inevitably "disturb the peace." Differences, especially religious differences with their ultimate claims, must be managed above all. So, there are three options: (1) insist that all have the same religion; (2) forbid religion from entering the public square; or (3) consign religion to the private sphere. Generally, it is options 2 and 3 that have characterized western democracies. In France and Turkey, for example, the practice of laicism has effectively excluded religion from public life. In the United States and other western democracies, freedom of religion may be guaranteed but ample social and legal strictures are present to consign religion effectively to the margins.

Conyers believes the modern doctrine of toleration is not sufficient in itself to create the social environment needed to establish and maintain peace because it bifurcates life into public and private spheres and assigns questions of ultimate concern a role only on the margins (Conyers 2001b, 43–44).[39] While the modern doctrine of tolerance pretends initially to support the place of religion in society, it almost immediately will neutralize any sincere expression of religious conviction. With the one hand the tolerant democracy gives—and it can afford to give because it is a powerful, prosperous state—with the other it takes away.

Reclaiming the Practice of Tolerance

Since the modern project of tolerance will likely fail and give rise ultimately to other kinds of intolerance (Marcuse 1969, 95–137), Conyers suggests that we must seek to reclaim the ancient practice of tolerance in order to meet the growing tensions apparent in our shrinking, global world. The practice of "high tolerance" or "authentic tolerance," as he refers to it, is natural inasmuch as it

39 Conyers recognizes that the privatization of religion was intended not only to protect the state, but religious life as well, but this resulted in the assumption that public life belonged ultimately to the state.

deals with ultimate questions of meaning and purpose. The modern strategy of tolerance, however, merely postpones those questions in order to privilege other, more manageable questions. However, according to Conyers, authentic tolerance must first be disentangled from the "questionable alliance with power and will to power ..." (Conyers 2001a, 229).

Conyers asks: Is there a practice of tolerance not based on indifference to the question of "the good"? Is there an authentic tolerance that does not privilege power and materialism over deeper, more abiding questions? Yes, he argues; and the answer is found in the central mystery of the incarnation (Conyers 2001, 231). For Conyers "the powerful fact of the incarnation" provides a basis sufficient to reorder human existence and establish peace amidst difference (Conyers 2001, 232). Conyers is quick to point out, however, that he is not talking about "the doctrine of the incarnation"; for it is in the nature of doctrines to develop over time and doctrines may or may not be true. Rather he is speaking of the central conviction that God became flesh in the particularity of Jesus of Nazareth and that He was in Christ to reconcile the world (Conyers 2001a, 232).

As a "fact" or "conviction" rather than a doctrine, it is not necessary that we grasp the reality of the incarnation or can explain it in some systematic fashion. It is more important, according to Conyers, that the reality grasps us and reorients our lives essentially toward a more tolerant and open attitude toward others who share the same enfleshed existence. Incarnation then becomes the basis for hope. A life shaped by the vigorous conviction of the incarnation recognizes that the world is not destined for suffering, nor is it beyond hope. If God has entered our world and dwelt among us, then our world must be good and our future hopeful. This stands in stark contrast to the modern notion that the world is to be feared, subdued, and made safe for power and profit.

If the fact of the incarnation provides hope, then the purpose of the incarnation provides reconciliation. Initially, that means reconciliation between God and humanity; but it also means reconciliation between people for whom differences have proven hard and often insurmountable problems. Reconciliation in practice manifests itself in tolerance and openness to "the other" (Conyers 2001a, 241). Conyers argues that the Church is "the natural culture" for reclaiming an authentic practice of toleration despite the impulses that have led some to legitimate violence through religion. If God was in Christ reconciling the world (2 Cor 5:16), then the reconciliation of all things (*ta panta*) becomes the *raison d'être* of the Church. Ultimately, the incarnation means that all things are interrelated. Therefore, all things must matter to God; and all things must include all people with their diverse cultures, ways, and worldviews (Conyers 2001a, 234).

The incarnation also reveals something hitherto unknown regarding God and humanity. In Christ's self-emptying and death on the cross (Phil 2:5–11), his followers see a "lordly example" of humility and are called to imitate it (Hurtado 1984, 113–126). Therefore, according to Conyers, the practice of the incarnation is first of all the practice of humility that manifests itself in listening to others. This does not mean listening for the sake of gaining advantage or seeking information; this is listening expectantly, waiting to hear the truth (Conyers 2001a, 233). Conyers surveys the biblical evidence for toleration and defines it as "a willingness to hear other traditions and learn from them" (Conyers 2001a, 33). Indeed, the fundamental virtue necessary for tolerance to exist and flourish is humility. This kind of authentic tolerance reflects a depth to humility that is willing to set aside the self to attend to the voice of "the other." Humility, then, for Conyers is what makes dialogue possible. Dialogue birthed in authentic tolerance is not content to dwell on similarities, agreements and surface issues; it begins with commonalities but does not stop until it has engaged the most cherished and deeply held convictions of a group, even when those convictions differ considerably from people to people. This kind of dialogue stands in sharp relief to the pseudo-toleration that makes "dialogue possible only so long as it conforms to certain 'rules' that preordain its result" (Conyers 2001a, 244). Conyers remarks:

> Just as pseudo-toleration answers power with power, it answers bigotry with bigotry. The hallmark of authentic tolerant practice should be the listening heart for which the wise king prayed and not the management of language and appointing itself the arbiter of all public discussions (Conyers 2001a, 244).[40]

Elsewhere Conyers refers to this tolerant disposition toward "the other" as *the practice of the open soul*. For him such tolerance "springs from a propensity toward magnanimity and a predisposition toward faith" (Conyers 2001a, 245).

The practice of the open soul is essentially the practice of hospitality. It involves "welcoming the stranger" and serving his or her physical, social and spiritual needs. In any cross-cultural exchange both parties are strangers, aliens to the other. So hospitality involves not only giving but also receiving in a way that gives dignity and honor to the other. As Amy Oden (2001, 14) has written, "Acts of inclusion and respect, however small, can powerfully reframe social relations and engender welcome."[41]

It is important to note that Conyers considers "high tolerance," as he refers to it, a recovery or reclaiming of what the Church practiced in earlier days. He finds significant evidence that Christian believers in earlier centuries did exercise tolerance and openness, though not universally. He notes in particular the writings of Justin Martyr (d. 165), Clement of Alexandria (d. 215) and Thomas Aquinas (1225–1274). According to Conyers, Thomas Aquinas' *Summa Theologiae*—one of the greatest achievements in Christian thought and history—"would never have seen the light of day but for a strong sentiment for a certain openness toward thinkers from other faiths and other philosophies" (Conyers

40 Most translations of 1 Kings 3:9 indicate that Solomon prays for "wisdom," but the Hebrew phrase means literally "listening heart."

41 See too Pohl (1999).

2001a, 43–46). In particular on the question of "truth" (*Summa Theologiae*, XVI "On Truth") Aquinas draws from Christian, Jewish, Muslim, and "pagan" teachers. But he does not draw on these thinkers in any sort of modern way. In Aquinas we find "no self-conscious celebration of diversity," nor a facile claim that everyone is entitled to one's own opinion; instead we find "the resolute pressing forward to an idea of truth that is common to everyone simply because it is *real* for everyone" (Conyers 2001a, 233).

Conyers, of course, is not alone in this assessment. David Burrell suggests that the doctrine of God inherited by the enlightened west was already an achievement of interfaith dialogue (Burrell 1986: ix).

Conyers and Gülen

Although A.J. Conyers and Fethullah Gülen were shaped in different worlds culturally and religiously, amazing resonance exists between them on this issue of tolerance. This resonance is located precisely in the vitality of their respective faiths. For both men, their deep religious commitments inform their unwavering dedication to tolerance.[42] Still, there are subtle differences between them based in large part upon the faith communities and worlds from which they come.

First, it must be acknowledged that both Gülen and Conyers are working from a similar definition of toleration. Gülen defines tolerance as embracing all people regardless of differences and having the ability to put up with matters we personally dislike by drawing upon the strength of convictions, conscience, faith and a generous heart (Gülen 2004, 46). One of the key concepts Gülen uses in discussions of tolerance is *hoşgörü* (*hoş* = good, pleasant; *görü* = view). Sometimes this word is translated into English as "tolerance" but conceptually it is probably best taken as empathetic acceptance.

42 On the paradox of commitment and tolerance in Gülen, see Kurtz (2005).

For Gülen, tolerance involves identifying with and accepting others. But one cannot identify with others without first listening to them and understanding the world from which they come. Conyers would agree with this construal of tolerance and go on to say that difference is what makes "high tolerance" possible. Unlike some moderns who may wish to eliminate differences and seek to assimilate minority groups into the powerful state, Gülen and Conyers argue that embracing differences ultimately serves the same goal and demonstrates respect for those who otherwise would be left out (Gülen 2004, 33).[43] Furthermore, both Gülen and Conyers locate the resources necessary to create an atmosphere of tolerance precisely in the particularity of each faith community. For Gülen, the essence of Islam—like the word "Islam"—involves surrender [to God], peace, contentment and security. He cites a well-known episode from the life of the Prophet. When asked what practice of the faith is most beneficial, Muhammad remarks that feeding the hungry and offering *salaam* (the greeting of peace) to both friend and stranger are the most beneficial (Gülen 2004, 58). Essentially, the pursuit of peace and seeking to establish peace are fundamental to Islam. If "peace is better" as the Qur'an teaches (4:128), then the true Muslim will work toward peace. Conyers, likewise, from a Christian perspective argues that the pursuit of peace via authentic tolerance is implicitly theological (Conyers 2001a, 25). If the modern project of tolerance sets aside faith and ultimate questions about humanity, the world and God because these questions cannot be easily resolved, authentic tolerance deals precisely with these questions and embraces those who answer the questions differently.[44] The pursuit of peace is therefore an essential call for any Christ-follower as it is for any Muslim.

---

43 Other words for tolerance include "respect," "mercy," "generosity" and "forbearance." Tolerance is the "most essential element of moral systems."

44 Within the Christian tradition, for example, Jesus is known as "the Prince of Peace" based primarily upon the strength of an intertextual appropriation of Isaiah 9:6 to him. Likewise, Jesus teaches his disciples: "Blessed are the peacemakers for they will be called the sons of God" (Matt 5:9).

For Gülen, tolerance is ultimately rooted in the attributes of God. God is All-Forgiving, All-Merciful, All-Compassionate. These attributes of God, while common to the teaching of all the messengers of the past, have been communicated most effectively through the Qur'an and the Sunna. In particular, the Qur'an calls all Muslims to engage in tolerance and forgiveness because of the nature of God (64:14). Although a true believer may defend himself from attack, God does not forbid showing kindness and acting justly to those non-Muslims who are willing to live in peace (60:8). True believers are called to forgive those who do not look forward to the Days of God (45:14). Likewise, they are to swallow their anger and forgive others when they have been harmed (3:134). Gülen cites these passages, along with many others, to show that the Qur'an itself is "the source of leniency and tolerance" (Gülen 2004, 37–38).[45] Additionally, Gülen relates a number of episodes from the life of the Prophet and his companions to show that he was a man of peace and demonstrated respect in his relationships with friends, enemies and People of the Book (Gülen 2004, 41–44).

The negative statements about Jews and Christians in the Qur'an, according to Gülen, are not universal injunctions. They are sourced in contingent circumstances of doctrinal controversies or active hostilities. Clearly, the Qur'an does criticize certain beliefs held by Jews and Christians (e.g., claiming God has a son and granting certain powers to the clergy). However, these critiques are leveled against ideas and attitudes not people. Furthermore, those verses that permit fighting are based on the active hostilities of particular Jewish, Christian, or pagan groups against the nascent Muslim community. On the whole, according to Gülen, the Qur'an is balanced toward civilized, peaceful coexistence while preserving Muslim identity.[46]

---

45 See the collection of Qur'anic passages cited by Gülen in Alp Aslandoğan. (2007).

46 I am grateful to Dr. Alp Aslandoğan for helping me understand this point of Gülen's teaching.

One of the strongest points of connection between Gülen and Conyers on tolerance resides in their conviction that faith in the One God reveals the interrelatedness of all things. Gülen begins with the idea that love is the reason for creation and existence, and that everything in the world is God's handiwork. Accordingly, if you do not approach all humans, who are creatures of God, with love, then you hurt those who love God and those whom God loves. Essentially, one cannot claim to love God without loving everything that God has made. Love, of course, is an essential pillar of tolerance (Kurtz 2005, 375–382). Conyers would agree with Gülen's teaching on love and the interrelatedness of all things, but once again, for him, the incarnation shapes the discussion because it reveals God's love for all things and ultimately reconciles all things back to God. If all things are destined to be reconciled to God, then the believers' vocation in this age consists of joining God in "the ministry of reconciliation" (2 Cor 5:16–20).

The interrelatedness of all things leads Gülen to practice what Conyers calls in his theology the "open soul." Gülen has famously said, "Be so tolerant that your bosom becomes wide like the ocean. Be inspired with faith and love of human beings. Let there be no troubled souls to whom you do not offer a hand, and about whom you remain unconcerned" (Gülen 2000, 75). For Gülen, faith in God and love for God's creation serve as twin pillars for a tolerance that makes one's heart as wide as the ocean. Practically, this is worked out in deeds of generosity, compassion and hospitality directed to everyone, regardless of their need. Similarly, Gülen has said, "Applaud the good for their goodness, appreciate those who have believing hearts, and be kind to believers. Approach unbelievers so gently that their envy and hatred melt away" (Gülen 2000, 75). Gülen does not limit the word "believers" to Muslims, but to People of the Book (Jews and Christians) and then by extension to all people. He bases this upon the Qur'anic injunction that calls Muslims to accept the earlier prophets and their books (2:2–4) and to act kindly and justly toward non-Muslims as long as they are not fighting against you (60:8). However, such openness must also be balanced when it comes to oppressors. Gülen warns that there are limits to tolerance and dialogue when he writes, "Being merciful to a cobra means being unjust to the people the cobra has bitten" (Gülen 2004, 75–76).

The practice of "the open soul" for both Gülen and Conyers depends upon humility. Humility for Gülen means judging "your worth in the Creator's sight by how much space He occupies in your heart and your worth in people's eyes by how you treat them" (Gülen 2004, 31). We see in this statement evidence of the spiritual side of Islam, a kind of mysticism typical of the Sufi tradition. The human heart is made for its Creator and is at its best (namely, humble and generous) when the All-Forgiving and All-Merciful One fills every corner. Gülen privileges the spiritual sphere of Islam over the institutional and political spheres. This means that one's commitment to vitality in one's spiritual life manifests itself in treating others with compassion, forgiveness, love and tolerance (Kurtz 2005, 376–378). Such treatment will be noticed, appreciated and result in kind treatment in return.

As we saw earlier in this essay, Conyers also considers humility fundamental to any authentic practice of tolerance, but as a Christian, Conyers locates that virtue in the example of Christ and the call to "follow" him. Additionally, Conyers finds that the reality of the incarnation challenges every idea and practice of *exousia* ("power" or "authority"). In the New Testament Jesus is clearly a prophet with authority and he shares that authority with his disciples, yet the teaching here is "not simply one of power distributed from on high but power exercised as a cosmic exchange. It is not the love of power but the power of love: God has become man, and that man, the representative of the race of men, is indeed God, so that human beings can participate in all that God is" (Conyers 2001a, 238). For Conyers, the coming of Christ into the world is a powerful demonstration of God's love for us, a love that ultimately exalts those who are truly humble. As the Scripture says, "God opposes the proud, but gives grace to the humble" (James 4:6; quoting Prov 3:34).

For both Gülen and Conyers, the practice of tolerance with roots firmly planted in their respective Scriptures and traditions finds its *telos* in dialogue, what Conyers calls "the listening heart." Gülen has been able to accomplish more than any leader or activist I know to inspire a generation of leaders who have taken the message of love, tolerance and dialogue to the nations. In particular, Gülen has urged his followers to found organizations committed to dialogue and tolerance. He has recommended that tolerance awards be given to encourage leaders from a variety of faith communities to work toward peaceful coexistence. He has warned that tolerance and dialogue will be costly ventures that will take decades to change the social landscape (Gülen 2004, 54–57). For Gülen interfaith dialogue involves people who are committed to their faith coming together and bearing witness to that faith for the express purpose of mutual understanding, empathy, appreciation, enrichment and cooperation. Dialogue is not about (1) proselytizing others, (2) debating the merits or various truth claims of each faith, or (3) attempting to unify all faiths or create a single, world religion. True dialogue does not mean that one must compromise one's own faith (Gülen 2004, 42). Those who approach dialogue with hidden agendas will find the engagement frustrating, polarizing and ultimately a failure. Successes in interfaith dialogue will come slowly as sincere individuals share the stories that have shaped their lives. By learning the truth about others and their faiths, by respecting the differences that exist between all of God's creation, we find our own faiths enriched, our commitments deepened, and perhaps we will create a world where peace reigns.

Conclusion

While Gülen and Conyers share much in common in relation to their theology of tolerance, I find one significant difference between them: Gülen understands the crucial role that forgiveness and non-retaliation play in creating sacred spaces where tolerance can flourish. He refers to forgiveness as a great virtue that is paramount to tolerance. Forgiveness restores us and our world in ways that no other action can. To be forgiven is to be repaired; and yet one cannot seek forgiveness for oneself without forgiving others for "the road to forgiveness passes through the act of forgiving" (Gülen 2004, 27–30). However, like tolerance, there are limits to forgiveness. To forgive "monstrous, evil" people who delight in suffering would be disrespectful to all humanity. We have no right to forgive such people for to forgive them is to dishonor the people who have suffered so much from them. Similarly, a person committed to tolerance must also be committed to non-retaliation. According to Gülen, tolerance will manifest itself in halting verbal attacks on or abuse of unbelievers. True Muslims will swallow their anger and forgive as the Qur'an teaches (3:134). Citing the Sufi poet Yunus Emre, Gülen encourages those who have been attacked to act as if they had no hand or tongue with which to strike back (Gülen 2004, 61). Clearly, for Gülen, forgiveness and a commitment to non-retaliation are foundational to tolerance.

I am unable to find an explicit discussion of forgiveness and non-retaliation relating to tolerance in Conyers' writings. While I think these two commitments may be implicit in his emphasis on humility, openness and the reconciliation that comes through Christ, the fact is that Conyers does not mention them unambiguously in his attempt to reclaim the ancient practice. This, in my view, is a significant oversight that may be credited to the insulated academic and ecclesiastical environments in which many European and American theologians have worked. Gülen, on the other hand, has labored in a world where injustice and suffering are the ambient reality, where retaliation is natural, and where forgiveness is only a distant hope.

If Conyers had ever spent time with Gülen, I am confident he would have come away from that conversation enriched, with a friend and co-worker in the cause of peace. Both men are effective advocates of dialogue and tolerance precisely because of the strength of their respective faiths.

References

Aslandoğan, A. 2007. "Interfaith Dialog and Tolerance in the Contemporary World: Fethullah Gülen." Paper presented to the Southwest Commission on Religion Studies, Dallas, TX.

Bonhoeffer, D. 1995. *Ethics*. New York: Touchstone.

Burrell, D. 1986. *Knowing the Unknowable God: Ibn-Sina, Maimonides, Aquinas*. Notre Dame: University of Notre Dame Press.

Conyers, A. J. 1988. *God, Hope and History: Jürgen Moltmann and the Christian Conception of History*. Macon, GA, Mercer University Press.

———. 2001a. *The Long Truce: How Toleration Made the World Safe for Profit and Power*. Dallas, TX: Spence Publishing.

———. 2001b. "Rescuing Tolerance." *First Things: A Monthly Journal of Religion and Public Life* 115, 43–46.

Gülen, M. F. 2000 *Pearls of Wisdom*. New Jersey: The Light, Inc.

———. 2004. *Toward a Global Civilization of Love and Tolerance*. New Jersey: The Light, Inc.

———. 2005. *The Statue of Our Souls: Revival in Islamic Thought and Activism*. New Jersey: The Light, Inc.

Helwys, T. 1612. *The Mistery of Iniquity*. London.

Hurtado, L. W. 1984. "Jesus as Lordly Example in Philippians 2:5–11." *From Jesus to Paul: Studies in Honour of Francis Wright Beare*, ed. P. Richardson and J. C. Hurd. Waterloo, Ontario: Wilfrid Laurier University Press.

Kurtz, L. R. 2005. "Gülen's Paradox: Combining Commitment and Tolerance." *The Muslim World* 95, 373–384.

Locke, J. 1950. *A Letter Concerning Toleration*. New York: The Liberal Arts Press.

Marcuse, H. 1969. "Repressive Tolerance." *A Critique of Pure Tolerance*, ed. R. P. Wolff, B. Moore, and H. Marcuse. Boston: Beacon Press.

———. 1969. *The Listening Heart: Vocation and the Crisis of Modern Culture*. Dallas, TX: Spence Publishing.

McBeth, H. L. 1987. *The Baptist Heritage*. Nashville: Broadman.

Mullins, E. Y. 1978. *The Axioms of Religion*. Nashville: Broadman.

Oden, A. G. 2001. *And You Welcomes Me: A Sourcebook on Hospitality in Early Christianity*. Nashville: Abingdon.

Pohl, C. D. 1999. *Making Room: Recovering Hospitality as a Christian Tradition*. Grand Rapids: Eerdmans.

Ünal, A. and A. Williams. 2000. *Advocate of Dialogue: Fethullah Gülen*. Fairfax, VA: Fountain.

Walzer, M. 1997. *On Toleration*. New Haven: Yale University Press.

PART 4

Peacebuilding in Global Action

Chapter 11

Phnom Penh's Fethullah Gülen School as an Alternative to Prevalent Forms of Education for Cambodia's Muslim Minority

Philipp Bruckmayr

Introduction

Religiously motivated educational efforts have been and are an outstanding feature of the worldwide Islamic resurgence in recent decades. To this, one has to add the unprecedented internationalization of such efforts in our rapidly globalizing world, first through organizations like the Muslim World League and then through Islamic charities. The case of the Gülen Movement is unique as it is an Islamically inspired international actor providing not religious but secular education. What is more, its activities are happening in a time of major transitions and upheavals in the Muslim world, contemporaneous with developments displaying common patterns such the growth of terrorism in the name of religion and the politicization of Islam from Trinidad to Maluku. Yet, these transitional processes have had very different outcomes. In 1998 the Taliban regime was firmly consolidating its rule over most of Afghanistan; the same year witnessed Indonesia's long-time ruler General Suharto being forced to give way to a pro-democracy movement largely supported by what was labelled as "civil Islam" (Hefner 2000). For the Chams of Cambodia the period following 1993 was also a major transitional experience, as long-enduring isolation from the wider Muslim world gave way to unprecedented international Islamic endeavors in the Khmer kingdom.

Gülen-inspired schools have been founded in a number of Southeast Asian states, namely in Cambodia, Vietnam, Thailand, Indonesia, Myanmar and in the Philippines.[47] Unlike the Muslim minorities of the Philippines and Thailand, Cambodia's Muslim minority is not confined to a specific geographical area, but is dispersed over all twenty-two Cambodian provinces.[48] Another major point of difference between the Cambodian Chams and other Southeast Asian Muslim minorities is their specific history in relation to the Khmer majority. As they were not conquered but instead came to Cambodia as refugees, there is no long history of inter-religious strife as in southern Thailand, the South Philippines and the Arakan region of Myanmar.

While taking into account, that Phnom Penh is not a potential interreligious powder keg like Zamboanga on Mindanao, which houses the Gülen-inspired Turkish-Philippine School of Tolerance (Michel 2003, 70), it is important to view the Movement's agenda of education and ethics across religious and ethnic boundaries in the contemporary Cambodian context, to assess its possible contribution to both the Khmers' and the Chams' plight in a country which still has to recover from the repercussions of Khmer Rouge rule (1975–1979). This is even more important if one considers that a prime field of the Movement's activities is in countries under former communist rule such as the Central Asian republics and Albania.[49] Although, as far as Central Asia is concerned, common Turkic-ness plays a major role in describing the motivations of both Gülen himself and of the Movement's activists there (Agai 2004,

47 References to these educational facilities are scattered throughout different sources. See Yılmaz (2003, 236); Agai (2004, 14–15); Michel (2003, 70–71).

48 However, a third of the Cham population resides in Kampong Cham province.

49 For these see Agai (2003, 66–68); Agai (2004, 272–280); Clement (2007); Keles (2007); Turam (2003, 184–207).

224–229; Turam 2003, 188–202), it is nevertheless often stated that "the moral vacuum left by communism" (Agai 2004, 344) is something to be confronted by the Movement's efforts in the field of education. Moreover, Gülen's thought on living in non-Muslim lands (Yılmaz 2003, 234–237) should be valuable for all Muslim minorities and immigrant communities around the globe.

As background to my assessment of Phnom Penh's Gülen-inspired school's presumed character as an appropriate alternative to other forms of education for the Cham minority, especially to similarly foreign–sponsored ones, in the first section of this study it will be necessary to present a concise overview of Cham history in Cambodia in relation to the Khmer majority and the field of education. For our purpose it is certainly most important to focus on the period since 1993, when Cambodia emerged from over twenty years of isolation to become a playground for numerous NGOs and private enterprises (as far as aid for the Chams is concerned) often originating from Muslim states and investing in educational programs. Thus, the next section will present an assessment of the different forms of schooling as well as of differing views on education that have emerged among the Chams since then. The third section then tries to detect convergences between Gülen's thought on the one hand and the efforts and self-images of Cham NGOs on the other. The following two sections deal specifically with the relation of Zaman International School to the Gülen Movement and to the Cham community. Finally, the concluding section will, apart from recapitulating prior findings, try to assess the relevance of Gülen's thought for the Cambodian Chams' case in the field of education and beyond.

The Chams in Cambodia and Education in Religious and Secular Spheres

Chams migrated to Cambodia in numerous waves between 1471 and the 1830s, as their homeland, the once powerful Champa, was gradually absorbed by the Vietnamese (Phoeun 1988). Close contact with resident Malays as well as the advance of Islam in Champa itself in the sixteenth and seventeenth century led to their Islamization. In Cambodia the Chams, with a population of between 400 thousand and 500 thousand people, constitute the only numerically important ethnic and religious minority, mostly adhering to the Shafi'i school of law and having undergone a significant Malay cultural influence. With Cham language as their native tongue, most Chams are also fluent in Khmer and, due to its traditional relevance in religious instruction, have a knowledge of Malay too.

A distinct minority within the Cambodian Cham community are the *Cham Sot* ("the pure Chams"), who display no traces of Malayization and profess a specifically Chamic form of Islam (De Feo 2005a; Baccot 1968).

For both Khmers and Chams, education had for centuries a purely religious character, provided in the Buddhist monasteries or in Muslim village schools or by itinerant Muslim teachers. However, in both the monasteries and the Muslim village schools, acquiring the ability to read and write was a prerequisite for further religious instruction. That Islamic education was a major ingredient of Cham village life in the middle of the nineteenth century can be inferred from European travel reports.[50] From the early twentieth century we are informed about textbooks used in Cham schools. Then, studies were confined to Qur'anic commentaries (*tafsir*)[51] and Malay translations of Arabic catechisms (Cabaton 1906, 43–44).

French rule, beginning in 1863, with education as "an area of colonial neglect" (Vickery 1999, 19), initially had virtually no impact on the Chams, who were observed to be still hardly participating in the French educational system in the late 1930s.

50 See for example the reports of Adolf Bastian visiting Cambodia in 1864 (Bastian 2005, 100 & 145).

51 Unfortunately there is no mention of the authorships of the commentaries in question. However, by the time of Cabaton's survey, there existed only two Malay commentaries on the entire Qur'an, namely the works by the Acehnese Abd al-Ra'uf al-Singkili (d. ca. 1700) and the Javanese Muhammad Nawawi Banteni (d. 1897) (Feener 1998, 52–55; Riddell 2001, 195–197).

They rather opted for their lively local religious education system and, at times, further studies in Kelantan (Malaysia) and even Mecca (Ner 1941, 188–190). Of major importance for our present discussion is the fact that the religious centre of Trea[52] already housed a *madrasa* providing a mixed curriculum of both religious and secular subjects in the 1930s. Throughout Southeast Asia, the introduction of such balanced curricula was among the major demands of the Islamic modernist movement as well as a symbol of it (Giora 2004, 1–8). However, this innovative institution in Trea was neither destined to last nor to serve as a model for other religious schools in Cambodia at that date.

Naturally, neither the low enrolment of Chams in the French schools nor the failure to establish a network of modern institutions of religious education, as was done by Indonesia's Muhammadiyah modernists in the same period (Ricklefs 2007, 223), served to uplift the Chams in a protectorate society, where upward mobility through education was very hard to achieve even for Khmers. In the late 1930s Cham enrolment in official schools was very low in the urban milieu and virtually non-existent in rural Cham strongholds (Ner 1941, 196). Accordingly, Chams were not to be found in any administrative positions, apart from that of district or village chief in Cham areas.

In independent Cambodia under King Sihanouk the overall educational situation changed dramatically, with a rapid increase in availability and attendance up to tertiary level. Yet, observers in the early 1960s still lament the Chams' preference for religious schools despite the progress of the public system (Delvert 1960, 23). However, Chams recalling the Sihanouk era, criticize the system's partiality in terms of availability to minorities and allocation of stipends (Front d'Union 1983, 50, 58)[53].

---

52 On Trea's history as a centre of Muslim learning in Cambodia see Bruckmayr 2007b.

53 Although the source of this information is a publication of the People's Republic of Kampuchea (PRK) government, which was certainly intended to present the condi-

When General Lon Nol deposed Sihanouk in 1970, the country was already a battlefield with both communist insurgency and US bombing in the countryside (Kiernan 1999, 18–19). As the war gradually intensified up to the Khmer Rouge's victory in 1975, Cambodians were generally occupied with more fundamental issues than educational reform. Subsequently, although the new regime did not completely dispose of education, only the lowest level of primary schooling, providing basic literacy and numeracy, was maintained (Vickery 1999, 183–186). Apart from the horrible death toll inflicted on the overall Cambodian population under Democratic Kampuchea (DK), as the Khmer Rouges dubbed their regime, its rule proved especially disastrous for traditional religious learning among the Chams. In 1979 they found themselves with hardly any teachers and almost all their mosques destroyed (Kiernan 1999, 271; Taouti 1982, 194–195), not to mention the deaths of probably a few hundred thousand Chams (Kiernan 1988, 30; Osman 2002, 1–3; Bruckmayr 2006, 4–7).

After the Vietnamese invasion ousting Democratic Kampuchea, the new People's Republic of Kampuchea (PRK) started to rebuild the country, with its educational efforts being considered as "one of the regime's greatest achievements" (Gottesmann 2002, 74) by posterity. Moreover, participants emphasized its non-discriminatory treatment of the Chams, whose participation in public schooling was then certainly greater than ever before.

These developments were paralleled by Cham efforts to re-establish their religious school system, although initially only achieved at a minimal scale, due to absence of experienced teachers and a chronic lack of funds. The community's calls for international aid went unanswered due to the international rejection of the regime, which came to be regarded as a mere puppet of communist Vietnam at a time which coincided with US and Saudi-Arabian

tions of the Chams under previous regimes as unfavorable, it would be misleading to regard the grievances described in the published interviews as mere inventions of the interviewees.

engagement in the anti-communist struggle in Afghanistan. Thus, the Chams' isolation from the wider Muslim world continued as a general pattern.

The first arrival of international Islamic aid used for education occurred in the early 1980s via the Islamic Development Bank (Taouti 1986, 200 n. 10). After the 1993 elections, which marked a late return to a certain degree of stability not experienced for more than two decades in Cambodia, a great number of Muslim charities started to operate in Cambodia, mainly financing mosques and religious schools, which led to an unprecedented increase in both (Bruckmayr 2006, 10–13; De Feo 2005b, 107–110).

Consequently, the percentage of Chams having access to religious education has risen dramatically. Yet, a number of Cham leaders are arguing that more is needed to uplift the still mostly rural, poor and uneducated minority, whose overall situation was apparently little affected by the promising restart of public education in the early 1980s, notwithstanding the obvious success of a small number of Cham politicians and businessmen. Moreover, Islamic resurgence and its side effects have also affected otherwise traditionally harmonious Khmer-Cham relations, and have, in some circles, brought forward the view, that too intimate relations with the Khmers are undesirable.

The Religious, the Secular, the Paralleled and the Combined: Schooling the Chams

Recent research among the Chams has shown that in the rural villages illiteracy in Khmer, Cambodia's official language, is still a major problem. As the religious schools are naturally not concerned with instruction in the Khmer alphabet and language, the over-concern of many Chams and Islamic charities with religious education does nothing to confront this deficiency (So 2005, 5). Moreover, it is obvious that the public school system has failed even in this basic aspect.

By now, Cambodia boasts around three hundred Islamic schools, most of which are teaching a purely religious curriculum. However, independent initiatives are also undertaken to provide useful extra classes to the pupils in several of these schools. Thus, in a school in a Cham village in Siam Reap, which, having the ruins of Angkor Wat in its vicinity, is the main tourist centre of Cambodia after Phnom Penh, English, no doubt of major importance in such an area, is also taught apart from the usual classes in Malay.[54]

Among many Chams the former rejection of public schools has given way to an embrace of secular education; however, a fear of assimilation to the Khmer majority through education remains. Therefore pupils often pursue parallel schooling. Enrolled in both public and religious schools, even children attending primary school spend a considerable amount of time at school "in a desperate attempt to ensure a better future [..] while retaining their identity as Muslims," as Milligan has put it observing a similar situation among the Maranao of the southern Philippines (2005, 139–140). Naturally, in rural Cambodia, where children are often needed by the family to participate in fishing, rice farming and the like, this educational double load is often not endurable for long. As the religious village schools are closer to home than the public ones, usually located in Khmer villages, the choice is often made in favor of the former, when attendance at both proves to be too exhausting or too time-consuming.

A possible solution to the problems posed by parallel schooling is the establishment of religious schools with a mixed curriculum including core subjects of the public syllabus. Thus, while explicitly Islamic in orientation, its students still have the opportunity to switch to, or to engage in further studies in the public system. A notable advocate of such institutions is the Cambodian Muslim Development Foundation (CMDF), a local NGO patronized by the Grand Mufti Kamaruddin Yusof, and headed by Oths-

54 Interview with the province imam of Siam Reap, Musa Soleh, in Stung Thmey (15.7.2005, 16.7.2005).

man Hassan, Secretary of State (Ministry of Labor and Training) and currently the most influential Cham in politics. Starting in 1999, the CMDF has embarked on building a network of secondary schools for boys and girls which rely on the same mixed syllabus employed at similar schools in Malaysia (CMDF 2004, 8–11).[55] Their goal is to provide, standardized Islamic education, otherwise unavailable in Cambodia, without barring their students' way to success through secular education.

Similarly, a number of schools founded and funded by Arab NGOs employ such a combined syllabus, and are generally credited with providing classical Islamic education as well as general subjects at a high level (De Feo 2004, 92). However, their funding is regarded as controversial as several of the operating NGOs feature on the blacklists of the Bush administration for suspected links to terrorism. Given the intricacies of the situation, a crackdown on and subsequent shutdown of a school of the Saudi Umm al-Qura International Organization in Kendal province caused fierce disputes, as the school was regarded as the only high-level institution affordable for Chams in its rural surroundings (Osman 2006). Additionally, it is a matter of doubt whether combined-curriculum schools are having a positive impact on national integration. In the Philippine context, the question has been raised whether they are not implicit symbols of "dissatisfaction, if not outright rejection, [...] of educational alternatives offered [...] by mainstream society" (Milligan 2005, 124).

Apart from those advocating parallel schooling or religious schools with balanced curricula, there are also currents within the Cham community which deliberately reject public schooling above the primary level to avoid Khmerization, while strongly opting for purely religious studies. This view is specifically expounded by members of the Cambodian branch of the *Tablighi Jamaat*,[56] an

55 In 2004 the foundation already had 14 schools in 8 provinces.

56 Naturally not all of the movement's members share this view.

Indian "evangelical" movement and offshoot of the Deobandi school (Metcalf 2002), which lays particular stress on individual conduct with regard to the Prophet Muhammad's example (Masud 2000; Sikand 2002). Since appearing on the local scene in the late 1980s, it has become a mass movement, especially among rural Chams (De Feo 2005b, 110–112; Bruckmayr 2006, 13–14). The centre of its activities is Trea in Kampong Cham province, which houses a big Tablighi boarding school attached to Cambodia's largest mosque (Bruckmayr 2007b).

Common Agendas of Gülen and Cham NGOs

Greg Barton has recently shed light on the similarities of the Gülen Movement in Turkey and the neo-modernist currents in Indonesia as so-called post-Islamist civil society forces standing out in the Muslim world (Barton 2005, 43). As such they might be rightfully regarded as illustrative, yet rarely recognized examples of the fact that Islam, civil society, and democracy are indeed compatible. Although taking Turam's (2003, 186–187) reservations about applying the label "civil society organization" freely to everything non-governmental and independent into account, I am suggesting that Cambodian Muslim NGOs should be regarded similarly as their agendas have many convergences with those of the two aforementioned movements. Organizations like CMDF and the Cambodian Islamic Development Association are indeed supporting democracy, the participation and interaction of the Chams with the Khmer majority, as well as secular education as a means of community empowerment without necessarily losing one's Islamic identity.

Although Gülen's ethos of education, with its outstanding element, the view of the acquisition of secular knowledge as an Islamic value per se (Agai 2004, 195–196), has so far found no effective counterpart or followers in Cambodia, the agenda and activities of an organization such as the Cambodian Muslim Student Association (CAMSA) bear many resemblances to Gülen's discourse on education (Michel 2003; Agai 2003). Indeed, according to its own presentation,[57] CAMSA offers its services to make sure that Cham youths complete their secular education. Another activity is the founding of hostels to accommodate students from the countryside for free or at low cost, in exchange for community work. Due to the fact, that businessmen sympathetic to its cause are instrumental in funding the Gülen Movement's activities, it is also of interest, that CAMSA organizes classes in business administration to foster entrepreneurial activities. Likewise also other Cham NGOs, for example the Cambodian Islamic Development Association, are actively supporting secular education (Collins 1996, 61; De Feo 2005b, 108).

Another important feature of Gülen's thought is his call to achieve intercultural and interreligious understanding by emphasizing common values rather than differences (Agai 2004, 256), the basis of which is seen to be knowledge of the other. In this respect, CAMSA pursues the translation of seminal works on Islam into Khmer and English for distribution to Islamic and public schools to be available to both Muslims and non-Muslims, apart from stressing interreligious and intercultural understanding. Whereas Gülen is mostly associated with dialogue among Muslims, Jews and Christians (Ünal & Williams 2000, 241–296), participants in the Gülen Movement are also cooperating and interacting freely with Buddhists in Buddhist countries such as Korea or Thailand (Yılmaz 2003, 236) and in Cambodia.

The Zaman International School (ZIS) of Phnom Penh and the Gülen Movement

The private Zaman International School was founded in 1997 by the Turkish journalist Attila Yusuf Güleker. With over 1,100 students enrolled from kindergarten up to high school, it is educating

57 The following information about CAMSA's agenda is derived from an unpublished document of the organization dating to the year 2005 and obtained thanks to Sos Mousine.

more boys and girls than similar Phnom Penh private schools such as the International School of Phnom Penh or Northbridge International School.[58]

Apart from education and media, business and finance networks are considered to be the third important sphere of the Gülen Movement's activities as exemplified by the business support agency PASIAD (Society for Social and Economic Solidarity with Pacific Countries), which serves to facilitate trade contacts between Turkish and Asian businessmen. In turn, those businessmen are often benefactors of the Movement's educational institutions (Barton 2005, 29–30), with PASIAD playing a supportive role also in the distribution of funds from businessmen to the institutions in question (Nawab Osman 2007, 338). In line with this approach Ali Kökten, director of the Zaman school, was likewise involved in PASIAD activities in Cambodia.[59] The same goes for both Kökten and principal Osman Karaca in relation to a similar organization named TUSKON.[60]

Apart from these typical intra-movement relations the connection between the Gülen Movement and the Zaman school can also be inferred from references from within, as reports about it appear in Gülen-related forums and websites.[61] Although the efforts of the Movement are widely appreciated (even in the West), persecution in Turkey, negative press and conspiracy theories surrounding Gülen's figure since 1999 (Agai 2004, 162–164) might have contributed to the silence concerning his person in communication with outsiders. Additionally, the great number of non-Muslim native

58 During the inauguration of the new ZIS kindergarten and primary campus in March 2008 Cambodian Deputy PM Sok An not only voiced his appreciation for the school but also suggested the opening of an affiliate private university. This project was scheduled for 2010.

59 See www.pasiad.org/haber.php?id=2269

60 See *Zaman International School Newspaper*, IV, no. 46 (5.3.07), p. 1.

61 See for example http:://en.fgulen.com/content/view/2171/20/. The same text also appeared in the E-Gazette of *Today's Zaman* (19-1-06).

teachers in the school might even be unaware that they are part of a process which owes so much to the thought of Fethullah Gülen.

The ZIS and the Chams

It is obvious that the ZIS was founded with the purpose of providing high level education for the Cambodian public and not specifically for the Muslim Chams. In line with Gülen's thought, activists in the Movement emphasize that good works cannot be limited to Islamic countries (Agai 2004, 335–336) or to Muslims for that matter. Thus, the schools opened by Movement participants are open to everybody, and although its members often espouse Islamic values motivated by Gülen behind their efforts (Agai 2003), this does not involve a distinct agenda towards Muslims in contrast to adherents of other religions in multi-religious societies such as Kazakhstan, South Africa or Cambodia. This equal treatment sets the Gülen Movement apart from Islamic charities in Cambodia, which are exclusively concerned with Muslim affairs. Moreover, Gülen himself stresses the importance of providing adequate education in accordance with local contexts and value systems by saying that "although education is undeniably important for a country's development, the expected results will never be achieved if the young people are not educated according to the country's traditional values," yet with each generation learning from its predecessors' experiences and following its own way (Gülen 2005, 54). The ZIS makes its open approach explicit by stressing that it pursues a strictly non-discriminatory policy regarding race, color, sex, national and ethnic origin, age, religion or disability in all school-administered programs. Moreover, it declares its aim to foster both "respect for people of a variety of cultural and social backgrounds and of various religious and political orientations [.., as well as] an understanding of the interdependence of individuals, groups and nations" as part of its mission (ZIS Student and Parent Handbook, 3–4).

While the Gülen-inspired schools do not rely on any confessional instruction, they seek to convey and expound ethical Islamic values like honesty, hard work, generosity and the like (Michel 2003, 71; Aslandoğan and Çetin 2006, 41) by exemplary conduct. Gülen and the Gülen Movement refer to this practice as *temsil* (representation of Islamic values by way of individual example) as opposed to common notions of *tebliğ*[62] (usually meaning propagation of Islam as such, or in the understanding of the Tablighi Jamaat, propagation of proper conduct and religious revival among Muslims). Interestingly, Gülen uses these two terms interchangeably in his religious works (Agai 2004, 235), which gives *tebliğ* a considerably broader meaning within the Gülen discourse than in common usage.[63] Obviously, the aforementioned values are far from being exclusively Islamic ones, but rather part of a universal ethical system and communicated to people through different cultural and religious traditions, which is also considered by Gülen (Michel 2003, 82).

Currently there are nine Chams enrolled at Zaman school according to its principal.[64] Apparently, the staff of the school is not particularly concerned with the Chams. Principal Karaca explains that he knows only little about them,[65] and references to the Chams are neither to be found in Yusuf Güleker's articles in *Zaman*, nor in the school's newspaper,[66] which is surprising as otherwise presents a wide range of cultural and historical information on Cambodia, including Buddhist and Khmer festivities as well as about those of the Chinese minority.

---

62 Derived from the Arabic *ballagha* (to relate, inform).

63 On the use and relevance of these terms in the Gülen discourse see Agai 2004, 235–243.

64 See n. 17.

65 See n. 17.

66 An article about the ancient kingdoms of Southeast Asia contains two references to Champa, without mentioning its descendents on Cambodian soil. See *ZIS Newspaper*, IV, no. 41 (22.11.06), p. 4.

However, as the school is open to every pupil who passes the entrance exams and whose parents' are able to pay the high, yet for quality education in Cambodia usual, entrance and tuition fees,[67] it is not surprising, that a mostly poor minority such as the Chams is not well represented in its ranks. To this one has to add the rejection of secular, or at least of purely secular education by minor parts of the Cham community. Naturally, for the limited number of Chams that both desires private secular education for their children and has the financial means to pay for it, ZIS should be the prime option, as they might find it desirable to have at least a number of coreligionists involved in imparting secular education to their children.

Although the school's self-presentation is explicitly secular, and also its newspaper is, in spite of its frequent treatment of Cambodian Buddhism, not concerned with Islamic religion at all, common religious values are emphasized by the school, as is common in institutions of the Gülen Movement. However, the Islamic background of parts of the staff at times reveals itself in the school's English newspaper. Thus, in an article about the relevance of reading for children, a story about Muhammad appears, in which the prophet's name is followed by the common abbreviation for "peace be upon him" (pbuh) without further explanation. This practice of calling blessings on the Prophet is most probably completely unknown to Khmer readers, but not so to the Chams. Moreover, the judgment attributed to the prophet in the story is presented as having been in the meantime confirmed by modern science.[68] Furthermore, sections about Turkish culture naturally at times contain information about Islamic culture, such as the history of calligraphy.[69]

---

67 Full scholarships are accorded every year to the five most outstanding students (starting from the 6th grade).

68 *Zaman International School Newspaper* III (31), 5. This is, of course, truly in Said Nursi's and Gülen's tradition of emphasizing the value of Qur'an and Sunna for science and vice-versa.

69 See issues III (27) and I (3).

Moreover, the fact that the Turkish staff at ZIS does not display specific interest in the Chams does not imply that the latter should not be able to appreciate the advantages of the school with regard to their special situation as a Muslim minority in the country,[70] especially once they have been exposed to Gülen's thought themselves. Thus, in our final section, we will assess the relevance Gülen's ideas could have in Cambodia, and their applicability among the Chams.

Concluding Remarks: Gülen's Thought and the Plight of the Chams

As far as Gülen's thought on secular education is concerned, it is obvious that the opposition between the secular and the religious is perceived in different terms by Gülen than by the minority of Chams that rejects secular education. Rather than seeing it as a threat to the believer, Gülen regards secular knowledge as prerequisite for better religious understanding and for the ability to refute the arguments of those who claim revelation and reason are irreconcilable (Agai 2004, 196). That Gülen is not an advocate of purely religious studies at all is evident from his view that the closing of Islamic educational institutions to positive sciences was a catastrophe for Islamic thought (Ünal and Williams 2000, 324–325). Moreover, he stresses that "avoiding the positive sciences fearing that they will lead to atheism is naiveté, and seeing them as contradictory to religion and faith and as vehicles for the rejection of religion is prejudice and ignorance" (Gülen 2005, 49), as the constructed conflict of religion and science is "a bitter struggle that should have never taken place" (quoted in Michel 2003, 75).[71]

70 Recent research has shown that Kenya's Muslim minorities are taking a keen interest in and identifying themselves strongly with the Gülen-inspired Turkish schools in the country, as they view Islam as their common denominator with the schools' Turkish staff (Kalyoncu 2008, 354–355).

71 Indeed there was originally no distinction between secular and religious schooling in Islam, but only between *manqulat* (transmitted sciences) and *ma'qulat* (rational sciences), both usually being taught in the same madrasas (Sikand 2005, xxxiii),

Another distinct problem, albeit also belonging to the education debate, is the situation of Cham women, among whom illiteracy and drop-out rates after primary school are even higher than among male Chams (So 2005). At the root of this dilemma lies not only the traditional role of women in Cham households, but also the recent spread of the *hijab* among the Chams. As the headscarf is forbidden in most secondary schools, many Cham females from conservative villages drop out of public schools to continue at purely religious ones (So 2005, 6). Especially in Turkey, but also in many European countries, the Islamic headscarf has proven to be a bone of contention. Gülen's view on the topic is strikingly simple and pragmatic. According to him, the Islamic headscarf belongs to the realm of secondary issues and not to the essentials of faith. Therefore, treating it as an essential part of Muslim belief would amount to "sacrificing the important for the trivial" (Ünal & Williams 2000, 63). Moreover, the sharp increase in participation in secondary and university education by girls from religious families in Turkey during the last decade, has also been partly attributed to Gülen's tireless efforts for equal education for both boys and girls in Turkey among the religiously minded (Yavuz 2003, 30).

It has already been stated above that Gülen's ideas about Muslims living in non-Muslim lands bear relevance for all Muslim minorities and immigrant communities outside the Muslim world. Given the Chams' history as descendents of refugees, and the long history of peaceful coexistence with their Khmer hosts, the term *dar al-harb* (country of war) seems to be very inappropriate for their place of residence, rather justifying refined Islamic legal terminology such as *dar al-aman* (country of security).[72] Similarly, Gülen stresses that local laws are to be obeyed by Muslim residents in non-Muslim (as well as in secular) states (Yılmaz 2003, 234). Thus, Muslim minorities such as the Chams should rather contribute to

---

which would nowadays, following our categorization, almost be labelled schools with balanced curricula.

72 On this terminology see Yılmaz 2003, 234.

peace within the country than jeopardize it by pressing for a special legal or political status. Given the importance of childhood and adolescence in identity formation, it is beyond doubt that Khmers and Chams being educated together in a non-discriminatory environment characterized by mutual respect, as embodied by the ZIS, is preferable to the denominational schooling of Islamic institutions to counter fears of a growing alienation of the Chams from Cambodian society. However, as long as public schools are often unable to provide high-quality education due to a chronic lack of funds, it is not only religious considerations which will draw Chams to comparably well-funded foreign-run religious schools with combined curricula. For those Chams primarily seeking high-level secular education for their children, ZIS should indeed be very inviting. The common Islamic faith with some of its staff and its embodiment of Muslim-Buddhist cooperation as daily practice due to its Turkish-Cambodian faculty should serve as a psychological incentive to choose this particular institution. In this context it is also noteworthy that the majority of Chams was always on good terms with the representatives of the Vietnamese-backed PRK regime and its political successors (e.g. the ruling Cambodian People's Party[73]), and is thus much less inclined to the anti-Vietnamese sentiments still wide-spread in Cambodian society. Certainly aware of this latter problem, the ZIS has recently started to organize school trips to Vietnam (including visits to local Gülen-inspired Turkish schools), once again testifying to its concern for peaceful coexistence and getting to know and respect each other.

Returning to Gülen's thought, the last factor to be discussed here in relation to the Chams is of special interest, as it appears to be both rather unique to Gülen and fitting perfectly into the Cham context. This concerns the relation between the Sunnite Cham majority and the *Cham Sot*. Albeit generally respected by the rest of the community, the latter minority group with its specific tradition-

73 On the CPP and its history see Vickery 1994.

al practices, at times in outright discord with what is generally regarded as standard Islamic ritual, is not accepted as truly Muslim. Therefore it is excluded from the benefits of international Islamic charities, which are tying aid to proper religious conduct, and have therefore refused to provide funds to *Cham Sot* villages (Collins 1996, 50–51; De Feo 2005a, 227). Local NGOs like CAMSA are not closing their doors to them, yet are allegedly also actively seeking to purify their religious practices (De Feo 2005a, 235).

The antagonism between the two Cambodian Muslim groups is of course reminiscent of Sunni–Alevi opposition in Turkey or Sunni–Bektashi opposition in Albania, Kosovo and Macedonia.[74] The issue of similar Muslim minorities, often regarded as divergent sects, has not been addressed by many Muslim writers so far, especially when compared to the issue of dialogue with other book religions. Given the similarity of the respective cases, what Gülen has to say about Sunni–Alevi relations appears to be very useful for the Cambodian case. He notes that the Alevis are in fact enriching Turkish culture, and that the two groups should open up to each other "for the sake of unity and enrichment." Moreover, he argues that Alevi prayer houses should be supported to reflect Islam's inclusiveness (Ünal and Williams 2000, 68–69). With regard to the two specific Cham groups in Cambodia, Gülen's references to inclusiveness and cultural diversity are particularly important, especially if one considers that the *Cham Sot* indeed represent traditional Cham culture in Cambodia, and that the eventual consolidation of the two factions as distinct religious groups is of very recent date, as this process only took place during the twentieth century (Bruckmayr 2007a, 103–107).

It appears that Gülen's thought could provide useful approaches to confronting various current problems among the Cambodian Cham community. Whereas acquaintance with Gülen's ideas is still lacking in Cambodia now, acknowledgment of the thought of

74 On these two groups see Yaman & Erdemir 2006.

Indonesian Neo-Modernists such as Nurcholish Madjid and Abdurrahman Wahid,[75] and its convergences with Gülen's positions (Barton 2005) might pave the way for the recognition of his efforts as universal and locally applicable instead of being specifically Turkish, something which is highlighted daily by the existence of ZIS. As far as the school is concerned, it is evident that it remains mostly rather a theoretical than an actual option for the education of Cham students. Yet, what is more, certain segments of the Cham community have agendas similar to those of Gülen and the Movement in the field of education. Certainly, home-grown efforts along similar lines would have a much bigger impact on the community than a single foreign-run school. In this respect it should be taken into account that erstwhile students of Gülen-inspired schools usually display an ongoing close attachment to their former schools and their respective approaches as well as a tendency to follow up this model with personal initiative, which has played a major part in the worldwide spread of the Movement and its schools. Thus, the currently small number of Chams being educated in this environment, combined with their presumed future elite status, could eventually have a disproportionate impact on the community too.

Evidently, the idea of secular educational endeavors being not merely for upward mobility, but also for the pursuance of an Islamic ideal, as expounded by Gülen and exemplified by the ZIS, is an entirely new factor in the education debate among the Chams. Although still widely unknown and still of small relevance in Cham discourse in comparison to the agendas of Cham, Arab, Malaysian and Tablighi institutions propagating their respective views and ideals, it is indeed important to note that the Gülen Movement has obviously arrived in Cambodia as a completely different type of Islamic internationalism. Its inclusive character is well-suited to the plight of a Muslim minority people with intra-community diversity, and would therefore likewise facilitate dealings with the Cambo-

75 On life and thought of Madjid and Wahid see Saleh 2001, 240-292 and Barton 2002.

dian government. In contrast, the activities of other foreign Islamic groups at times rather serve to provoke intra-community strife between Sunnis and *Cham Sot* as well as between modernity-oriented Muslims and Tablighi traditionalists, and are moreover in certain instances at odds with governmental demands, whenever pragmatism is sacrificed to matters of principle.[76] Moreover, in a discussion strongly informed firstly by a perceived rigid distinction between religious and secular learning (and a likewise inherent—though not as conflicting pattern—in balanced/combined curricula) and secondly, by a view of public secular education as possibly leading towards loss of identity, especially concerning its religious component, the ZIS represents a strand of secular schooling devoid of both spiritual emptiness and attempts at assimilation to the majority population, but rather conducive to community empowerment and an inclusive, spiritually grounded cosmopolitanism combined with identity preservation.

References

Agai, B. 2003. "The Gülen Movement's Islamic Ethic of Education." *Turkish Islam and the Secular State: The Gülen Movement*, ed. M. H. Yavuz and J. L. Esposito, 48–68. Syracuse: Syracuse University Press.

Agai, B. 2004. *Zwischen Netzwerk und Diskurs. Das Bildungsnetzwerk um Fethullah Gülen (geb. 1938): Die flexible Umsetzung modernen islamischen Gedankenguts*. Hamburg: EB-Verlag.

Aslandoğan, Y. A. & M. Çetin. 2006. "The Educational Philosophy of Gülen in Thought and Practice. *Muslim Citizens of the Globalized World: Contributions of the Gülen Movement*, ed. Robert A. Hunt and Y. A. Aslandoğan, 31–54. New Jersey: The Light, Inc.

Baccot, J. 1968. *On G'nur et Cay à O Russey: syncrétisme réligieux dans un village cham du Cambodge*. Paris: Faculté des Lettres et Sciences Humaines.

Barton, G. 2002. *Abdurrahman Wahid, Muslim Democrat, Indonesian President: A View from the Inside*. Honolulu: University of Hawai'i Press.

76 For example, a teacher at a Phnom Penh school and orphanage run by the Kuwaiti *Jami'at Ihya' al-Turath al-Islami* (Revival of Islamic Heritage Society) was reprimanded by his superiors for attending a government AIDS prevention workshop for teachers (personal conversation, Kampong Cham, 1.8.2005).

———. 2005. "Progressive Islamic Thought, Civil Society and the Gülen Movement in the National Context: Parallels with Indonesia." Paper presented at the Conference on Islam in the Contemporary World: The Fethullah Gülen Movement in Thought and Practice, Rice University Houston.

Bastian, A. 2005. *A Journey in Cambodia and Cochin-China (1864)*. Bangkok: White Lotus Press.

Bruckmayr, P. 2006. "The Cham Muslims of Cambodia: From Forgotten Minority to Focal Point of Islamic Internationalism." *American Journal of Islamic Social Sciences* 23(3), 1–23.

———. 2007a. "The Islamization of Champa." M.A. thesis, University of Vienna.

———. 2007b. "Cambodia's Phum Trea as Mirror Image of Religious Change." *ISIM Review* 20, 48–49.

Cabaton, A. 1906. "Notes sur l'Islam dans l'Indochine française." *Revue du Monde Musulman* 1: 27–47.

Cambodian Muslim Development Foundation. 2004. *CMDF Serves the Muslim's Community*. Phnom Penh: CMDF.

Clement, V. 2007. "Turkmenistan's New Challenges: Can Stability Co-exist with Reform? A study of the Gülen Schools in Central Asia," 1997–2007. *Muslim World in Transition: Contributions of the Gülen Movement*, ed. I. Yilmaz et al., 572–584. London: Leeds Metropolitan University Press.

Collins, W. 1996. *The Chams of Cambodia*. Phnom Penh: Center for Advanced Studies.

De Féo, A. 2004. "Les Chams, l'islam et la revendication identitaire." Mémoire de DEA, Paris EPHE IVe section.

———. 2005a. "Les Chams sot, dissidence de l'islam cambodgien." *Les Cahiers de l'Orient* 58: 115–124.

———. 2005b. "Le royaume bouddhique face au renouveau islamique." *Les Cahiers de l'Orient* 58: 99–114.

Delvert, J. 1960. *Le paysan cambodgien*. Paris: Mouton.

Feener, R. M. 1998. "Notes towards the History of Qur'anic Exegesis in Southeast Asia." *Studia Islamika* 5(3), 47–76.

Giora, E. 2004. *Islam in Indonesia: Modernism, Radicalism, and the Middle East Dimension*. Brighton: Sussex Academic Press.

Gottesman, E. 2002. *Cambodia after the Khmer Rouge: Inside the Politics of Nation Building*. New Haven: Yale University Press.

Gülen, M. F. 2005. *Pearls of Wisdom*. New Jersey: The Light, Inc.

Hefner, R. W. 2000. *Civil Islam: Muslims and Democratization in Indonesia*. Princeton: Princeton University Press.

Kalyoncu, M. 2008. "[Gülen-inspired schools in East Africa] Secular Alternative in Kenya and Pragmatist Approach to Development in Uganda." *Islam in the Age of Global Challenges: Alternative Perspectives of the Gülen Movement.* Washington DC: Rumi Forum, 350–373.

Keles, I. 2007. "The Contributions of the Sebat International Education Institutes to Kyrgyzstan. *Muslim World in Transition: Contributions of the Gülen Movement*, ed. İhsan Yilmaz et al. London: Leeds Metropolitan University Press, 362–376.

Kiernan, B. 1988. "Orphans of Genocide: The Cham Muslims of Kampuchea under Pol Pot." *Bulletin of Concerned Asian Scholars* 20(4), 1–33.

———. 1999. *The Pol Pot Regime: Race, Power, and Genocide in Cambodia under the Khmer Rouge, 1975–79*. Chiang Mai: Silkworm Books.

Le Front d'Union pour l'Edification et la Défense de la Patrie Kampuchéenne. 1983. *La communauté islamique au Kampuchea*. Phnom Penh.

Masud, K. M. ed. 2000. *Travelers in Faith: Studies on the Tablighi Jama'at as Transnational Islamic Movement for Faith Renewal*. Leiden: Brill.

Metcalf, B. D. 2002. *Islamic Revival in British India: Deoband, 1860–1900*. New Delhi: Oxford University Press.

Michel, T. 2003. "Fethullah Gülen as Educator." *Turkish Islam and the Secular State: The Gülen Movement*, ed. M. H. Yavuz and J. L. Esposito. Syracuse: University Press, 69–84.

Milligan, J. A. 2005. *Islamic Identity, Postcoloniality, and Educational Policy. Schooling and Ethno-religious Conflict in the Southern Philippines.* New York: Palgrave MacMillan.

Ner, M. 1941. "Les musulmans de l'Indochine française." *Bulletin de l'Ecole Française d'Extrême-Orient* 41: 151–200.

Osman, Y. 2002. *Oukoubah: Justice for the Cham Muslims under the Democratic Kampuchea Regime.* Phnom Penh: Documentation Center of Cambodia.

Osman, M. N. M. 2007. "Gülen's Contribution to a Moderate Islam in Southeast Asia." *Muslim World in Transition: Contributions of the Gülen Movement*, ed. İhsan Yılmaz et al. London: Leeds Metropolitan University Press, 334–346.

Osman, Y. 2006. "War against terrorism: Response from a Cambodian Muslim." Paper presented at the Conference on War against Terrorism: People's Response, Malaysia.

Phoeun, M. 1988. "La communauté cam au Cambodge du XV au XIX siècle." *Actes du Séminaire sur le Campa organisé à l'Université de Copenhague, le 23 mai 1987*. Paris: Centre d'histoire et civilisations de la péninsule indochinoise, 83–93.

Ricklefs, M. C. 2007. *Polarising Javanese Society. Islamic and Other Visions (c. 1830–1930)*. Leiden: KITLV Press.

Riddell, P. 2001. *Islam and the Malay-Indonesian World: Transmission and Responses*. Honolulu: University of Hawaii Press.

Saleh, F. 2001. *Modern Trends in Islamic Theological Discourse in Twentieth-century Indonesia: A Critical Survey*. Leiden: Brill.

So, F. 2005. "The Study of the Qur-an vs. Modern Education for Islamic Women in Cambodia." Paper presented at the short course on Islam, Gender, and Reproductive Rights, Sunan Kalijaga University Yogyakarta.

Sikand, Y. 2002. *The Origins and Development of the Tablighi Jama'at (1920–2000): A Cross-country Comparative Study*. Hydarabad: Orient Longman.

Taouti, S. 1986. "The Forgotten Muslims of Kampuchea and Viet Nam." *Readings on Islam in Southeast Asia*, ed. Ahmad Ibrahim et al. Singapore: Institute of Southeast Asian Studies, 193–200.

Turam, B. 2003. "National Loyalties and International Undertakings: The Case of the Gülen Community in Kazakhstan." *Turkish Islam and the Secular State: The Gülen Movement*, ed. M. H. Yavuz and J. L. Esposito, 184–207. Syracuse: University Press.

Ünal, A. and A. Williams, eds. 2000. *Advocate of Dialogue: Fethullah Gülen*. Fairfax: The Fountain.

Vickery, M. 1994. "The Cambodian People's Party: Where Has It Come from, Where Is It Going?" *Southeast Asian Affairs* 21, 102–117.

———. 1999. *Cambodia 1975–1982*. Chiang Mai: Silkworm Books.

Yaman, A. and A. Erdemir. 2006. *Alevism-Bektashism: A Brief Introduction*. London, England: Alevi Cultural Centre and Cem Evi.

Yavuz, M. H. 2003. "The Gülen Movement: The Turkish Puritans. *Turkish Islam and the Secular State: The Gülen Movement*, ed. M. H. Yavuz and J. L. Esposito, 19–47. Syracuse: Syracuse University Press.

Yılmaz, I. 2003. "*Ijtihad* and *Tajdid* by Conduct: The Gülen Movement." *Turkish Islam and the Secular State: The Gülen Movement*, ed. M. H. Yavuz and J. L. Esposito, 208–237. Syracuse: Syracuse University Press.

Yılmaz, I. et al (eds). 2007. *Muslim World in Transition: Contributions of the Gülen Movement*. London: Leeds Metropolitan University Press

Zaman International School. n. d. *Student and Parent Handbook*. Phnom Penh: ZIS.

CHAPTER 12

Investigating the Contribution of Fethullah Gülen through the Activities of a Gülen-inspired Religio-cultural Society Based in Ireland

Jonathan Lacey

INTRODUCTION

Fethullah Gülen motivates his sympathizers to mobilize by insisting that the mere avoidance of transgressions is not sufficient to be a "good Muslim." One must also become active in order to improve the conditions in the world. Islam, according to Gülen's articulation, is action-oriented. This principle has inspired the establishment of a multitude of organizations around the world devoted to interfaith dialogue and peaceful coexistence. This article focuses on a Gülen-inspired society based in Ireland, namely the Turkish Irish Educational and Cultural Society (TIECS). This society provides a range of interfaith and intercultural activities. From my study of this group, I hope to shed light on the real and practical contribution of Fethullah Gülen.

Ireland provides an interesting site for this study because unlike Holland, France, Britain and Germany, inward migration is a relatively new phenomenon in Ireland and likewise debates on multiculturalism and integration. Piaras MacEinri and Paddy Walley (2003,

18) argue that Ireland can now be understood "as a microcosm of the realities of globalisation" and Fintan O'Toole (2003, 4) insists that "the Republic of Ireland is the most globalised country on earth." Trade and finance pass fluently in and out of the territorial boundaries of Ireland. As of 1993, Ireland received 25% of all new US investment into Europe, employing 94,000 people in 2002 (O'Toole 2003, 6). This inward investment since the early 1990s along with EU contributions over the last two decades has resulted in Ireland's economy flourishing, making it one of the strongest economies in the world (O'Toole 2003).[77] This effervescent economy is necessarily coupled with inward migration to Ireland. Since 1997, Ireland, for so long suffering from an emigration hemorrhage, became an immigration destination (Lentin and McVeigh 2002; Ruhs 2005). Immigrants were courted by Irish companies and the government to fill job shortages. Consequently, we have witnessed unprecedented levels of immigration in Ireland and likewise an unprecedented mixture of cultures and religions. Irish culture has moved from one defined by Catholicism, nationalism and economic isolationism, to one oriented towards economic and cultural liberalism. Ireland has moved from a nation that largely perceived itself as homogenous to one that is renegotiating its identity on the recognition of heterogeneity.

Irish culture has been steeped in the Catholic tradition for centuries and though there has been a decline in practicing Catholics in Ireland (see Inglis 1998; Tovey and Share 2003), over 3.6 million of the total population of nearly 4.2 million in Ireland still claim to be Catholics (Central Statistics Office (CSO) 2007). The Irish state still pays great deference to religion in Ireland, inviting religious groups to perform prayers at state events. The most recent example of this was the National Day of Commemoration, an event that pays tribute to all the Irish people who died in wars or on

77 However, a recent decline in the house building coupled with problems in the global financial markets means that in the short term Ireland is likely to experience recession for the first time since 1983 (see Barrett, Kearney and O'Brien 2008).

United Nations duty. Leaders of the Jewish, Christian and Islamic communities were invited to say a prayer peculiar to their faith tradition at this event (O'Reagan 2007).

Until recent years interfaith dialogue in Ireland was dominated by Catholicism and Protestantism and the dialogue was often focused on crisis intervention. Islam is now the fastest growing religion in Ireland, with over 31,000 subscribers (CSO 2007) and has now become part of the national conversation vis-à-vis Irish identity. Muslims living in Ireland originate from a multitude of nations, counting Ireland, and from a number of Islamic zones. I maintain that for historical, geographical and cultural reasons, we can talk of Islam in the plural sense. Drawing on the work of M. Hakan Yavuz (2004), I argue that TIECS and the Gülen Movement practice "Turkish Islam"[78] which has Sufi principles at its core, promoting tolerance and reason as the keys to peaceful coexistence. This article illustrates how Fethullah Gülen's principles are practiced in a European context.

I begin this paper by surveying the various Islamic institutions in Ireland. I describe the multiple and diverse expressions of Islam practiced by Muslims living there and issues arising vis-à-vis integration into Irish society. This is followed by an articulation of the need to talk about Islam in the plural sense and a description of one expression of Islam, namely, Turkish Islam. Subsequent to this I introduce the Gülen-inspired TIECS. I firstly focus on its members' attitudes towards integration in Ireland before analyzing their principal pursuits, namely, conferences celebrating the commonalities amongst the Abrahamic religions and fast-breaking Ramadan dinners. I show how members implement the thought of Fethullah Gülen in these symposiums and evaluate their effect in the Irish context.

78 This expression of Islam has also been referred to as "Anatolian Islam." However, for consistency's sake I will use the term Turkish Islam throughout this paper.

Islam in Ireland

Islam is the fastest growing religion in Ireland. Census figures indicate that in 1991 there were only 3,873 Muslims in the population. The 2006 Census shows a massive increase with over 31,000 Muslims now living there (CSO 2007). The activities of Muslims in Ireland have, however, attracted little academic attention. An exception is Kieran Flynn (2006) who offers a timely survey of Muslims in Ireland. Importantly, he notes the diversity of practices amongst Muslims and observes that despite its small size, the Muslim community is quite fragmented.

Flynn notes that whilst the early Muslims living in Ireland were typically students or working in the textile or catering industries, Muslims are now predominantly middle class and involved in a much wider range of professions, including medicine and information technology. There appears to be a strong Arab influence amongst Islamic institutions in Ireland. One of the most prominent establishments, the Sunni-oriented Islamic Cultural Centre of Ireland (ICCI) based in Dublin, is run by the Al-Maktoum Foundation and directed from the United Arab Emirates. This has caused some tension amongst the Islamic community, some of whom feel disturbed by the fact that they do not have control of their local centre. Flynn astutely recognizes that the heavily subsidized ICCI cannot be considered independent given the fact that it is fiscally dependent upon this Arab Foundation. Despite this, he insists that the ICCI is an important organization for Muslims all across Ireland, playing a vital role in civil society by hosting politicians and religious groups, and operating several Qur'anic schools, with hundreds of students attending. Though there are several state-recognized Muslim primary schools in Ireland (though no secondary schools), most Muslim pupils in Ireland attend mainstream schools.

Surveying the various Islamic communities in Ireland, Flynn notes a wide diversity. Besides the Sunni-oriented ICCI, there is also a strong Shi'a presence in Ireland with up to 2,000 members originating predominantly from the Middle East and Pakistan. The year 1996 saw the official opening of the Shi'a Ahlul Bayt Islamic Centre in Milltown, Dublin. Flynn pays tribute to this organization claiming, "The Shi'a community and its leadership have emerged as the voice of moderation within the Irish Islamic community, representing an Islam that is at once tolerant, progressive and in tune with the challenges of a modern society" (2006, 227). Flynn cites its endorsement of democracy and human rights in the Middle East as evidence of its commitment to moderation, noting that this has also gained the group positive regard vis-à-vis the media in Ireland.

Flynn (2006) also notes the emergence of the Urdu-speaking Islamic communities in Ireland and points to the opening of two prayer rooms as evidence of this. The numbers attending Friday prayers reach 1,000 and members originate from Pakistan, Bangladesh and India. This group has courted a degree of scandal in relation to some of their "more radical and reactionary members" (Flynn 2006, 227). There are also a number of other Islamic communities around the country, notably in Cork (which hosts the second largest Muslim population in Ireland) and Mayo. Writing in *The Irish Times*, Mary Fitzgerald (2006) notes that around the country there are many different prayer rooms subscribing to different schools of thought within Islam, including several different Sufi-inspired groups.

Flynn argues that the greatest challenge to Islam in Ireland is its diversity. This is supported by Fitzgerald who notes that one of the newest Muslim communities in Ireland is that of Nigerian Muslims, led by an imam originating from Lagos, who claims to preach "African Sufism." The preacher argues, "It's a real Nigerian community thing. Islam as a religion is based on unity, and we recognize that, but we are different in some respects to Arab and south Asian Muslims" (Fitzgerald 2006). I believe this statement, describing the specificity of culture and geography is the key to understanding Islam in Ireland. This will be discussed in greater detail in the next section, when I introduce the concept of Turkish Islam.

According to Fitzgerald (2006) there has been thus far no comparable institution to the Muslim Council of Britain, with a "clearly defined leadership" in Ireland. This has led to a spate of squabbling between different groups and personalities vying for control. The outspoken South African, Sheikh Shaheed Satardien argued that Muslim leaders in Ireland were "in denial" regarding a growing number of extremist Muslims here. These claims have been denied by most Muslims and remain largely unproven. The South African sheikh gained a lot of media attention for his outburst and has subsequently been "ostracized" by some members of the Muslim community in Ireland (Fitzgerald 2006).[79] This incident is an illustration of the lack of consensus amongst Muslims in the country.

This brief survey of Islamic communities in Ireland is an explicit illustration of their diversity and indicates the desire of different groups to organize societies peculiar to their faith and culture. According to the National Consultative Committee on Racism and Interculturalism (NCCRI) (2007), most Muslims living in Ireland have successfully integrated. However, they have faced some difficulties due to racism/Islamophobia from members of the host society.

Until recent years there was a fallacious notion that Ireland was free of racism. Given that Ireland was a post-colonial state, it was argued, how could Irish people be racist? Ronit Lentin and Robbie McVeigh led the charge in 2002 illustrating that racism has been present in Ireland for a long time, noting that anti-Traveller racism and anti-Semitism were seen as "common sense" and unproblematic. With the dramatic increase in migrants over the last fifteen years, racism has become far more conspicuous to the point whereby there is a general acceptance of the problem of racism by the state and civil society. There has been quite a lot written in recent years about racism in Ireland (see Lentin and McVeigh 2002;

79 However, his views gained him popularity in other circles, and he was unanimously elected Chairman of the European Muslim Council for Justice, Peace and Equality (Horan 2007)

2006; Fanning 2002; Garner 2004), though little attention has been given to the topic of Islamophobia (exceptions include NCCRI 2007; Lentin and McVeigh 2006). In this regard, Flynn argues that "Muslims in Ireland tend to experience racism through avoidance and indifference" (2006, 235). There may be some truth in this, though the NCCRI argue that there have been more explicit forms of Islamophobia in Ireland, especially in the immediate aftermath of the terrorist attack on the "twin towers" in New York on September 11, 2001. These incidents have included physical and verbal abuse. The NCCRI (2007) also note that "typical" Islamophobic abuse reported to them includes "verbal abuse, other forms of harassment and disrespect rather than physical assaults or criminal damage." They also draw attention to some recent hyperbolic headlines in major Irish newspapers that help create a milieu whereby Islamophobia can thrive. Examples include "Fascist fundamentalism is rife among young Irish Muslims" (cited in NCCRI, 2007) and "The green jihads" (cited in NCCRI, 2007).

The NCCRI notes that while the actual article may be balanced, these sensationalist headlines can have a powerful impact on the reader, leading to irrational fear of Muslims. Wilson and Gutierrez (1985) take this point up in a more general context, arguing that because there is a lack of positive portrayals of minority ethnic groups in the media, it is quite conceivable that in the minds of the audience, this partial representation of minority ethnic groups becomes accepted as the reality (cited in Campbell 1995, 83). It becomes the taken for granted expression of "how things really are." It thus enters into the realm of "common sense" and largely goes unchallenged (Hall 1982). The race theorist Teun Van Dijk (2000, 48) insists that this systematic negative representation of the "Other" leads "indirectly to the enactments and reproduction of racism." Stuart Hall (1982) contends that this reproduction of the ideology of racism often takes place on the unconscious level. He does not believe that there is a group of media elite who consciously and malignly promote their version of reality to the explicit exclusion of others. Rather he argues that "statements may be unconsciously drawing on the ideological frameworks and classifying schemes of a society and reproducing them—so that they appear ideologically 'grammatical'—without those making them being aware of so doing" (Hall 1982, 72). In other words, when journalists and broadcasters frame media narratives, they do so drawing on classifications signified by the ruling group in society. Those working in the media therefore unconsciously reproduce these categories as if they were natural and immutable. Returning specifically to the Irish context, despite some Muslims in Ireland experiencing Islamophobia, the NCCRI note that the majority of Muslims in Ireland have integrated successfully and Islamophobic incidents are isolated.

Fethullah Gülen and Turkish Muslimness

Edward Said (1997) argues, rightly in my view, that the majority of opinion-makers in Europe and America, both journalists and academics, have predominantly portrayed Islam as a monolithic group determined to challenge the West through terrorist activities. This articulation has intensified in recent years due to high-profile terrorist attacks by so-called Islamic fundamentalists. Said points out that many Western scholars understand Western civilization as complex and heterogeneous and have devised a multitude of theories in an attempt to understand its multifaceted nature. Yet when it comes to Islamic society, it is treated as a single undifferentiated group. Aziz Al-Azmeh (1993, 1) is critical of this view and rightly argues that "there are as many Islams as there are situations that sustain it" (cited in Yılmaz 2005, 385). Too often ignored are the distinguishing factors of geography, culture and history. These features are integral to accounting for the manifold differences across borders (both territorial and symbolic). This point is supported by the Turkish sociologist Talip Küçükcan, who argues (1999, 191) that "Islamic movements are very diverse in terms of their clientele, origins, ideology and composition. This leads us to conclude that one should talk about 'Islams' in the modern world rather than one bounded and fixed 'Islam.'" Social, historical and geographical conditions must be taken into consideration when discussing what one means by "Islam."

Yavuz (2004) concurs with Küçükcan's position regarding the existence of multiple "Islams." He maintains that there are seven different "ethno-cultural" zones of Islam: Arab countries, Persia, Turkey, South Asia, Malay-Indonesia, Africa and places where Islam is a minority faith (Yavuz 2004, 215). Each zone is peculiar to a particular region and its interpretations of Islam differ due to a variety of factors: "Each zone's understanding of Islam is primarily informed by its own national culture and by diverse historical and economic factors" (Yavuz 2004, 215). He argues that Turkey has its own zone that offers something unique regarding Islamic thought. This zone, however, is not restricted to the territorial boundaries of Turkey but rather refers to the Turkic people. Yavuz argues that Turkish Islam differs vastly from Arab and Persian Islam regarding "the interpretation of Islamic principles" (Yavuz 2004, 218). He argues that Sufism is an integral part of Turkish Islam and the "Turkish understanding of Islam is very much punctuated by the tolerance of Rumi, love of Yunus and reasonability of Hacı Bektasi Veli" (2004, 219). Rumi, Yunus and Hacı Bektasi Veli are all Turkish Sufi mystics, who according to Yavuz have been extremely influential to Turkish Islam.[80]

Writing in the *Journal of Muslim Minority Affairs,* Ünal Bilir (2004) attributes the popularizing of the concept of Turkish Islam to Fethullah Gülen. Narrating the history of Islam in Turkey, Gülen, of course, recognizes that Islam emerged from Mecca and Medina, but goes on to insist that Islam did not come directly from these areas but was routed through Central Asia. The Turkic people of Central Asia adapted Islam to their own culture before exporting

80 For a more comprehensive discussion on the origins of the concept of Turkish Islam, see Uğur 2004; Bilir 2004; Küçükcan 2004

it through migration to the Anatolian region. A key point, according to Gülen, is the fact that Islam was not forced on the Anatolians but they embraced it freely and wholeheartedly in great numbers. The corollary of this, he maintains, is that Islam in Turkey has remained "tolerant, open, and un-dogmatic" (Bilir 2004, 267). Gülen calls himself a Muslim Turk because he sees the two as inseparable, noting that "the Turkish nation put its true values on a solid foundation after becoming Muslim" (Ünal and Williams 2000, 56). Islam in Turkey has gone through many phases since the founding of the Turkish Republic and abolition of the caliphate in the 1920s. It has, however, undoubtedly remained a constant feature of identity formation amongst Turks, despite the various state and military interferences in people's practice of Islam (privately and politically) over the years. The discursive construction of Turkish Islam may be understood as an attempt to enshrine a sense of national patriotism within Islam in order to conjure up consensus as Turkey continues to modernize.

Gülen acknowledges that some may see a contradiction in his articulation of Turkish Islam, given the importance of universality in Islam. He responds:

> Islam is universal with respect to its principles. Details can be interpreted differently. It's my humble opinion that the Turkish nation has interpreted those interpretable matters quite well. If Ottoman tolerance existed today in the world, I believe there would be a very good basis for dialogue not only among Muslims but also humanity. In a world that is becoming more and more globalized, being open to dialogue is very important. (Ünal and Williams 2000, 56)

Gülen clearly recognizes the universal principles of Islam, though he importantly notes the differences in interpretation. As I argued above, based on geographical, cultural and social elements Islam is interpreted and expressed in different ways which leads us to talk about Islam in the plural sense. Gülen draws on the Ottoman legacy as an example of tolerance and relatively convivial relations between various religious groups further noting, "In our history, a synagogue, a church, and a mosque stood side by side in many places" (Yılmaz 2005, 395). Sarıtoprak and Griffith echo this sentiment:

> The Empire was composed not only of Muslims, but of many Christian and Jewish groups, and Zoroastrians. Until the emergence of modern nationalistic ideas, Muslims, Christians and Jews had managed to live together more peacefully and productively in Ottoman times than has been possible more recently in the twentieth century (2005, 332).

Though this is a largely uncritical view of the Ottoman Empire, it is still fair to claim that relative to most other empires of this period, the Ottoman Empire had a comparatively tolerant attitude towards minority religions.

In recent years, Fethullah Gülen has become renowned for his work on dialogue between different monotheistic faith groups and met a number of world leaders. He has also inspired the establishment of countless dialogue groups and schools throughout the world. All of these activities come out of Gülen's articulation of Turkish Muslimness as grounded in openness and tolerance. It is my intention to analyze the practical contribution of Gülen's work by focusing on a society inspired by him, based in Dublin.

TIECS' Attitudes to Integration

According to the 2006 Census, there are only 766 Turkish migrants living in Ireland. However, this is contested by Turkish migrants themselves who suggest it is closer to 3,000. Regardless of the exact figure, it is clear that there are relatively few Turks living in Ireland.

The Turkish Irish Educational and Cultural Society (TIECS) was established by members of the Turkish diaspora (who are inspired by Fethullah Gülen) present in Ireland. The precursor to TIECS involved gatherings of Turkish migrants congregating in order to deal with common bureaucratic issues such as visa problems. Another issue discussed amongst these migrants at this early stage concerned the socialization of their children in a society dominated by a culture different from their own. The most prominent members of the Turkish community in Ireland are men and several members claimed to have difficulties gaining a visa that would allow them to bring their families to Ireland.

As these Turkish migrants settled down, after a few years bureaucratic issues became less urgent. They began to focus on developing a social and cultural society. This culminated in the establishment of TIECS in 2004. Though TIECS was established by members of the Turkish diaspora living in Ireland, its composition has changed, and it now includes temporary migrants from Turkey and Turkmenistan. These migrants were recruited in order to build up an affiliate of the Gülen Movement in Ireland. With the growth of the organization and the lack of manpower, other members of the Gülen Movement contributed.

It appears then that Gülen Movement participants help set up organizations where members of the Turkish diaspora have already established a base. Active Movement participants periodically travel to Gülen-inspired organizations and share information on the best way to implement the objectives of the Movement. Ireland has become an important European centre for business and culture, and the initiation of the Gülen-inspired TIECS may be seen as a strategic move in order to make an impact in Europe. There appears to be a concerted attempt to gain influence in Europe by the Gülen Movement in recent years with the initiation of other Gülen-inspired associations not only in Dublin, but also in Belfast (NITECA), Edinburgh (Dialogue Society for Scotland) and Brighton (Interfaith Dialogue Society) all opened in 2004/5. The Dialogue Society in London preceded these and was established in 1999. One cannot fail to notice that the mushrooming of these organizations is concurrent with the opening up of talks between Turkey and the European Union (EU) regarding Turkey's possible accession.

The political scientist Hasan Kösebalaban draws attention to some interesting insights in the context of Gülen's views on European integration. He argues, "Fethullah Gülen is the leader of a formally apolitical social movement who nevertheless has influenced Turkish political debates, including those related to international relations" (Kösebalaban 2003, 171). This has particularly been the case regarding EU accession. Kösebalaban (2003) notes the polarization of opinion regarding Turkey's relationship with Europe. Some argue that European integration will lead to the loss of Turkish-Muslim identity. However, Gülen has been an avid supporter of EU accession (Gülerce 2004; Yılmaz 2003, 235). He maintains that Islamic identity and European identity are not necessarily incongruous but can be complementary. Given Gülen's support for European integration of Turkey, it is plausible to view the emergence of Gülen-inspired organizations as a concerted attempt to promote a positive image of Turkey in an attempt to gain support for European accession.

TIECS members developed a variety of pursuits. These include Turkish language classes, interfaith dialogue conferences, fast-breaking Ramadan dinners and annual trips to Turkey for Irish people and others. It is important to note that TIECS members do not appear to be involved in any sustained transnational economic activity. Nor are they involved in any political quests. Indeed, several members of TIECS noted that both TIECS and the Gülen Movement are apolitical. TIECS endeavors appear to be purely of the "socio-cultural" type.

TIECS website gives a summary of its aims and objectives:

> It is the mission of Turkish Irish Educational and Cultural Society (TIECS) to serve societal peace, love, and friendship by striving to bring forth the common values of humanity; values such as tolerance, respect, and compassion. TIECS acknowledges the importance of spreading these most significant values within Dublin's diverse communities, hoping for all to take them on as a common virtue. In order to build a better future, TIECS will work hand in hand with Irish and other communities and groups that recognize the same mission and uphold the same values (TIECS Homepage)

From their earliest meetings, members of TIECS were adamant that they did not want to assimilate into Irish society. They rather intend to simultaneously integrate while preserving their own culture and traditions and passing these down to their children. Integration according to these early members was the key to successful settlement. This is echoed in their Mission Statement above, which emphasizes "values such as tolerance, respect, and compassion." It is furthermore consistent with the wider goals of the Gülen Movement. This is a useful starting point to outline the principal goals of TIECS. However, by interviewing various members of this society, I was enabled to explore these goals in more depth and establish the principles adopted from Fethullah Gülen.

It is useful to look a little deeper at the views of TIECS on integration into Irish society. TIECS members that I spoke to insisted that they had learned from the mistakes of other Turkish migrants abroad who made little attempt to integrate in the early years, which led to subsequent generations of Turks feeling displaced and isolated from mainstream society. Several participants pointed to Germany as the principal site where Turkish migrants were caught in an "in between" or liminal space. The majority of these Turks are a legacy of the "guestworker" system established in the 1960s.

One member of TIECS said:

> ...what happened to the Turkish people in Germany? They didn't start to do volunteering work or social work thirty years ago and now they have big problems with the young generation because they have a kind of dual identification, actually not dual identification, no identity. They don't feel they belong to any society. They don't describe themselves as German. It is not easy to say, "I am Turkish." So they are kind of in the middle somewhere. And this is not integration, not assimilation even, just standing in the middle of somewhere and you don't know where you are, who you are. And we want to stop this because we were lucky here, our generation, our children are very small at the moment, so if we start now we can provide them with a healthy environment.

Though the TIECS member quoted above referred to Turks in Germany in a stereotypical fashion, his main point is that members of TIECS want to avoid the problems of integration that did indeed face many Turkish migrants in Germany. Later in the interview, he says,

> And also, we are part of this culture. We are not just here for doing this work. We are living here and we are contributing as part of society.

This is an interesting example of the promotion of integration of the Turkish community in Ireland. The interviewee insists that they are not just here as representatives of Turkey but they are now also part of Irish society and they are keen to contribute. They are part of the broader Irish society and not just part of the diaspora community. However, they have no intention of assimilating but instead intend to integrate, whilst simultaneously showing their culture and learning others' culture. I now look at one of TIECS main activities in order to evaluate the contribution of Fethullah Gülen in a very real and practical way.

TIECS, Dialogue, and Turkish Islam

TIECS has initiated a variety of social and cultural events. This section focuses on two such events, namely a series of conferences celebrating the Abrahamic Religions and a "Dialogue Night and Ramadan Dinner," organized by this society. I have chosen to discuss these events as I believe they best illustrate TIECS' relationship with the work of Fethullah Gülen and his promotion of Turkish Islam. TIECS has held two conferences celebrating the Abrahamic Religions—Judaism, Christianity and Islam. In 2005 the conference was staged in University College Dublin (UCD), and in 2006 it was held in Trinity College Dublin (TCD). There were speakers from each of the three religions, and all were interested in promoting interfaith dialogue. The Jewish and Christian speakers were residents in Ireland, while the Muslim speakers were rather of Turkish origin, living in London, and related to Gülen-inspired organizations in England. In 2005 Kerim Balcı, a journalist with the Gülen-inspired *Zaman* newspaper, represented the Muslim view of interfaith dialogue. In 2006, Özcan Keleş, of the Dialogue Society (a Gülen-inspired organization promoting interfaith dialogue), spoke on the theme of compassion in Islam. Admission to these conferences was free and the attendees included representatives of different faith groups, academics, students and local politicians.

I asked one member of TIECS why the society organized these conferences:

> The conferences are so important to introduce...the correct Islamic views to the society, because nowadays Islam is one of the main religions, which is ... [misunderstood] by the people, especially in the Western world. There are many reasons and also because of the mistakes of some Muslims... Also because of bias and prejudices by some of the intellectuals in the Western world. So as a Muslim, we believe we have some responsibility to introduce our belief to the society... some people have forced it to be recognized as a kind of religion for violence. And it was not easy for us to accept this without doing anything. The conference series is one of the projects which we would like to tackle this misunderstanding problem.

From this excerpt we can see that the main aim of the interfaith conferences organized by TIECS is to "introduce the correct Islamic views." It may be argued that interfaith dialogue is of secondary importance to members of TIECS, while promoting a tolerant understanding of Islam is the main objective. This is understandable given the unbalanced nature of reports regarding Muslims in both academia and the mainstream media. The above respondent maintains that Islam has been largely misunderstood in the Western world. He blames both the "prejudices" of various intellectuals towards Islam and indeed some Muslims who "misinterpret" the Qur'an and engage in violence. Edward Said takes up this point, claiming:

> Malicious generalizations about Islam have become the last acceptable form of denigration of foreign culture in the West;

> what is said about the Muslim mind, or character, or religion, or culture as a whole cannot now be said in mainstream discussion about Africans, Jews, other Orientals, or Asians. (1997, xi/xii)

In any other context, such denigration would be rightly regarded as racism. However in the context of Islam, such vilification appears acceptable as it has become part of the "common sense thinking" of many people in the Western world. In the absence of a collective effort to portray positive representations of Muslims by Western opinion-makers, it is only the negative depictions that filter down to the general media consumer. Said (1997) notes that for every book written fairly on the subject of Islam, there are numerous written with an unbalanced orientation towards depicting Muslims as terrorists. The corollary of this, according to Said, is that "the average reader comes to see Islam and fundamentalism as essentially the same thing" (1997, xvi). For the average person, Islam becomes synonymous with terrorism, violence and atavism. Said's position was articulated before the terrorist attacks in New York in 2001. A variety of authors have since shown that the denigration of Islam by Western opinion-makers has intensified since the attacks in New York (Modood 2005; Anwar 2005; Parekh 2006; Ishay 2004; Wu 2004). The objective of TIECS in this context is to illustrate that not only is Islam not synonymous with violence, but on the contrary, the religion is tantamount to peace.

Another member of TIECS explained other reasons for holding these conferences:

> It is...good to show the similarities between the Abrahamic religions, Christianity, Islam and Judaism...this really builds a bridge in society between believers and it really brings a kind of synergy between the people, breaking prejudices and biases. And it is good for a healthy society because when Irish society knows what Islam is, what true Islam is: when they deal with the Muslim people in Ireland, they have more open and healthy perspective because of the information and knowledge they get. So conferences help us to achieve this goal... and also it helps us to make good friendships and to collaborate with other

> groups... And we are focusing on the common point between us. All of us believe that there is one God. And this is the main moving point for us and when you put common points on the table, you see more common points than which you conflict on and you can just focus on the common points. This doesn't mean we are all the same. That is normal, the differences, but respect and tolerance [are] the magic words if you live. So conferences help us to succeed these goals.

By illustrating the parallels amongst the Abrahamic religions, members of TIECS are attempting to find common ground with other monotheistic religions in Ireland. The reasons for this are twofold. Firstly, as mentioned previously, to educate people of other faiths on the tenets of Islam in order to dispel the malign myth that Islam is tantamount to brutality. Secondly, the above TIECS member believes that it will aid the integration process for Muslims and serve to prevent them being isolated from mainstream society. He recognizes that people are different but stresses that "respect and tolerance [are] the magic words."

The words spoken above and actions taken through the conferences are entirely consistent with Fethullah Gülen's articulation of Turkish Islam, grounded in the Sufi principles of tolerance and dialogue. Members of TIECS use the same strategy as Gülen to bring apparently irreconcilable groups together around the one table. The focus on building a secure foundation on commonalities is the key to their success, ignoring or suspending the dogma of each sect, faith or cultural group.

Through TIECS interfaith conferences, members attempt to promote Islam as they understand it. In the two conferences they have held so far, the Muslim speakers were of Turkish origin and members of Gülen-inspired institutions. They emphasized "tolerance," "love," and the "reasonability" of Islam as promoted by Gülen and other Turkish Sufi mystics. There is, however, competition regarding the interpretation of Islam in Ireland. As previously mentioned, Islam is the fastest growing religion in Ireland today, and these followers of Islam come from many different regions in the world, including Ireland, and from all the Islamic zones mentioned by Yavuz (2004). TIECS is now involved in a competitive market with other interpretations of Islam.

I now turn my attention to another event organized by TIECS, namely the "Dialogue Night and Ramadan Dinner." In early 1995, the Journalists and Writers Foundation (JWF) initiated a Ramadan fast-breaking dinner which included representatives from many different strata of Turkish society. "In terms of diversity of the participants, it was the first of its kind" (Yılmaz 2003, 230). Following the lead of Fethullah Gülen and the JWF, TIECS organizes annual Ramadan fast-breaking dinners to which they invite different groups to share a meal together hosted by TIECS. In 2007, TIECS held the event in a south-side Dublin hotel. The event was sponsored by the Gülen-inspired *The Fountain* magazine, *Zaman* daily newspaper and Dublin City Council. As is typical with TIECS events, attendees included academics, local politicians, clerics and community workers. The sponsoring of the event by Gülen-inspired organizations is testament to its transnational nature, while the contribution by the Dublin City Council is a small but important acknowledgment from the state that it supports TIECS aims and objectives and has the added advantage of legitimizing the organization in the eyes of the Irish public.

The emphasis on this dialogical engagement was slightly different to the annual conferences. They were interested in promoting interfaith dialogue but also in emphasizing the need for immigrant integration in Ireland. Members from TIECS sister organizations, the Northern Irish Tolerance, Educational and Cultural Association (NITECA) and the Dialogue Society of London, all spoke about the compatibility of the Abrahamic religions and a clip from the movie *The Message* (1976) was shown to illustrate this point. Speakers also explained to the audience of about fifty people the meaning of Ramadan and fast-breaking for Muslims.

In a previous discussion with a leading member of NITECA, he had claimed that many Muslims believe that Ramadan is only about sharing with other Muslims but he insisted that those people misinterpret the spirit of the festival. He further maintained that the Qur'an specifically calls the "People of the Book" (i.e. Jews, Christians, and Muslims) to come together and contended that the initiation of events like these consolidates this position.

Instead of different faith leaders speaking at this event, local politicians and community workers were invited to talk about the need for integration in Ireland. Declan Hayden of the Intercultural Relations Unit of the Dublin City Council and Councilor Michael Donnelly spoke on this need and paid tribute to TIECS for their dialogical activities.

This event was evidence of TIECS commitment to integration in Ireland and supports TIECS' stated position on integration, discussed in a previous section. There were also Turkish crafts and books by Fethullah Gülen and other Turkish Muslim scholars on sale at the event, encouraging people to appreciate both Turkish culture and the Turkish expression of Islam. This further illustrates TIECS' refusal to assimilate and pronounces their strong ties to Turkish culture.

I maintain that TIECS is first and foremost a Turkic religio-cultural society, with an emphasis on Turkish culture and the Turkish understanding of Islam. It is too much to ask this small organization to solve the problems of multiculturalism in Ireland. Indeed, it is too much to ask that this group resolve the complexities of even Muslim integration in Ireland. What this society has, however, accomplished is a small platform, whereby they promote a positive and moderate image of Islam, countering the overwhelmingly negative portrayal of this religion by leading opinion-makers in the West. They have further contributed to Irish society by engaging in dialogue with different faith groups and cultures. Indeed, the efforts of this group are an example of how migrants with different cultural, linguistic and religious differences can adapt and integrate into a host society dominated by a very different culture. Furthermore, the presence of this Gülen-inspired organization is an illustration of the very real and practical contribution of the thought and action of Fethullah Gülen. The fact that such an organization is present in Ireland (a country that up until fifteen years ago was understood by many outsiders as a backwater of Britain), is indicative of the reach of the thought of Fethullah Gülen. Their various activities, inspired by Gülen, are an example of how peaceful coexistence is possible amongst different ethnic groups in a diverse society in a European context.

Conclusion

This article began by surveying the various Islamic communities living in Ireland. I noted that there has been an academic deficit in this field of study in Ireland, though Kieran Flynn (2006) must be commended for his work. My principal aim in this section was to illustrate the diversity and different expressions of Islam practiced in Ireland and support my argument that based on geographical, cultural and social differences we can talk about Islam in the plural sense. This section also served to contextualize TIECS in the Irish setting. Subsequent to this I introduced the theme of Turkish Islam as one expression of Islam, before evaluating Fethullah Gülen's contribution to the popularizing of this concept. I then moved to the heart of this article by introducing the Gülen-inspired TIECS and exploring its members' attitudes to integration. They appear to show a commitment to becoming part of Irish society, while simultaneously maintaining their Turkish identity. They refuse to isolate themselves, arguing that they have learned from the mistakes of other Turkish migrants, especially those in Germany. Drawing on Yurdakul's (2006) work I also noted the active role Turkish associations in Germany play in promoting integration and lobbying for better conditions for Turkish settlers in Germany. This section then showed how TIECS serves as a good representative of Gülen's thought regarding openness and tolerance to different faith groups.

The final section focused on TIECS's very practical and visible contribution to integration and interfaith dialogue in Ireland. I examined its motivations for organizing a series of conferences devoted to exploring the commonalities between the Abrahamic religions. I argued that one of the main reasons for these conferences was to counteract the overwhelmingly negative media portrayal of Muslims as violent and atavistic. Drawing on the work of Said, I contended that in any other context such denigration would be referred to as racism but in the context of Islam, such denigration appears uncritically acceptable to many in the West. This section also showed how TIECS adopts Gülen's articulation of Turkish Islam grounded in the principles of openness, tolerance and reason and promotes these in its conferences.

Despite the lack of consensus amongst Muslims in Ireland, Flynn (2006) points out several positive points, arguing that both the main Shi'a and Sunni institutions in Ireland have made attempts to engage with the Irish public and civil society through a variety of activities. It is my contention that TIECS will become another major player in the debate about the role of Islam in Ireland.

In conclusion, this article has attempted to show the real and practical contribution of Fethullah Gülen by focusing on a society inspired by his thoughts. By analyzing the motivations and activities of TIECS, I illustrated how a group of Turkish Muslims have comfortably settled into a country with a very different culture and contributed in a very meaningful way. This can be understood as a good example of peaceful coexistence amongst different ethnic and religious groups in a European context.

References

Anwar, M. 2005. "Muslims in Britain: Issues, Policy and Practice." *Muslim Britain: Communities under Pressure*, ed. T. Abbas. London: Zed Books.

Atalik, G. and B. Beeley. 1993. "What Mass Migration Has Meant for Turkey." *Mass Migration in Europe: The Legacy and Future*, ed. R. King. New York: John Wiley & Sons.

Azmeh, A. 1993. *Islams and Modernities*. London: Verso.

Barrett, A., I. Kearney and M. O'Brien. 2008. *Quarterly Economic Commentary* (Summer Edition). Economic and Social Research Institute (ESRI). http://www.esri.ie.

Barry, M. 2006. *We Are Workers Not Slaves: The Story of the GAMA Struggle*. Dublin: The Socialist Party.

Bilir, Ü. 2004. "'Turkey-Islam': Recipe for Success or Hindrance to the Integration of the Turkish Diaspora Community in Germany?" *Journal of Muslim Minority Affairs* 24(2):259–283.

Campbell, C. P. 1995. *Race, Myth and the News*. London: Sage Publications.

Central Statistics Office (CSO). 2007. www.cso.ie.

Fanning, B. 2002. *Racism and Social Change in the Republic of Ireland*. Manchester: Manchester University Press.

Fitzgerald, M. 2006. "Ireland's Muslims Forging an identity." *The Irish Times* 13/10/2006.

Flynn, K. 2006. "Understanding Islam in Ireland." *Islam and Christian-Muslim Relations* 17(2):223–238.

Garner, S. 2004. *Racism in the Irish Experience*. London: Pluto Press.

Gülerce, H. 2004. Gülen's message to the European Union. http://en.fgulen.com [Accessed 1/1/2006].

Hall, S. 1982. "The Rediscovery of 'Ideology': Return of the Repressed in Media Studies." *Culture, Society and the Media*, ed. M. Guvrevitch, T. Bennett, J. Curran and J. Woollacott. London: Routledge.

Horan, N. 2007. "Irish Muslim Gets Top Role in Fight to Counter Extremism." *The Sunday Independent* 23/11/2007.

Inglis, T. 1998. *Moral Monopoly: The Rise and Fall of the Catholic Church in Modern Ireland*. Dublin: Gill and Macmillan.

Ishay, M. 2004. *The History of Human Rights: From Ancient Times to the Globalization Era*. London: University of California Press.

Kösebalaban, H. 2003. "The Making of Enemy and Friend: Fethullah Gülen's National-security Identity." *Turkish Islam and the Secular State: The Gülen Movement*, ed. M. H.Yavuz and. J. L. Esposito. New York: Syracuse University Press.

Küçükcan, T. 1999. *Politics of Ethnicity, Identity and Religion: Turkish Muslims in Britain*. Aldershot: Ashgate Publishing.

Lentin, R. and R. McVeigh, ed. 2002. *Racism and anti-Racism in Ireland*. Belfast: Beyond the Pale.

———. 2006. *After Optimism? Ireland, Racism and Globalisation*. Dublin: Metro Eireann Publications.

MacEinri, P. and P. Walley. 2003. *Labour Migration into Ireland: Study and Recommendations on Employment Permits, Working Conditions, Family Reunification and the Integration of Migrant Workers in Ireland*. Dublin: Immigrant Council of Ireland.

Modood, T. 2005. Foreword. *Muslim Britain: Communities under Pressure*, ed. T. Abbas. London: Zed Books.

National Consultative Committee on Racism and Interculturalism (NCCRI). 2007. *The Muslim Community in Ireland: Challenging Some Myths and Information.* http://www.nccri.ie.

O'Reagan, M. 2007. "Leaders in Tribute to Irish War Dead. *The Irish Times* 9/7/2007.

O'Toole, F. 2003. *After the Ball*. Dublin: New Island Books.

Parekh, B. 2006. "Europe, Liberalism and the 'Muslim question'". *Multiculturalism, Muslims and Citizenship: A European Approach*, ed. T. Modood, R. Zapate-Barrero and A. Triandafyillidou. New York: Routledge.

Ruhs, M. 2005. *Managing the Immigration and Employment of Non-EU Nationals in Ireland*. Dublin: The Policy Institute, Trinity College

Said, E. 1997. *Covering Islam: How the Media and the Experts Determine How We See the Rest of the World*. London: Vintage.

Sarıtoprak, Z. and S. Griffith. 2005. "Fethullah Gülen and the 'People of the Book'": A Voice from Turkey for Interfaith Dialogue." *The Muslim World* 95(2):329–340.

TIECS Homepage. http://www.tiecs.ie.

Tovey, H. and P. Share. 2003. *A Sociology of Ireland*. Dublin: Gill and Macmillan.

Uğur, E. 2004. "Intellectual Roots of 'Turkish Islam' and Approaches to the 'Turkish Model.'"*Journal of Minority Affairs* 24 (2).

Ünal, A. and A. Williams. 2000. *Advocate of Dialogue: Fethullah Gülen*. Virginia: The Fountain.

Van Dijk, T. A. 2000. "New(s) Racism: Racism: A Discourse Analytical Approach." *Ethnic Minorities in the Media*, ed. S. Cottle. Buckingham: Open University Press.

Wu, F. H. 2004. "Profiling in the Wake of September 11: The Precedent of the Japanese American Internment." *Civil Liberties vs. National Security in a Post-9/11 World*, ed. M. K. B. Darmer, R. M. Baird and S. E. Rosenbaum. New York: Prometheus Books.

Yavuz, M. H. 2004. "Is There a Turkish Islam? The Emergence of Convergence and Consensus." *Journal of Muslim Minority Affairs* 24 (2).

Yılmaz, İ. 2003. "*Ijtihad* and *Tajdid* by Conduct: The Gülen Movement." *Turkish Islam and the Secular State: The Gülen Movement*, ed .M. H. Yavuz and J. L. Esposito. New York: Syracuse University Press.

———. 2005. "State, Law, Civil Society and Islam in Contemporary Turkey." *The Muslim World* 95 (2).

Yurdakul, G. 2006. "State, Political Parties and Immigrant Elites: Turkish Immigrant Associations in Berlin." *Journal of Ethnic and Migration Studies* 32(3):435–453.

CHAPTER 13

Building Civil Society in Ethno-religiously Fractured Communities: The Gülen Movement in Turkey and Abroad

Mehmet Kalyoncu

INTRODUCTION

Civil society is generally associated with the presence of voluntary civic and social organizations that function as the basis of a given community. Run by informed citizens or groups, these non-governmental organizations assume responsibility for monitoring governmental organizations and mobilize available resources to maintain order and efficiency in the functioning of not only governmental organizations but also of society in general. According to Alexis de Tocqueville, the civic organization, or the ability of the citizens to organize through associations for common purpose, constitutes the basis of civil society. A critic of American individualism, Tocqueville suggested that coming around common causes would create a civic consciousness for American nationhood far more important than fulfilling selfish individual desires. Moreover, Gabriel Almond and Sidney Verba (1989) found a direct correlation between civil society and democracy, arguing that political civil society organizations increase civic awareness which generates informed voting choices, participation in politics and holding the government more accountable. Along similar lines to Almond and Verba, Robert Putnam (1993) argues that not only political but also non-political civil society organizations are crucial to democracy because they build social capital, trust and shared values, which are transferred into the political sphere and help to hold society together, facilitating an understanding of the interconnectedness of society and interests within it. What is common to all four students of civil society is their conviction that the coming together of citizens within either political or non-political organizations for a common purpose is crucial to achieve a fully functioning civil society and as such a healthy democracy. They all compare the merits of civic organization over its absence in terms of achieving a stable and functioning democracy.

What if the community does not have the ability to organize in the first place? What if there are ongoing intra-communal conflicts stemming from deeply entrenched ethno-religious differences? How is it possible to convince the different ethno-religious groups within a community to come together around a common cause as Tocqueville suggests, which would eventually generate a common identity and, as Almond, Verba and Putnam suggest, a functioning democracy? The very fact that contemporary societies still suffer from ethno-religious conflicts makes it imperative for students of civil society to reformulate their strategies for attaining civil society in ethno-religiously fractured communities, where what divides different segments of the community is more than what unites them.

I argue that it is possible to develop common practical methods to foster civil society and democracy in communities that are traditionally divided along ethno-religious fault lines and have been experiencing conflict over those ethno-religious differences. My own field research in the city of Mardin, which is located on the Syrian border of Turkey and populated by ethnic Turks, Arabs, Kurds and Assyrian Christians, about the Gülen Movement, a faith-based civil society movement, suggests that the Movement is able to develop common strategies to bring together different ethno-religious groups within a community to organize toward building civil society. Addressing the common problems facing the different ethno-religious communities within a given society, providing solid services to eradicate those problems, and seeking collaboration of those ethno-religious communities along the way constitute the crux of mobilizing social potential which it is possible to channel toward adopting a civil society's values and practices.

A Glance at the Gülen Movement in Southeast Turkey

The Gülen Movement has been able to mobilize Turks, Kurds, Arabs, and Assyrian Christians in Mardin to cooperate in tackling their common problems. The city has been heavily affected by insecurity, and infrastructural and economic deprivation due to conflicts between the Turkish security forces and terrorist organizations such as the Marxist PKK and the Islamist fundamentalist Hezbollah respectively since the early 1980s and 1990s. The ongoing conflicts and insecurity have not only deprived the city of basic infrastructure, investment and educational facilities, but also deepened the ethnic fault-lines, though less so the religious ones.

Against this background, participants in the Gülen Movement first established personal contact with local people from different ethnic groups in the late 1980s. Their conversations focused on common problems facing all groups regardless of their ethno-religious allegiance, such as the lack of education of the youth, increasing unemployment, the consequent tendency of the youth to fall prey to recruitment into either the PKK or Hezbollah, and the ensuing problems of terrorism and economic deprivation. The Movement has not only preached about these issues but also mobilized the local people to tackle these problems together. The local people's cooperation seems to have yielded tangible outcomes which have changed the earlier attitudes and practices of the ethno-religious groups in Mardin, thereby preparing the ground for fostering participative civil society. These tangible outcomes include educational and cultural institutions which continue to build the human capital for a stable and democratic Mardin.

Institutions Inspired by the Gülen Movement in Mardin[81]

Sur Dersanesi: University Preparatory Courses

Sur Dersanesi is a pioneer in Mardin in preparing the local youth for the national university entrance exam. Before Sur Dersanesi, a few organizations had attempted to run university preparatory courses in Mardin. However, they had ceased their operations either because of financial hardship or the security problems caused by the PKK and Hezbollah in the 1980s. In other words, they fled Mardin without fulfilling their promises to the local people to prepare their children for the national university entrance test.[82] This unfortunate precedent made it difficult for the movement's local representatives to obtain the necessary official endorsement from the local government. The Gülen Movement opened its first university preparatory course, which was also its first local institution, in Mardin in 1992. Ever since then, the movement's expansion in Mardin has been focused on opening university preparatory courses. Currently, the movement runs four university preparatory courses in the surrounding counties of Kızıltepe, Derik, Nusaybin, and Midyat. These courses serve the students not only in their own counties but also in nearby counties. For instance, since there is no university preparatory course in Dargeçit yet, the students commute to the closest county (Midyat) to attend the course. Opening another branch of Sur Dersanesi is always one of the top items on

81 For further information on the Gülen-inspired schools and cultural initiatives in Mardin, see Kalyoncu, Mehmet. 2008. *A Civilian Response to Ethno-Religious Conflict: The Gülen Movement in Southeast Turkey*, New Jersey: The Light, Inc. This particular part of this chapter about the Gülen-inspired institutions in Mardin is based on that book.

82 I obtained this information through my interviews with the local people who helped the movement open its first university preparatory course in Mardin in 1992.

the movement's agenda in Mardin. In that regard, Mardin's *mütevelli* (board of trustees composed of local Mardinian businessmen) is currently negotiating with the local authorities of Savur, another county in Mardin, to obtain a license and rent a building to open a university preparatory course there.

The growth of Sur Dersanesi in Nusaybin is similar to that of its branches in the other counties. According to Murat Salim, a local store owner and resident of Nusaybin, the city has been heavily influenced by both the PKK and Hezbollah: "Between 1989 and 1993, the region was under the complete control of the PKK. For instance, if there was an incident that required a judicial process, the parties had to first see the regional administrator of the PKK. If they went directly to the official court, then the PKK punished them for that wrongdoing."[83] He suggests that Hezbollah, the counter-PKK organization, took over control of Nusaybin from the PKK after 1993. About this time, the Gülen Movement opened its first university preparatory course in Nusaybin. Murat Salim notes: "Sur Dersanesi in Nusaybin had about ten to fifteen students in 1996, but the number of the students has grown every year. The number was 280 in 2004, 480 in 2005, and 900 in 2006."[84] This growth has mirrored the growth in the other counties, such as Kızıltepe and Derik, which are under heavy PKK influence. Today, even though Kızıltepe is still a PKK stronghold, the local people send their children to Sur Dersanesi to prepare for the national college entrance test.

ATAK Koleji - Private School (Elementary-Secondary-High School)

Atak Koleji is the first and only private school in Mardin. Its construction started in 1996. In the meantime, however, the school

83 Excerpt from the author's interview with Murat Salim on February 9, 2006, in Nusaybin, Mardin.

84 Excerpt from the author's interview with Murat Salim on February 9, 2006 in Nusaybin, Mardin.

has registered students and provided an education. The school's construction has been funded solely by a wealthy Mardinian family (the Ataks) that has been residing in Istanbul since 1974. The family decided to build the school upon the encouragement of a group of Mardin's local businessmen and a teacher who share Gülen's educational vision and believe that increased educational facilities are the only remedy for Mardin's underdevelopment and the way to solve southeastern Turkey's terrorism problem. When the Atak family visited Mardin and saw that non-Mardinian teachers, despite all the deprivations they suffered there, were dedicating themselves to educating Mardin's children and youth at the university preparatory courses, the family was stimulated to contribute to the Movement's educational projects in Mardin. They are still contributing.

Just as it is the first institution being funded solely by a civic initiative, Atak Koleji is a pioneer in terms of other characteristics. It has become a meeting place for the area's different ethno-religious groups, most notably Kurds and Arabs. The school is located halfway between Kızıltepe (Mardin's largest county) and the city center of Mardin, both of which are, respectively, strongholds of ethnic Kurdish and ethnic Arab populations. According to reports made by Atak Koleji teachers, even if the Kurds and Arabs have not engaged in an active conflict, they have not quite intermingled either.[85] In addition to Kurdish and Arab students, the school also has Assyrian Christian students and follows a secular curriculum approved (and periodically inspected) by the Turkish Ministry of Education. Atak Koleji is a co-ed school and has about three hundred and fifty students taught by thirty teachers, fourteen of whom are women.[86]

---

85 This information is based on my interview with the Atak Koleji teachers on February 3, 2006, in Mardin. Several other respondents of both Kurdish and Arab origin confirmed this information at different times and places.

86 This information is based on my notes from my trip to Atak Koleji on February 3, 2006.

The school is unique in Mardin for its education system and the opportunities it provides to its students. Beside teaching natural sciences and math, English as a second language, computer science as well as arts and humanities, the school prioritizes the students' development in terms of not only academic skills, but also of social and physical skills. Throughout the year, the students organize science fairs, exhibitions, theater plays, music performances, chess tournaments, and such sporting events as soccer and basketball tournaments. The teachers encourage each student club to organize own event and participate in those of the other clubs. The school principal Oğuz Ozan explains: "At the end of every school year, a fair is held among the student clubs; these clubs present the activities and accomplishments they have achieved in that year. The local people are invited to the fair and are asked to vote for the best clubs. The students are free to invite as many people as possible, including those with no affiliation to the school, in order to increase the number of votes for their club. Last year, the students brought about five thousand people from the city to visit the fair, and sought to increase the number of their votes."[87] Ozan believes that this voting application helps familiarize students with democratic election practices.

Moreover, the school organizes public seminars and social gatherings with the local people. Through these public seminars, the school shares its future projects with the local people, and seeks their involvement in carrying out these projects. The schools engagement with the local people has not only changed some rooted traditions such as not sending girls to school, but also attitudes toward them. A mother from Surgucu village laments, "I was not allowed to go even to elementary school and was married at a very early age." She continues, "I did not have much say in my immediate family, let alone the extended one, but I am quite happy for Hatice [her daughter] because she is going to high school now in Balıkesir [a western city]. Even now, her father consults her for her ideas on issues. She

87 Excerpt from the author's interview with Oguz Ozan at Atak Koleji on February 3, 2006.

has the opportunity to influence her father's decisions. She will be a strong woman and a good mother."[88]

MOSDER (Mardin Reading Halls Association)

MOSDER has several branches in Mardin, one of which is in the highly impoverished and isolated Dargeçit province. Dargeçit does not even have a bank despite its more than seven thousand inhabitants, and has one entrance, which also serves as an exit and a military checkpoint. The main reason for such deprivation and heavy military control seems to be a combination of the local people's implicit support for the PKK terrorist organization, frequent clashes between the PKK and the Turkish security forces in the vicinity of Dargeçit, and the resulting absence of investment. MOSDER's reading hall opened in February 2005 and serves about one hundred and fifty students. The students are encouraged to spend as much time as possible there reading or studying for the national college entrance test. The students stress that the reading hall has helped them organize their preparation for the university admissions test by providing them with a study place and test books, and that without these they would not be able to prepare very well in their impoverished houses. While the ultimate goal of the reading halls is to help local students get educated and go to college, the most immediate function is to keep them off the street where they easily fall prey to either PKK or Hezbollah recruitment.

MARKOYDER (Mardin Village Development Association)

Compared to MOSDER, MARKOYDER has a more comprehensive scope for its activities, from providing educational facilities to distributing food and clothing to poor villagers. The operational

88 Excerpt from the author's interview with a groups of women from Surgucu village on February 2, 2006.

relation between the two organizations is such that MOSDER goes into a village if MARKOYDER identifies a need for a reading hall in that village, and they cooperate in opening the reading hall. In addition, MARKOYDER, in partnership with the teachers from Atak Koleji, visits families in the villages and tries to convince parents to send their children to school, especially their daughters, since the indigenous conservative culture impedes girls from going to school. MARKOYDER has reportedly been in contact with hundred and fifty villages so far.

What the Movement's Institutions Mean to the Local People

According to my interviewees' responses, Atak Koleji seems to be matchless in Mardin in terms of the education it provides the students. Similarly, Sur Dersanesi, the university preparatory courses, and the reading halls seem to provide the locals with opportunities that the state cannot offer and that perhaps only a small percentage of Mardinians could afford on their own. The material value of these services is clear. However, the local people also seem to attribute a special meaning to these institutions, for they view them as being more than just schools. There are contextual reasons for this special meaning: the local realities of severe unemployment, terror, a conservative culture, and a chronic shortage of schools and teachers. These correspond almost perfectly with what Atak Koleji and the university preparatory courses are committed to eradicating. Therefore, the fact that each of these contextual reasons is important to the parents, although to varying degrees, makes Atak Koleji, as well as other movement-associated educational institutions, something more than what such institutions, by common definition, are.

The local people who have placed their children in these institutions comment that they see the Gülen Movement institutions as a way to keep their children immune to the influence of both the PKK and Hezbollah. Although they do not reflect the entire Mardin community, those parents who send their children to the university preparatory course view it as a way to rescue their children from the recruitment pool of both the PKK and Hezbollah. Based on this proposition, one cannot argue that the movement's activities have decreased local support for the PKK and Hezbollah, but we can conclude, based on the parents' statements, that their main motivation is not necessarily to help their children go to university but to keep them away from the streets, which constitutes the main recruitment pool for both the PKK and Hezbollah.

Is the Gülen Education Model Applicable to the International Arena?

So, the question is whether the sociological approach introduced and practiced by the Gülen Movement in Mardin, which focuses on communal perfection through individual perfection, and mobilizes different segments of society to tackle their common problems putting aside their differences, is applicable to alleviating ethno-religious conflicts in diverse communities around globe, and to fostering civil society within these communities.

My field research about the impact of the movement's services in Mardin, a place which is not only ethno-religiously divided but also suffers from terrorism and economic deprivation, suggests that the movement is able to prepare the preliminary conditions for a civil society to flourish in that community. First, the educational facilities established and run by Turks, Arabs, and Kurds together have minimized, if not eradicated, the perception of Turk–Kurd enmity through which the PKK garnered popular support. Second, these institutions, be they college prep courses or reading halls, take off the streets the unemployed youth who constituted otherwise the main recruitment resource for both the PKK and Hezbollah. Third, Gülen's ideas about Islam conveyed through both human interactions and media have convinced the public that radicalism conflicts with the very essentials of Islam. Fourth, the Gülen Movement's sound education services help rationality override nationalist and ethno-religious sentiments, and create a public opinion opposed to violent means such as terrorism.

I argue that with its proven capabilities in Mardin, whose ethno-religious diversity and socio-economic problems are representative of the global map where similar problems are experienced, the Gülen Movement can contribute to eradicating ethno-religiously driven conflicts and to fostering civil society by mobilizing the different indigenous ethno-religious groups to tackle their common problems. That is, the reconciliatory approach of the Gülen Movement can help to greatly appease, if not totally eradicate, social conflicts continuously experienced in various parts of the world provided that the following hypotheses are true for any given community.

1. The parties of a given ethno-religious conflict are rational actors. As such, they recognize their interests in peace and stability and in obtaining tangible results that better their socio-economic situation.
2. The Gülen Movement's philosophy is that the absence of education, dialogue and tolerance is the source of all likely conflicts.
3. The movement envisions societies that consist of idealistic and patriotic individuals who share common values with their counterparts with different ethno-religious backgrounds. These values are mainly dialogue, tolerance, individual perfection through education, and altruism.
4. The movement's vision of dialogue, tolerance, and search for common grounds between different cultures is what enables the movement to communicate with a wide range of different communities.
5. The movement's strict avoidance of politics and from being politicized makes it able to communicate with communities that are radically distant from each other on the political spectrum.

6. The movement's activities within any community start with personal contacts with the individuals in that community. That is, the participants in the movement share the vision of the movement with individual(s) in the given community.
7. Once inter-personal relations are established between participants in the Gülen Movement and local figures, and the necessity of dialogue and education is agreed upon in a particular community, the schools and related educational institutions become means whereby a vision of dialogue and tolerance are realized through raising individuals who believe in the importance of intercultural dialogue and tolerance.
8. The quality education provided by the schools and the joint-cultural activities held in cooperation with the local people become non-relational channels for communicating the vision of the Gülen Movement, and they help the movement take further root in a given society.

Based on my field research about the impact of the Gülen Movement, a faith-based civic movement, on the ethno-religiously highly fractured and socio-economically deprived community of Mardin, I contend that examining the Gülen Movement's educational activities in global conflict zones would enable us to develop strategies that may be helpful in minimizing ethno-religious conflict and fostering civil society in those very zones. Such case studies, which would include the movement's impact on conflictual communities in Kenya and the Philippines and which will be further discussed in the following section. The case studies, each of them unique in the sense of their socio-political context and their underlying cause of conflict, present a representative sample of the population of ethno-religious conflicts around the globe.

The Gülen Movement has been actively operating in all these four places for more than a decade, and has been successful in mobilizing the indigenous ethno-religiously distinct communities to put aside their differences and cooperate to tackle their common problems. Identifying the norms and practices that enable the movement to accomplish such an endeavor may help us identify common and effective strategies to minimize, if not eradicate, ethno-religious conflicts in general.

The Gülen Movement in Conflict Zones

In order to fully assess the ability of the Gülen Movement to ease social conflicts and contribute to building civil society in ethno-religiously fractured communities, it is imperative to select a sample or a set of samples, which reflects the notion of ethno-religious fracture in all aspects. That is, the sample examined should be representative of communities that are divided along the lines of ethnic differences, religious differences, and ethnic and religious difference. Similarly, the set of samples should also take into account the political framework of the ethno-religiously fractured community under scrutiny. Since it affects the concept of civil society and a social movement's ability to contribute to building civil society in a given community, the indigenous political culture of the local people should be taken into account as an indicator of availability of the pre-conditions for civil society to develop. In this regard, Kenya and the Philippines provide a unique combination of various sorts of ethno-religiously fractured communities.

In terms of empowering individuals in Africa through education and inspiring them with hope for what they can achieve, the Gülen-inspired schools in Kenya present a unique example. In this ethno-religiously diverse country, the first Gülen-inspired school, the Light Academy was opened in 1998 by a handful of Gülen-inspired Turks and a few local Kenyans who helped them. Mr. Verre teaches business studies at the Light Academy. After growing up and being educated in an impoverished eastern province of Kenya, Verre joined his Turkish colleagues in the early years of the school: "I have been working here now for some seven years. I have good relations with my students and colleagues. They are from a different culture, which creates a multicultural environment on the campus. The school has exchange programs with Turkey, though I have never been to Turkey so far. So it has been quite a good experience for me."[89] Verre takes a rightful pride in the Light Academy's accomplishments: "I remember, when it started about 10 years ago, our school's space was very limited and in an impoverished building. Now, when I look around, I see a modern and huge campus with different facilities. This is the most important accomplishment of the school, I believe. Secondly, when we did our first national KCSE (Kenya Certificate of Secondary Education) exam in 2002, we were nowhere on the map of Kenya. However, when we look at it today, we can say that the Light Academy is likely to be the light of this country, because the success graph is always showing a positive trend. We ranked tenth, then eighth and then seventh. Finally this year [2007], we ranked second among some 5,000 private schools in Kenya." As he speaks of every success of the Light Academy as if his own, Verre's words explain not only what sort of impact the Gülen-inspired initiatives in Kenya may have had already, but also what the local people can accomplish for their own societies in Africa.

The improvement and reform of the education system with a great emphasis on secondary and post-secondary education is crucial to civil society building in any given country according to the World Bank civil society development program. Unlike early civil society theoreticians who associated the possibility of civil society formation with the will of the people, the World Bank civil society program recognizes the reality that will itself does not suffice to form civil society if the human capital to do so is not present. With its proven experience and capability in Mardin and Kenya as well as other conflict zones to help the ethno-religiously diverse local population develop human capital, the Gülen Movement and its schools can contribute to developing human capital not only in

89 Excerpt from the authors interview with the respondent (Nairobi, Kenya. 23 April 2008).

Nigeria but also in other African countries which possess a similar demographic and socio-economic structure.

The Philippines provides a unique example of a community which is scarred by enduring Muslim-Christian fighting. Like the Christians of Northern Iraq, the Moro Muslims constitute the minority in the Philippines and are concentrated in the autonomous region of Mindanao in the Southern Philippines. The Moro Muslims have politically organized themselves as a Muslim nationalist movement, which they describe as both Islamic and anti-colonial. As such, the main mobilizing force for the Moro Muslims has been their historical resistance to Spanish colonialism, and that resistance currently continues as their struggle against Christian Manila's attempts to assimilate the Muslim Philippines. In a way, after the end of the threat of colonialism, the conflict in the Philippines has transformed into an enduring one between the Muslim minority and the Christian majority. Yet, despite earlier attempts to form a unified nationalist Muslim identity (Bansgsamoro), the Philippine's Muslims have organized as three distinct political groups, which are respectively the Moro National Liberation Front (MNLF), the Moro Islamic Liberation Front (MILF), and Abu Sayyaf. Despite their different political orientations, what brings these distinct groups together is their common uprising against their common "other"—the Christian majority.

What is interesting about the Philippines, where Muslim-Christian conflict is still vivid, and the contribution of the Gülen Movement in the Philippines is articulated by Thomas Michel, the former Vatican representative for interfaith dialogue for Northern Africa and the Middle East. Michel emphasizes that the Gülen schools in the Philippines bring together in a peaceful atmosphere Christian and Muslim students whose fathers have been fighting each other for more than two decades because of their religious differences (Michel 2003). It is certainly interesting to see a platform in the Philippines where Christians and Muslims peacefully join together. What is more interesting is to see that it is a platform brought about by Muslims affiliated with a faith-based civil society movement while the local Muslims are party to the conflict. The situation is very similar in Bosnia, Northern Iraq and Afghanistan. In spite of sharing an ethnic and/or religious background with parties in the ongoing conflict in these places, supporters of the Gülen Movement tend not to take part, or not to continue if they have taken part previously, in the conflict. Instead, they prefer to identify common grounds where they get together and cooperate to tackle common problems.

Conclusion: Gülen Schools as a Means to Social Development and Civil Society

Finally, given the specific example of what the Gülen Movement has achieved in the ethno-religiously diverse city of Mardin in building and maintaining social consensus among different communities which were previously engaged in a conflict and in mobilizing them to counter common challenges, what are the prospects that the movement and its schools may do the same in other communities in ethno-religious conflict? I have argued that analysis of the Gülen Movement's activities in cases as Bosnia, Northern Iraq, Afghanistan and the Philippines would demonstrate that the movement is able to bring together the various indigenous ethno-religious communities in these respective countries by addressing their common problems, providing a solid vision and services to address those problems and mobilizing the local people to cooperate in solving those problems. It is certainly necessary to conduct field research in all these countries to verify whether the Gülen Movement is able to achieve what it did in Mardin. Already accounts of those who have visited the schools in these countries just like Thomas Michel's account of his visit to the schools in the Philippines, suggest that the movement is able to bring ethno-religiously varied communities together in a peaceful environment.

This observation entails a broader question about the Gülen Movement's ability to contribute to developing human capital, the fundamental pre-condition of civil society formation, in socially deprived countries with ethno-religious conflicts such as some countries in Africa. The continent provides several examples of countries which have plunged into ethnic, religious or ethno-religious conflict and chronic political turmoil due to the lack of social capital which enables civil society, political stability and economic prosperity.

The case of Mardin has demonstrated that the Gülen Movement has been able to mobilize individuals of Turkish, Kurdish, Arab and Assyrian origins, who were previously fractured and isolated from one another, to tackle their very own common problems with their own resources. Similarly, the case of Kenya illustrates the ability of the Gülen-inspired initiatives, most notably of the schools, to contribute to building self-confidence in individuals and developing human capital through education. Based on this example, one can deduce that the Gülen Movement emphasizes the role of human agency and the autonomy of society and individuals from the state. That is, individuals organize together and mobilize their resources to meet their common needs. Consequently, the necessity for law and order to sustain what has been achieved as a result of the collective action cultivates both the individual and communal quest and respect for the rule of law, which constitutes the backbone of a sustainable civil society.

References

Almond, G. and S. Verba, ed. 1989. *The Civic Culture: Political Attitudes and Democracy in Five Nations*. Sage Publications.

CIA World Factbook – Nigeria. https://www.cia.gov/library/publications/the-world-factbook/geos/ni.html#People.

DK Publishing. 2006. *How Governments Work: The Inside Guide to the Politics of the World*. London, New York, Melbourne, Munich and Delhi: Dorling Kindersley Limited.

Kalyoncu, M. 2008. *A Civilian Response to Ethno-religious Conflict: The Gülen Movement in Southeast Turkey*, New Jersey: The Light, Inc.

Michel, T. 2003. "Fethullah Gülen as Educator." *Turkish Islam and the Secular State: The Gülen Movement*, ed. M. H. Yavuz and J. L. Esposito. Syracuse: Syracuse University Press,

Putnam, R. 1993. *Making Democracy Work: Civic Traditions in Modern Italy*. Princeton: Princeton University Press.

Chapter 14

Towards a Middle Way: Islam in Southeast Asia and the Contributions of the Gülen Movement

Mohamed Nawab bin Mohamed Osman

Introduction

The emergence of Islam as a political force is a recent development in Southeast Asia. Earlier, the impact of the resurgence of Islam had been felt both in the social and cultural realms through the mushrooming of Muslim organizations attempting to promote a "purer" form of Islam in the region. In more recent times, however, the expression of religious practice has been enacted by way of participation in political parties and groups. More shockingly, some of these groups, such as the terror network known as Jemaah Islamiyah, have sought to use violence to achieve their aims. This has had severe ramifications for both intra-Muslim relations and Muslim–non-Muslim relations in the region. In this chaotic socio-political climate, a group has emerged in the region advocating peace, tolerance and understanding between people of different races and religions. This group is known as the Gülen Movement, or is commonly referred to as *hizmet* in Turkey.[90]

90 *Hizmet* literally means "service to humanity" in Turkish and is often used by participants in the movement to describe their activities.

This chapter is intended to demonstrate how the Gülen Movement has addressed the issues facing them and remained relevant by developing a counter-trend through proactive measures to oppose extremist ideology and enhance peacebuilding in the Southeast Asian region. Its key thrust is to show that the Gülen Movement can reverse the current distorted state of Islam back to its original form and thus promote peace in the region. The teachings of Islam can accommodate cultural differences in Southeast Asia and enhance peace between Muslims and non-Muslims in the region. This chapter first examines case studies of organizations inspired by Gülen in Singapore and Indonesia and how these organizations have utilized his ideas to enhance peacebuilding and interreligious dialogue and provide an alternative to the legalistic discourse on Islam. The study also attempts to compare and contrast the approach of the organization in a Muslim-majority country (Indonesia) and in a Muslim minority country (Singapore). The paper concludes by charting a trajectory of the movement's role and its potential contributions to the development of moderate Islam and peace-building in Southeast Asia. It argues that these contributions will become important counters to extremist ideologies and enhance peace among Muslims and between members of different faiths in the region.[91]

The Gülen Movement in Southeast Asia

Individuals from Turkey who were influenced by Gülen's ideas first arrived in the region in the 1980s. But it was only in 1993 that the first school was started in the region. Today, the movement has schools in virtually all the Southeast Asian countries. Interestingly, the Movement started a school in Cambodia in the late 1990s,

91 The research for this paper combines field and documentary research methods with a qualitative approach. The field research component is based on data gathered through participatory observation (in the case of Singapore) and interviews with key figures of Gülen-inspired organizations as well as local partners of these organizations. The documentary research component of the paper gathers data from the movement's publications, including books, newspaper articles and online materials.

when the country was just recovering from the political turmoil following the genocide perpetrated by its dictator, Pol Pot, against the Cambodians. Participants of the Gülen Movement, through the encouragement of peers, made their way to certain cities after first assessing their needs. The Movement in Southeast Asia adopts the same method of spearheading and promoting its activities as in other parts of the world. Businessmen from a particular city in Turkey would concentrate their efforts on a particular Southeast Asian city. For instance, the city of Gaziantep in southeastern Turkey partially supports the activities in certain cities in Southeast Asia, such as Singapore and Manila. The Movement participants who came to Southeast Asia did so mainly due to self-motivation or to a sense of duty to serve in places that badly needed assistance. This sense of duty motivated a follower of Gülen from Malaysia to subsequently leave for Papua New Guinea to set up a school. An organization that plays an important role in the development of the movement in the region is the Pacific Countries Social and Economic Solidarity Association (PASIAD). PASIAD plays an important linking role, assisting Turkish businessmen and students who are interested in investing or studying in a particular Asia-Pacific country by linking them up with the local Gülen Movement operating in a particular country. PASIAD does not, however, oversee or direct activities of the local service projects. Its role is merely a supportive one. The role of PASIAD will be further explained in the analysis of case studies of Gülen-inspired organizations in Singapore and Indonesia.

The arrival of the movement participants in Southeast Asia has also enhanced peace in the region. The Gülen-inspired schools played an important role in peacebuilding efforts in the region. The success of these schools in peacebuilding is best encapsulated in the observations made by Thomas Michel, the secretary for Inter-Religious Dialogue of the Society of Jesus in Rome. He remarks that the Philippine-Turkish School of Tolerance in Zamboanga, the Philippines, offers Muslim and Christian Filipino children a positive way of living and relating to each other (Michel 2003, 71). This is especially important in a country bogged down by more than three hundred years of conflict between Christians and Muslims. The school also marks an important step in countering terrorism, as the value system taught in the school prevents students, especially those from the Muslim community, from being influenced by Muslim terrorist groups in the region. Such examples can be seen in other parts of the region including Singapore and Indonesia.

The Turkish Cultural Centre in Singapore

Context and Historical Background

Singapore is a small country of four million people. Muslims make up about 14 percent of the population while the rest consists of Buddhists, Christians, Hindus and Jews. Most Muslims in Singapore are ethnically Malay. For historical and political reasons, the Muslim minority in Singapore is often seen to be a "problematic" community.[92] Their increased adherence to Islam and the emergence of a more puritan version of Islam among Singaporean Muslims is often viewed with trepidation by the Singaporean government. Since the 1990s, several controversies—such as the banning of the headscarf in schools, the government's attempt to reform *madrasahs* in Singapore and the arrests of several members of the Jemaah Islamiyah network—had created tensions between the Muslim and non-Muslim communities.[93] There was little effort made to formulate any form of interreligious dialogue between the different religious communities. Ignorance of one another's religion only went on to exacerbate the uneasiness between Muslims and non-Muslims in the country. The emergence of the Gülen Movement was timely in easing some of these tensions.

92 For more on the problems of Malays in Singapore, see Rahim, L. Z. 1998. *The Singapore Dilemma: The Political and Educational Marginality of the Malay Community.* Kuala Lumpur: Oxford University Press.

93 For more on these issues, see Mohamed Osman, M. N. 2004. *Activism of Ulama in Singapore.* Unpublished academic thesis. National University of Singapore.

The Gülen Movement first found a foothold in Singapore when Sadık Yıldız first came to the island state in 1997. Just like other participants in the Gülen Movement elsewhere in the world, he began to establish relations with members of the Singaporean community. In particular, he made important contacts with members of the ethnic Chinese and Indian communities, who are mostly non-Muslims, as well as with several important politicians including Sidek Saniff, then Senior Minister of State for Education. In addition, he built strong relations with several Singapore-based Turkish businessmen, including İsmail Cem, owner of a prominent Turkish restaurant (Candemir 2007). These important links facilitated the work of the Gülen Movement in the country. Yıldız, with the assistance of the local Turkish community and Singaporeans, formed the Turkey-Central Asia Cultural Centre on 3 April, 1999. Later, the centre was renamed the Turkish Cultural Centre (TCC).

Yıldız also encouraged students from Gülen-inspired schools in Turkey to further their studies in Singapore. These students began to enroll in several universities in Singapore from 2001 (Eskici 2007). These students, including Dr. Erkan Polatdemir, were to later form an important component of the movement in Singapore. The TCC grew in prominence after Turkey's 1999 earthquake, when it coordinated the assistance that Singapore gave to Turkey. In more recent times, the TCC assisted students from Turkey and Central Asia, most of whom were studying in Gülen-inspired schools, to acclimatize to Singapore life (Polatdemir 2007). The support for its activities comes mainly through PASIAD, though in recent times the TCC has successfully obtained help from local businessmen and partners to support some of its activities.

Encouraging Tolerance and Dialogue

At the initial stages, the TCC, under the leadership of Yıldız, worked with the Inter-Religious Organization (IRO) to promote interreligious dialogue in Singapore. However, due to the limited reach of the IRO, the TCC started its own initiatives (Polatdemir

2007). The flagship event that the TCC organizes annually is the *iftar* dinner, held during the holy month of Ramadan. The first such dinner was organized in 1999, when about a hundred people, one third of whom were non-Muslims, attended. A large number of the Muslim attendees were members of the Turkish community in Singapore. The event served as a platform for the community to gather and enhance their relations. Some Singaporean Muslims were also invited. These were often family members or friends of Turks staying in Singapore. Among the non-Muslims, the attendees comprised members of the IRO, including its then chairman, the Venerable Gunaratna, Christian community leaders, Buddhists and Hindus. The guest of honor was Mr. Sidek Saniff, then Senior Minister of State for Education. The *iftar* dinner was a watershed event, given the context of the time when it was organized (Eskici 2007). Firstly, the Muslim community in Singapore was divided along religious and ideological lines. Several issues, such as the ban on the wearing of the headscarf and the perceived attempt by the Singaporean government to ban Islamic religious schools, had given rise to differing opinions among Muslims. Secondly, these issues had resulted in tensions between Muslims and non-Muslims in Singapore. Both the Singaporean government and the non-Muslim communities perceived Muslims as being exclusive and failing to integrate with the larger Singaporean society. Most importantly, the *iftar* was often seen to be an exclusively Muslim event and most Singaporean Muslims were not comfortable with inviting non-Muslims to it. The smooth running of this annual event thus served as an important milestone in bridging the gap between the communities, which otherwise would have widened. This initiative was a replica of the larger Abant platform that the Gülen Movement had initiated and utilized in Turkey. The Journalists and Writers Association, an organization inspired by Gülen, first initiated the Abant platform in 1998.[94] It was a platform to discuss issues considered

94 For all the declarations for the various Abant meetings, visit www.gyv.org.tr.

to be sensitive and divisive in Turkey. İhsan Yılmaz (2007) noted that the Abant Platform has shown the Turkish public that it is possible to bring together intellectuals, academics and civil-society leaders from all walks of life, discussing and, in most cases, agreeing on every single sensitive issue in the country.

The TCC's *iftar* dinner attendance has since grown and now includes more non-Muslims. When I attended the *iftar* dinners of 2006, 2007, and 2008, the diverse backgrounds of the attendees pleasantly surprised me. The Muslims who attended the dinner were of different ideological types—from those influenced by puritan Salafi teachings to those who are more inclined towards Sufism.[95] Despite their different religious ideologies, they sat at the same table and interacted well. The leaders of all major Muslim organizations were also invited to this function. More interestingly, members of the various religious communities were also present, including members of the Jewish community and various church communities such as City Harvest Church, a church known for its staunchly conservative and evangelical position. The fact that representatives of the church even came to the function was a matter of amazement for many of the attendees, and was a great achievement for the TCC.[96] The programs of these *iftar* dinners also feature non-Muslim speakers, such Michael Broughten from the Catholic community and Hsieh Fu Hua from the Methodist community. Even the masters of ceremony for these *iftar*s were non-Muslim students (a Sikh in 2007 and a Christian in 2008). The success of these *iftar* dinners was acknowledged even by the Islamic Religious Council of Singapore (MUIS), a government statutory board dealing with the affairs of Muslims in Singapore when they decided to partially sponsor the 2006 and 2008 *iftar* dinners (Eskici 2007).

95 Personal observation of author at the TCC *iftar* dinner at the Hilton Hotel, October 2006.

96 The church has been at odds with the Muslim community and other communities for its aggressive proselytizing techniques. For more on this church, visit the website of City Harvest Church at www.chc.org.sg/main_landing.htm.

Perhaps the most important impact of these *iftar* dinners is the fact that following the events of September 11, other Muslim organizations and several mosques have begun inviting non-Muslims to their own *iftar* dinners. This used to be seen as a taboo but, learning from the example of the TCC, they began to realize the importance and value of this endeavor. For instance, as a student leader leading the National University of Singapore Muslim Society, the author himself also organized *iftar* dinners like those organized by the TCC and invited non-Muslim students to the function. As such, one could argue that the efforts of the TCC have been significant in creating a new way of interreligious dialogue. At the same time, many of the attendees, including prominent religious and community leaders of the Singaporean society, continue to come and even look forward to the *iftar* dinners. This is a reflection of the importance of the event in building peace between Muslims and non-Muslims.

Intra- and Interfaith Dialogues

The TCC's interfaith engagements go beyond *iftar* dinners. Imbued with the spirit of Gülen's teachings, they also collaborate with various local partners to organize seminars and talks aimed at creating a better image of Islam. One such event was a seminar on Islam and Modernity jointly organized with the Ba'alwi Mosque in April 2006. The seminar featured several prominent academics. The key message of the speakers was that Islam is a religion of the Middle Way which is against terrorism and extremism. They also spoke about the ideas of Fethullah Gülen in countering extremism and building peace. The session, attended by many non-Muslim Singaporeans, was significant in trying to create a better image of Islam post–September 11. Another approach undertaken by the TCC to enhance peace between Muslims and non-Muslims is to invite non-Muslim Singaporeans to Turkey for a "cultural introduction" program. These trips are not only important insofar as they contribute to a deepening understanding of Turkey and its culture but also enhance the participant's knowledge of Islam. In December 2006, the TCC facilitated a trip to Turkey organized by the National University of Singapore's Scholars Program.[97] The students, who were mostly non-Muslims, visited various historical sites. They were also introduced to Turkish Muslimness. Upon their return to Singapore, a seminar was organized at the Harmony Centre, a centre for interfaith activities, and they presented their impressions of Turkey. It was obvious that their knowledge of Islam had been greatly enhanced, and many were clearly moved by the experience. One of the non-Muslim participants mentioned in his presentation that the teachings of Gülen would shape a positive perception of Islam.

The TCC also organized another trip to Turkey in June 2007 for Christian community leaders in Singapore. They also met and had dinner with supporters of the Gülen Movement. During those events, they developed an understanding of the Middle Way Islam that Gülen is advocating and gained an insight into why many people devoted their time and effort to the movement (Yap 2007). One of the participants, Reverend Yap Khiam Hoe, the former Bishop of the Methodist Church in Singapore and Malaysia, said that Gülen is indeed a gifted Muslim renewer who would change the world's impression about Islam through his enlightened ideals (Yap 2007). After the trip, Reverend Yap became an even stauncher supporter of the TCC. He has promoted the ideas of Gülen to his Muslim friends, and has requested the author to address members of the Contemporary Centre for Islamic Studies on Gülen's ideas and the movement. In 2007, the TCC started giving out awards to individuals for their contribution to enhancing interreligious ties and building peace between different communities in the country.

The efforts of the TCC to enhance intra- and interreligious dialogue are indeed commendable. Besides being a trendsetter in interreligious dialogue, the TCC is also at the forefront of organizing various events to improve the understanding of Islam. Its efforts

97 Students who are selected for this program are among the best students in Singapore and often occupy important policy-making positions upon their graduation.

have led to better relations among Muslims and between Muslims and non-Muslims in Singapore and enhance peace in the country. The TCC's next stage of its intra- and inter-religious dialogue effort is to start a Turkish school in Singapore in 2010. Indeed, there is little doubt that the Turkish school in Singapore will lead to creating better relations between Muslims and non-Muslims in Singapore. This will in turn contribute to better inter-ethnic ties and enhance peace in the country.

PASIAD Indonesia

Context and History

Indonesia is the world's largest Islamic country, with 190 to 200 million Muslims out of a total population of around 240 million. Historically, Islam in Indonesia is moderate and is known for its pluralistic nature. Yet, since the fall of President Suharto in 1998, a more radical form of the religion has emerged. While the vast majority of Indonesian Muslims are moderate, some are now pushing for an Islamic state to be established, through violence if necessary. Religious conflict between Muslims and Christians in some parts of Indonesia has led to thousands of lives lost. The proliferation of Islamic groups and political parties in the country also means that Muslims are increasingly divided along the lines of religious ideology.[98] In these difficult times, the Gülen Movement in Indonesia remains one of the few moderate Islamic voices advocating for both intra- and inter-Muslim tolerance and dialogue as well as contributing to peacebuilding efforts.

The Gülen Movement arrived in Indonesia in 1993 when three students from Turkey came to study in the country. One of these students, Hakan İslamoğlu, is still in Indonesia at the time of writing this chapter. The other two students were Kerim Tursun and

---

98 For a better sense of Indonesian politics and history, see Ricklefs, M. 2001. *History of Indonesia since c.1200*. Hampshire: Palgrave.

Galip Kayar. The decision of these students to go to Indonesia was indeed strange, given that none of them could speak Indonesian or even knew anyone in the country. They made their approach through contact with an Indonesian friend (who studied in Turkey). This person, Haji Alwi, was initially rather surprised to see the Turkish boys, but nevertheless assisted them to obtain places in various universities in Indonesia. İslamoğlu secured a place at the University of Indonesia, in the Department of Indonesian Literature. In 1994, after about a year of studying in the university, İslamoğlu told Haji Alwi about the Gülen Movement and expressed his desire to start a school in Indonesia (İslamoğlu 2007). Haji Alwi introduced him to Burhanuddin Abdullah, the Governor of Indonesia's state bank, who assisted İslamoğlu in setting up the first school in Indonesia, the Pribadi High School in Depok. Another person instrumental in the setting up of the school was Dr. Aip Syarifuddin, an Indonesian politician (İslamoğlu 2007). To ensure that the administration of the school was managed professionally, İslamoğlu and his friends joined with several Indonesians, including Dr. Syarifuddin and a Firman Kartiman, to start the Yenbu Indonesian Foundation (İslamoğlu 2007).

In 1997, another organization, PASIAD Indonesia, was formed to facilitate the administration of the school. In 1996, İslamoğlu decided to transfer his studies to the Gadjah Muda University in Semarang, a city located in the centre of the island of Java. İslamoğlu quickly became close to the dean of the university, Professor Siti Chamamah Soeratno, and invited her to visit the school in Jakarta. Upon seeing the quality of its education, Professor Soeratno was impressed and inspired to start a similar school in Semarang. This led to the setting up of the Al-Firdaus Semarang Foundation, which then worked closely with PASIAD Indonesia to start the SMP-SMA Semesta Boarding School (PASIAD 2006, 18). In 2002, a school was built in Bandung. Another school was built following the tsunami of 2005 in Aceh. The school built most recently is the Kharisma National School. This school was built with the support of a rich and prominent Indonesian family (Altun 2007).

Besides educational activities, PASIAD Indonesia also played an important role in promoting cultural ties between Turkey and Indonesia. Since 2001, it has published several books with local partners promoting the Turkish language, including the publication of a Turkish-Indonesian dictionary in 2006 (PASIAD 2006, 62). They have also played an important role in charity. Since 1998, PASIAD Indonesia has organized the donation of frozen meat from the Turkish community in Australia to poor Indonesians during the festival of Eid-ul-Adha. During the tsunami crisis that hit the province of Aceh, PASIAD Indonesia coordinated relief work in the region, which included rebuilding schools and houses, assisting in healthcare and providing food for the victims (PASIAD 2006, 50–51). In the cultural realm, PASIAD was also involved in organizing a Turkish film festival as well as in several international cultural festivals (PASIAD 2006, 60–61).

Building Peace and Tolerance through Education

As highlighted earlier, Gülen believes that it is through education that extremism will be curbed and tolerance promoted. It was this understanding that motivated his followers in Indonesia to build schools in the country. İslamoğlu noted that intolerance occurs between the different religious groups in Indonesia due to lack of education.

In its initial stage, there were only fifteen students in the school, many of whom were from a rural and poor background. Today, the number of students has increased to about 2,000, with many from a more privileged background.[99] This does not mean

99 The changing profile of these students is due to the high fees that the school charges. Parents pay an average of US$100 per month in the school. See Radio Singapore International, "Turkish Delight," 3 July 2007. Accessed on 4 July 2007 from www.rsi.org.sg.

that the schools are elitist in any way. The fees charged to the more privileged students are partly used to provide scholarships for students from poorer backgrounds to study in these schools (PASIAD 2006, 20). The diverse backgrounds of the students allow for interaction between them, many of whom would not otherwise meet due to the segmented nature of the different class groups in Indonesia. This allows the richer student to understand better the challenges faced by his fellow student from a less privileged background. At the same time, about 10 percent of the student population is not Muslim. PASIAD Indonesia also does not discriminate in the allocation of scholarships, and about 20 percent of those who receive scholarships from PASIAD Indonesia are non-Muslim students.[100] The presence of non-Muslim students allows for interaction and the building of trust and tolerance between Muslims and non-Muslims in an otherwise stratified society where there is little interaction between the two communities. The universal values taught to the students meant that they tend to look beyond ethnic or religious cleavages in dealing with others. Turkish schools in Indonesia are an important platform. At another level, these schools serve as an excellent cultural bridge between Turkey and Indonesia. The students are exposed to aspects of Turkish culture such as its food and language. Due to this exposure, the schools have become an important ambassador for Turkey in Indonesia.

For many parents, the attraction of these schools lies in their high standard of education, which has produced students who have won international physics and mathematics competitions (Republica, July 2006). More importantly, many parents are aware that the teachers in these schools are good role models for their children and that the schools give the students a good education without inducing any ideological leanings. Moreover, tolerance and an appreciation for what others do are also values advocated in these schools.

---

100 About 13 percent of Indonesia's population are non-Muslims. Generally, non-Muslims are stronger economically, which explains the relatively low number of non-Muslim students receiving scholarships from PASIAD Indonesia.

In an interview, an alumnus of the school echoed Gülen's vision of peace and tolerance when he said that Muslims should cease to have an "us-against-them" mindset. There must be a shift in their paradigm to start thinking of everyone as fellow human beings rather than of their religious affiliations (Riaz 2007). Mahmud Riaz is an example of the kind of educated, cultured Muslim, described by Gülen, who will never resort to terrorism or turn to extremism to pursue his aim. The Indonesian government has acknowledged the importance of these schools in countering extremist ideologies. A government leader to whom the author spoke indicated that the Department of National Education and local governments want more such schools built in Indonesia.[101] This is because they recognize that the Islam that Gülen advocates is an important antidote to the extremism promoted by radical groups in Indonesia. Interestingly about 70 percent of the school's alumni, including many non-Muslim students, have volunteered to teach in the schools despite their often prestigious educational backgrounds, which could allow them to obtain more lucrative jobs (Altun 2007). This development would mean that more schools could be built in future as the movement receives more staff support from within its alumni.

In Aceh, a war-torn region of Indonesia, the Turkish school played an important role in building peace in the region. The Acehnese had fought against the Indonesian authorities since 1953 in their attempt to seek independence from Indonesia due to differences in politics, economics and religion. The conflict led to worsening relations between the Acehnese and people from other parts of Indonesia such as the Javanese and Batak who were also living in Aceh. It was not until 2006 that peace was finally achieved in the region. The founding of the Aceh Fatih School has assisted in the peacebuilding efforts in the region. Students of various ethnic groups study together in the school leading to better ties between the different ethnic groups. The fact that many children

101 Conversation with a government leader who had interactions with participants in the Gülen Movement.

of the Acehnese and Javanese elites have been studying together also means that they will become an important bridge between the two communities.

Intra- and Interreligious Dialogue

Understanding the factional nature of Indonesian Islam and politics, PASIAD Indonesia has sought to maintain good relations with all Muslim groups and political parties in the country. PASIAD Indonesia has paid courtesy visits to the president, vice-president, and various cabinet ministers, as well as major Muslim organizations and political parties such as Muhammadiyah, Nahdatul Ulama, the Justice and Prosperous Party (PKS) and Golkar (PASIAD 2006, 69–82). It is also interesting to note that despite the constant changes of leadership in Indonesia, PASIAD Indonesia has been able to maintain warm ties with all the different leaders of the country. Building intra-Muslim dialogue remains an important focus for PASIAD Indonesia due to the fact that the country is overwhelmingly Muslim.

PASIAD Indonesia does this by initiating various programs such as *iftar* dinners and *Halalbihalal* functions. *Halalbihalal* is a unique Indonesian Muslim cultural practice where Muslims seek forgiveness from one another for mistakes committed against one another in the course of the year. This often occurs at the end of the fasting month. PASIAD Indonesia has adopted this practice and has been organizing *Halalbihalal* functions annually. Staff members of the different PASIAD Indonesia's schools as well as local partners of PASIAD are invited for the functions. Interestingly, PASIAD also invites various Islamic community leaders, despite differences in their religions and political ideology. The *iftar* dinner is another annual event organized by PASIAD Indonesia. Similar to the ones in Singapore, *iftar* functions in Indonesia are overwhelmingly Muslim events. The invited guests include prominent politicians and Muslim community leaders. The event is often graced by the presence of an Indonesian cabinet minister or the

Vice-President of Indonesia, Yusuf Kalla. Like the *Halalbihalal* functions, one can find politicians from secular political parties such Golkar as well as those from the more religious parties such as the PKS at the *iftar* dinners. They are also from different religious orientations. Non-Muslims were often not invited to *iftar* functions in the past. Breaking these norms, PASIAD invites non-Muslim community leaders such as leaders of various churches, Buddhist monasteries and Hindu temples to these events so as to bring about interreligious harmony between the different religious communities (İslamoğlu 2007). For many of these non-Muslim leaders, it is the first time in their lives that they have attended such a function, and it is important in enhancing their understanding of Islam.

In another effort to increase both intra- and interreligious tolerance, PASIAD Indonesia organizes overseas trips to Turkey. Once again, the leaders of different Muslim organizations are invited to enhance their relations with one another during such trips. Several non-Muslim leaders also accompany the delegation to Turkey (PASIAD 2006, 88–89). In these trips, delegates are taken to various historical sites and to meet supporters of the Gülen Movement to allow them to gain insight into the movement in Turkey. Such trips are important in cementing ties between these community leaders and PASIAD Indonesia. Perhaps the most important trip organized by PASIAD Indonesia was a trip to Moscow to attend an International Symposium titled "From Terrorism to Global Ethics: Religions and Peace" (PASIAD 2006, 90). The fact that a leader of an Islamic party, PKS, known for its conservative Islamic leanings, such as the imposition of Islamic criminal laws, decided to attend an interreligious symposium is remarkable. Several leaders of the Hindu, Christian and Confucian communities also attended the event. The participants in the event were exposed to the importance of interfaith dialogue in a climate where terrorism and extremism can weaken ties between faith communities (Altun 2007). The dialogue efforts of PASIAD Indonesia have been crucial in enhancing ties among Muslims and between Muslims and non-Muslims. It is an important platform for peacebuilding especially in a climate where conflict between the different faiths in Indonesia is prevalent. This is particularly so at the elite level of Indonesian society. Such efforts have become essential, especially given the threat of religious strife and extremism that Indonesia faces.

Conclusion

The Muslim world is today in a transition phase. This is clearly seen in the intolerant and extreme acts of some marginal Muslim groups. Historically, all major civilizations have undergone this phase, where members of these civilizations are insular and weak. Yet, in the midst of these uncertainties, the ideas of Fethullah Gülen have emerged to reverse the thinking and attitudes of Muslims. The Gülen Movement is a trendsetter movement that has sought to create intra- and inter-religious understanding and improve education standards in the world. As Gülen has highlighted time and again, improving educational standards in the Muslim world is likely to change the mindset and thinking of Muslims, leading them to have a more enlightened approach in dealing with their coreligionists and non-Muslims. This development is especially important where Muslims are in the minority, such as in Singapore and Europe. In Europe, the misconceptions and prejudices held by Muslims and non-Muslims towards each other have led to worsening relations between the two parties. Yet, if Gülen's ideas are imbibed and practiced by Muslims, such misconception and prejudices will slowly be eradicated. This will lead to peace in the world. The case studies of the Gülen Movement in Indonesia and Singapore are reflective of how a small group of Gülen followers have successfully impacted the society they live in. They are also reflective of the important impact Gülen's ideas have had for people around the world. Acting upon his vision of tolerance and dialogue, his followers in both countries promote this vision by encouraging dialogue among Muslims and between Muslim and non-Muslims. In the case of Singapore, such dialogues are especially encouraged between Muslims and non-Muslims, given that Muslims are seen as a problematic minority in the country. The efforts of the TCC have proved significant, as they have been able to change the perceptions of Islam and even gained supporters among non-Muslims for their cause. In Indonesia, PASIAD Indonesia focuses on the development of relations among Muslims due to the overwhelming number of Muslims in the country. In the process, they are not only able to reduce tension and build peace among Muslims but also to enhance ties between Muslims and non-Muslims through the Turkish schools and their interreligious activities. The schools in Indonesia are likely to chart a new course for Islam in Indonesia—a moderate and tolerant one. The precedence given to universal values in these schools, inherent in all religions, is important in shaping the educated, cultured Muslim who is tolerant and progressive, as Gülen envisages. The common values which the Gülen Movement emphasizes are also likely to renew the shape of Islamic understanding in Southeast Asia, and make it once more tolerant and accommodating to other religions.

References

Michel, T. 2003. "Fethullah Gülen as Educator." *Turkish Islam and the Secular State*, ed. H. Yavuz and J. L. Esposito. New York: Syracuse University Press, 69–84.

Osman, M. N. M. 2004. *Activism of Ulama in Singapore*. Unpublished academic thesis, National University of Singapore.

PASIAD Indonesia. 2006. *Mengenal lebih dekat PASIAD Indonesia*. Jakarta: PASIAD.

Radio Singapore International, "Turkish Delight," 3 July 2007. Accessed from www.rsi.org.sg on 4 July 2007.

Rahim, L. Z. 1998. *The Singapore Dilemma: The Political and Educational Marginality of the Malay Community*. Kuala Lumpur: Oxford University Press.

Republica, Indonesia-Turkish Schools Mewujudkan Pendidikan Masa Depan, 3 July 2006.

Ricklefs, M. 2001. *History of Indonesia since c.1200*. Hampshire: Palgrave.

Sarıtoprak, Z. and S. Griffith. 2005. "Fethullah Gülen and the People of the Book: A Voice from Turkey for Interfaith Dialogue. *The Muslim World*, 95 (July), 329–340.

Ünal, A. and A. Williams. 2000. *Advocate of Dialogue: Fethullah* Gülen. Fairfax: The Fountain.

Yavuz, M. H. 2003. "The Gülen Movement: The Turkish Puritans." *Turkish Islam and the secular state*, ed. H. Yavuz and J. L. Esposito. New York: Syracuse University Press, pp. 19–46.

Yılmaz, İ. 2005. "State, Law, Civil Society and Islam in Contemporary Turkey." *The Muslim World*, 95 (July), 385–411.

———. 2007. "Abant Platform, Alevis and Diaspora." *Today's Zaman*, 23 March 2007.

Interviews

Necmettin Eskici, Chairman of Turkish Cultural Centre. Interview by author, note-taking. Turkish Cultural Centre Singapore, #07–02, Golden Mile Plaza, Novena Square, 2 August 2007.

Dr. Erkan Polatdemir, Member of Turkish Cultural Centre. Interview by author, note-taking. Turkish Cultural Centre Singapore, #07–02, Golden Mile Plaza, Novena Square, 2 August 2007.

Serdar Candemir, Member of Turkish Cultural Centre. Interview by author, note-taking. Turkish Cultural Centre Singapore, #07–02, Golden Mile Plaza, Novena Square, 2 August 2007.

Yap Khiam Hoe, former Bishop of Singapore and Malaysia Methodist Church and supporter of Turkish Cultural Centre. Interview by author, note-taking. #16–02, Braddell Heights, Braddell Road, 3 August 2007.

Hakan İslamoğlu, founder of PASIAD Indonesia. Interview by author, note-taking. Pribadi High School, Jalan Margonda Raya, No. 229, Depok, 10 August 2007.

Mahmud Riaz, from the first batch of students of Pribadi High School and currently teacher at the Kharisma Bangsa School. Interview by author, note-taking. Pribadi High School, Jalan Margonda Raya, No. 229, Depok, 10 August 2007.

Mahmud Altun, staff of PASIAD Indonesia. Interview by author, note-taking. PASIAD Indonesia, Grha Diandra, Jalan Warung Buncit Raya, No. 2, Jakarta, 13 August 2007.

Chapter 15

The Role of Turkish Schools in Building Trusting Cross-ethnic Relationships in Northern Iraq

Harun Akyol

Introduction

Without any doubt ethno-nationalism as a movement and ideology has played a crucial role in world politics since the French Revolution. For some, it has been the only legitimizing source for exercising power over a nation, and for others, it is an evil ideology causing the most human catastrophes in history (Ross et al. 1999, 1). Social scientists had not shown a great deal of interest in ethnicity and ethno-nationalism until the world witnessed a new wave of ethnic conflicts and cleansing from Rwanda to Bosnia. In the Cold War era, conventional ethnic conflict prevention approaches can be summarized in four groups: (Hamburg et al. R 1997, XXI)

- Early warning and early response
- Preventive diplomacy
- Economic measures such as sanctions and inducements
- The use of force

Despite some variations, they are all mainly based on the concept of post-Westphalian state centric notions of sovereignty, which can only be claimed by national states. The issue of sovereignty is creating a complicated predicament in the uneasy relationship between Turkey and the autonomous Kurdish Regional Government in Northern Iraq (KRG). On the one hand, the KRG claims that they are the legal representatives of the Iraqi Kurds and should be recognized as a partner of Turkey; on the other hand, in the Turkish government's view, there is a dilemma: while there is a de facto recognition of the KRG,[102] officially Turkey denies the KRG's existence and strongly reaffirms Baghdad's authority over the regional affairs (Lundgren 2007, 73–74). Moreover, Turkish officials claim that there is a political vacuum in the north of Iraq, a problem that should be solved by Iraqis.[103] Iraqi Kurdish leaders are always addressed indirectly. The Turkish press and officials refer to these leaders using terms such as the "administration in northern Iraq" or "Tribal leaders" [Aşiret Reisi].[104] The Turkish government prefers a foreign policy and ethnic conflict resolution operating at the level of the nation states; therefore, conventional ethnic conflict prevention approaches are not the most effective tools for any improvements. Radical changes in international relations and a balance of power in favor of regional players have made this particular perception highly problematic for regional states (Natali 2005, 188). In particular, the military elites and Kemalist bureaucracy in Turkish politics have resisted reading this change and adopting new conditions (Kramer 2000, 52-53). In the post-Cold War period, the main question for the Turkish policy makers must not be the

102 David McDowal states that "Ankara withheld de jure recognition of the Kurdish government; its reliance on Iraqi Kurds implied de facto acceptance of realities" (McDowall 2004, 384).

103 According to one Turkish official, "We don't recognize them as political partners. There is nothing political about them [...] they are the elements at the moment filling the power vacuum and with whom we have to cooperate in the fight against PKK" (Lundgren 2007, 87).

104 For example, the well-known Turkish journalist Mehmet Ali Birand criticises this approach in his column. See "Our tribal chieftains are at the White House." http://www.milliyet.com.tr/Yazar.aspx?aType=YazarDetayArsiv&ArticleID=1009386&AuthorID=86&b=Bizim%20asiret%20reisleri%20Beyaz%20Sarayda%20&a=Mehmet%20Ali%20Birand&ver=84 accessed on 19 April 2010.

geo-strategic position and importance of the Iraqi Kurds to maintain indivisibility of nation and state, but rather who *they* are and how can *we* live together within a regional perspective.

Due to limitations, this chapter will only focus on a single concept: contact and its most basic principle that the "more contact, between ethnic groups, under the right conditions, even if it increases ethnic consciousness, need not increase conflict" (Forbes 1997, 2). Although at first glance it might seem very logical to claim that more contact will help to establish a sustainable conflict resolution, there are two important points need to be explored in detail. The first is the concept of the contact. What exactly constitutes contact? In the wider literature, it is generally perceived as commercial growth between conflicting parties. Are there any other possible ways to establish a contact in potential conflict cases? The second question is: what are the right conditions that make contact more effective and efficient in moving towards a sustainable conflict resolution and that take an existing conflict to a more constructive and peaceful stage? This paper offers answers to these questions with a special focus on the Gülen Movement schools in the region.

Problematizing Problematization

At the bottom of a whole range of theories on ethnic conflict prevention, there are different "*problematizations*"[105] of the initial dispute. Campbell argues that "a problematization is something that has made possible to think in terms of problems and solutions" (Campbell 1998, x). It is about how different parties perceive or interpret the conflict in order to create an imaginary resolution. In other words, in Foucauldian terms, it is about the "problematiza-

105 The term was originally used by Foucault. He defines this particular terms as "the proper task of a history of thought [is] to define the conditions in which human beings 'problematize what they are, what they do, and the world in which they live,'" (Foucault 1991, 389).

tion of a present" by the actors' point of view. It is a kind of narrative that the actors believe is the only representation of truth; therefore, ethnic conflict is not always in a direct "cause and effect" relationship for conflicting parties. Sometimes this misinterpretation or misperception over the cause of conflict itself might be the potential conflict (Ross et al. 1999, 4). So instead of the clashing interests of the actors, conflicting problematizations of present history define and determine criteria for any success or failure of the ethnic conflict resolution. Problematization defines the nature and characterization of a conflict, whether it is an economical, political, or ideological conflict. It is the creation of possibilities that makes particular ethnic conflict and potential solutions sustainable.

As noted above, there are three main pillars of the Turkish government's foreign policy: unity and sovereignty of the Iraqi government, the prevention of any potential political development which would lead the KRG to full independence, and the PKK problem.[106] Whilst the KRG administration admits that there is a security issue and an ethnic terror problem, it claims that these problems can only be solved through a political process that recognizes the KRG as a legitimate power.[107] Furthermore, Prime Minister Nechirvan Barzani gave a statement in November, 2007 making it clear that "for us, there is no alternative to dialogue and discussion. We believe there is an opportunity for a political solution, and we urge the dis-

106 Official Turkish Foreign policy states that "Iraq's preservation of its territorial integrity and national unity is of paramount importance for peace, stability, and prosperity in the Middle East. These are the priorities of our policy." From http://www.mfa.gov.tr/turkish-foreign-policy-on-iraq.en.mfa (accessed 08/25/2008).

107 Prime Minister Nechirvan Barzani states: "We understand Turkey's frustration with the actions of the PKK, and we share the grief and sadness over the loss of life that has taken place. We believe that the only solution to this long-running problem is to be found in negotiations and compromise, not further violence. We are willingly a part of Iraq, and we intend to remain so. The people of Turkey should not fear our progress along the road toward freedom and prosperity. We want to be a safe and responsible neighbour to Turkey. We threaten no one, not today, or in the future.' From http://www.krg.org/articles/detail.asp?lngnr=12&smap=02040100&rnr=268&anr=21122 (accessed on 08.26.2008).

tinguished group of Foreign Ministers to work with us to find that solution."[108] In this statement, he implicitly demands to be recognized as a political actor, which would stabilize and strength the KRG's position in both national and international politics. In addition to these concerns, the KRG administration also recognizes the need to unite its deeply fragmented political structure for its strategic aims to ensure that there will be no more tragic "*Halabja*" for Kurds (Bruinessen 1992, 43; Romano 2006, 211). We can now highlight the problems of these contesting problematizations of a protracted ethnic problem. Both parties do not trust each other, and there exists an important fear factor and misinterpretation of the others intentions on both sides. For Turkey, there is always the risk of an independent Kurdish state which might potentially lead to a "Great Kurdistan," separating the eastern part of Turkey (Barkey and Fuller 1998, 204-205). For the KRG, Turkey poses a potential threat to their hard fought political gains and improvements The KRG also fears Turkey's strong claim on Kirkuk and Mosul, where a considerable portion of the Turkmen population lives (Olson 2005, 98-102).[109] Each party problematizes the issue at the macro-narrative level of security or recognition. Turkey will not recognize the Kurds until its security concerns, the PKK and indivisibility of the nation, are met at least to some degree and at least enough to allay its fears. From the opposite point of view, the KRG will not fully and willingly cooperate with Turkey on security issues unless Turkey initiates an official recognition process.[110] This situation constitutes a typical dead lock which at present time cannot be bro-

108 http://www.krg.org/articles/detail.asp?lngnr=12&smap=02040100&rnr=268&anr=21122 (accessed on 08.26.2008).

109 The president of the KRG Barzani states, "I don›t want you to be misused by sides that have other agendas. You will achieve more with your understanding [agreement] with Kurds. You are our brothers. We have no issues with you; our sensitivities are with external agendas." His full press statement is available from http://www.iraqupdates.com/p_articles.php/article/34873 (accessed on 08.28.2008).

110 For further discussion, see Patrick Mac Manus, "The PKK and the Kirkuk" at http://www.puk.org/web/htm/news/nws/news080821.html (accessed on 11.27.08).

ken. However, I offer an alternative problematization of the protracted ethnic tension between Turkey and Iraqi Kurds. I am suggesting that by addressing the issues at the micro level, that is at the level of the individual within the community, it is possible to make significant changes towards a sustainable conflict resolution. A lack of understanding of each others' needs exists at the grass roots of this ethnic conflict. The inability to accommodate different social, political, and religious differences is perhaps caused by, in a wider and deeper sense, a lack of a strong democratic culture (Kirisci and Winrow 1997, 204). More importantly, at the core of this ethnic conundrum lies a fear of otherness which eventually turns this unwanted other into an imaginary enemy (Gunter 2006, 231). Yavuz points this out: "For instance, Turkey's own Kurdish problem shapes its policy toward Iraqi Kurds. Thus, Turkey has no Iraq policy, but rather an 'anti Kurdish policy' that is guided by the fear of being portioned" (Yavuz 2005, 164).

Despite all difficulties presented by different problematizations, the main question is: will it be possible to develop a strategy which will enable us to claim a sustainable resolution and to prevent potential conflict in future? This paper argues that if the conditions for such possibilities were created, then it would be possible to reach a common understanding towards a sustainable and peaceful ethnic conflict resolution (McDowall 1992, 31). In order to create such conditionality, a strong and effective communication between these conflicting groups is needed. With such, all conflicting parties will be able to reach a common understanding of the roots of the ethnic conflict and will begin the negotiation processes, an act that presupposes a recognition, respect, and understanding that the other needs. As Ross and Rothman point out, "They [non-governmental organizations] are far more likely to focus on creating the preconditions which might move the parties to the table where more formal negotiations can take place or encourage acceptance and implementation of an existing agreement and achieving reconciliation among disputants. Such work may emphasize intense contact between small groups of people, cooperative projects of joint interest, [and] building channels of communication" (Ross et al. 1999, 2).

Even though the authors strongly emphasize the importance of cooperation and common interest, they give no clear indication as to what kind of NGO activities might provide preconditions for a sustainable conflict resolution. It might be argued that there is no general rule applicable to all conflicts because each and every conflict is a unique case with unique historical and political specificities. As social researchers, it is our duty to find that historical and political specifity between Turkey and Iraqi Kurds.

Although some criticize the nature and definition of NGOs,[111] the importance and role of NGOs in preventing ethnic conflict is an undeniable fact.[112] Educational institutions are considered powerful functional mechanisms that have some clear advantages in comparison to the other mechanisms. According to Hamburg and Cyrus (1997, 120), "much of what schools can accomplish is similar to what parents can do—employing positive discipline practices, teaching the capacity for responsible decision making, fostering cooperative learning procedures, and guide children in prosocial behavior outside the schools as well as in them. [The schools] can convey the fascination of other cultures, making understanding and respect a core attribute of their outlook on the world—including the capacity to interact effectively in the emerging global economy, a potentially powerful motivation in the world of the next century. They can use this knowledge to foster sympathetic interest across cultures, recognition of shared and valued goals, as well as a mutual aid ethic" (Hamburg and Cyrus 1997, 120).

In this study, I rely on the definition of an NGO as a voluntary union which is legally constituted by private persons or orga-

---

111 For a detailed comparative analysis on different accounts and types of NGOs, see Turkone 2005.

112 The number of internationally operating NGOs is estimated around at 40,000, see in detail Helmut et al 2001.

nizations with no participation or representation of any government. In this sense the Fezalar Educational Institutions (FEI) associated with the Gülen Movement that operate in Northern Iraq fit into the definition of an NGO. FEI has been operating in Iraq, particularly in the northern Iraq, since 1993. The General Director of FEI, Talip Büyük points out an increasing demand for Turkish schools over the years in the region.[113] He also stated: "We love Kurdish people. Our love and loyalty have been tested many times [referring to hard times in Kurdistan, Gulf wars, and internal conflicts between rival Kurdish parties] and Kurdish people love us too." He denies the charges that Turkish schools are brainwashing Kurds, stating that "we have never ever imposed any ideology or hidden agenda other than love, tolerance, and peace. Furthermore, unlike some private institutions we follow the local and national curriculum in our schools." There are currently 12 Turkish schools in Iraq,[114] ranging from the nursery school to the university level. Eleven of these schools are in Suleymaniye (3), Arbil (5), Kirkuk (2) and Duhok (1). Ishik University also opened in September 2009 and has 4 faculties and 6 departments. In total, around 4000 students have attended these schools, and for 2010–2011, the FEI is targeting to accommodate 6000 students. General Director Talip Büyük emphasizes the fact that there was no school fee until 2001. They were funded by volunteers and businessmen. Currently the school fee is between $1500 and $1950 per year.[115] Like many other Turkish schools around world, the admission selection process is highly competitive. In order to apply for any of these schools' admission tests, students first should have an 85% overall mark from their local schools. Approximately 500 students enroll for the

---

113 For full report please see http://www.aksiyon.com.tr/detay.php?id=29041 (accessed 12.10.2007).

114 During my fieldwork, the General Director of Fezalar Education Mr. Talip Büyük showed me further 3 schools under construction which will bring the number to 15 schools.

115 This is relatively more affordable prices for local Kurds compared to some other private educational institutions such as SABI schools which charge $ 3900.00 per year.

first stage selection; then according to the test results, the first 90 students have to take another test consisting of logic and mathematics. Only 60 of those students are then accepted into each school. At the end of the selection tests, schools offer scholarships ranging from full funding to a 25% discount for the first 100 students. 210 teachers in total are employed at these schools; 120 of them are Turkish citizens and 19 of those teachers are the graduates of Fezalar schools.[116] Beside its educational and cultural activities, the FEI acts as a financial investment advisor for those companies who want to invest in the region. I witnessed one clear example of this practice. Two Turkish businessmen[117] presented themselves as representatives of one of the leading automotive companies, explained their intention to enter into Iraqi Kurdish market and their $20 million investment plan. Although they had their initial market research and feasibility reports, they asked Mr. Büyük for advice and help on establishing their business in Erbil. They believed that the FEI would provide the best local and financial information for their company and direct them to right sectors.

Commercial Growth and Ethnic Conflict

It is a very popular argument that we now live in a global village, with mass communication technologies, immigration, and global commerce.[118] All of these have increased or changed enormously in the past century and continue to grow, bringing different cultures and groups of people into more complicated networks of exchange. Borders have become less visible among nations and ethnic groups. Contact between different peoples or ethnic groups is increasing.

---

116 In an e mail message to the author on 23.08.2008, Mr. Büyük presented all the information about Fezalar Education Institutions detailed above.

117 This particular event happened during my interview with Mr. Büyük on the 6th of March 2010 in Erbil. These two businessmen wished to remain anonymous.

118 World trade was around $11.8 trillion in 2006. In the last seven years world trade grew approximately %7. From http://www.dtm.gov.tr/dtmadmin/upload/IHR/2007 yillik.doc (accessed on 09.25.2008).

Forbes claims that "economic development, it is often thought, should undermine narrow ethnic loyalties and thus ultimately reduce ethnic conflict and increase respect for individual rights. After all, the growth of commerce brings previously isolated groups into closer contact and gives them incentives to cooperate with each other in new ways" (Forbes 1997, 4). But can we draw a conclusion that this huge growth of commerce and intense contact between different ethnic groups will help us to prevent ethnic conflicts on the globe? Is there a real correlation between these variables? If there is, to what extent can the growth of commerce affect ethnic conflict?

Forbes attempts to answer these questions by saying that "more contact between individuals belonging to antagonistic social groups tends to undermine negative stereotypes and thus to reduce prejudice and improve intergroup relations. In relations between groups, familiarity can breed friendliness and appreciation. Commercial exchange, to the extent that it promotes personal acquaintance, should cure destructive prejudices" (Forbes 1997, 7). There is no doubt that familiarity of language, culture, and religion between antagonistic groups plays a strategic role in the prevention of ethnic conflict. Indeed, Turkish and Kurdish cultures have many common social practices such as kinship, a common history, and a common religion - Islam. For more than a thousand years, Turkish and Kurdish communities lived in peace and harmony (Romano 2006, 201–207). Although Forbes does not explain to what extent precisely commerce can be a useful tool and under what conditions, he offers commerce as another preventative element.

Due to the UN economic sanctions in 1990 following Iraq's invasion of Kuwait, trade volume between Turkey and Iraq has been in a long stagnation period. As Olson points out: "During the 1990s, around 500 to 1500 trucks a day used the border port of Habur/Ibrahim al-Khalil. After the US invasion of Iraq in March 2003, the truck traffic rose to some 2000 trucks a day" (Olson 2005, 25). Furthermore, the Turkish government is targeting to increase trade to $20 billion over the next two years compared with just under $4 billion in 2007 (Ibid.). He also claims that this enormous growth of commerce will restrain the aspirations of Kurdish hardliner nationalists and eventually establish strong cooperation towards regional peace and stability.[119]

In order to present my argument effectively, it is necessary to make a few remarks about the true nature of this commercial growth. First, according to the Turkish Foreign Economic Relations board's statistics, there was a steady rise in the volume of trade between Iraq and Turkey from about $370 million in 2000 to $2.75 billion in 2005.[120] However, the strongest objections and hostile comments[121] on Turkey's contribution to the allied forces for Iraq War came from Kurdish leadership in 2003 (Olson 2005, 29). It is very clear that Iraqi Kurdish politicians were gravely concerned about heavy Turkish military presence in Iraq and perceived this as a potential threat to their national politics. Second, according to Serpil Yılmaz of *Milliyet* newspaper, several Turkish businessmen were held in prison in Northern Iraq without being officially charged. In many cases, their contracts were terminated without negotiation or consent.[122] Finally, whenever an ethnic tension rises between Turkey and Iraq, whether this is due to PKK's terrorist activities or Kirkuk, the very first foreign policy decision is to close the border

119 Olson particularly claims that "the economic development of the Kurdish area will prevent any secessionist movements and radical demands of Kurdish nationalism such as the independence or annexation of Kirkuk" (2005, 244).

120 http://www.deik.org.tr/Lists/DisTicaretIstatistikleri/Attachments/2/200719155651ocak202007_TR.pdf(accessed on 03.20.2010).

121 According to *Zaman* newspaper, Mesud Barzani stated that 'Turkey constitutes a bigger threat for Kurds than Iraq." For the full article, see 02.26.2003. http://www.zaman.com.tr/arsiv.do (accessed on 03.20.2010).

122 There are 3 journal articles in this particular issue written by Serpil Yilmaz on 16.04.2002, 19.04.2008, 22.04.2008 available at: http://www.milliyet.com.tr/Yazar.aspx?aType=YazarDetayArsiv&ArticleID=517859&AuthorID=103&b=Kuzey%20Irakta%20ekonomik%20zorbalik&a=Serpil%20Yilmaz&ver=32 (accessed on 19 April 2010).

for trade and punish Kurdish politicians for their actions.[123] For instance, in October 2007, PKK terrorists attacked a Turkish military point and killed 12 soldiers. After this attack, both in parliament and on the street, the first reaction was to close the Khalil border crossing. This has been evidenced many times in the past.[124]

Evidently, the reliability and sustainability of commercial improvements in the long term will be important for achieving ethnic harmony because this policy can easily be turned into a strategic weapon for imposing one party's terms on the other. Therefore, instead of jumping to a very quick conclusion and establishing a direct correlation between growth of commerce, contact, and ethnic conflicts, we should focus on the nature and quality of contact and possible effects on ethnic conflict resolutions. Perhaps we should treat every individual case as *sui generis* and attempt to explain its historical and political specifities.

Kurds and Background of Kirkuk Crisis

The main characteristics of the Kurdish national movement in the 1990s were its dual structure and multiple antagonisms between rival parties. There were several reasons for the violence between early 1993 and 1998; however, most academics agree that the main reason for this internecine civil war was an unequal economic distribution of the custom revenues between the KDP (Kurdistan Democratic Party) and the economically deprived PUK (Patriotic Union of Kurdistan).[125] The postponement of the Kirkuk

123 This is also true for Iraqi domestic politics. During my field study in Iraq in March 2010, I interviewed several Turkish businessmen, and they all complained about the late payment due to political tension between Iraqi central government and the KRG which receives 17% of the National revenue.

124 For further information and the full story, see http://www.iraqupdates.com/p_articles.php/article/23620 and "Turkey Battles PKK, Considers Sanctions Against Iraq" http://www.turkishdailynews.com.tr/article.php?enewsid=87438 accessed on 19 April 2010.

125 Romano 2006, 209.

referendum,[126] status and funding of *Peshmerge* forces, and the strong opposition to the oil search contract made with international companies without the central government's approval raised serious concerns amongst Iraqi politicians. Kirkuk is located in the middle of an ocean of oil, holding 40 percent of Iraq's total and 6 percent of world's total reserves.[127] As Martin Chulov noted in an *Observer* article on June 14, 2009, "sitting on vast untapped oil fields, the northern city of Kirkuk has the natural resources to become one of the wealthiest places in the Middle East. But a standoff has developed between local Kurdish leaders and Baghdad over rights of ownership. And in Kirkuk itself, ethnic tensions are rising." The ethnic mix of the population in Kirkuk is one of its most contested issues, particularly in relation to which group has the majority in the city and therefore has right to be the dominant voice in politics (International Crisis Group 2006, 2). According to the U.N. special representative Staffan de Mistura, Kirkuk is "the mother of all crises" in Iraq (Tosh and Ahmed 2008). Prior to the invasion of Iraq, greater Kirkuk's total population was around 800,000.[128] Despite the fact that no accurate data on population exists, the current population of Kirkuk is estimated to be around 1.3 million (Ferris and Stoltz 2008, 11). The majority of the new comers are Kurdish, and they claim that they are originally from Kirkuk and were deported during Saddam's Arabization period (International Crisis Group 2006, 12).

---

126 It is stated in article 140 in the Iraqi constitution that "*in accordance with this Constitution, provided that it accomplishes completely (normalization and census and concludes with a referendum in Kirkuk and other disputed territories to determine the will of their citizens), by a date not to exceed the 31st of December 2007.*" In addition to that in the James-Baker report, it has been suggested that the Kirkuk referendum should be postponed and special status should be given to Kirkuk.

127 Vesely, Milan, 2004. "Iraq's Oil Wealth Fuel Fires of Discontent."*Middle East* 351 (3).

128 Soner Cağaptay and Daniel Fink, 2007. "The Battle for Kirkuk: How to Prevent a New Front in Iraq" http://www.washingtoninstutie.org/templateCO5.php?=2552 (accessed on 01.05.08).

Although each one of the ethnic groups recognizes the multi-ethnic composition of the city of Kirkuk, they each provide different narratives and claims on the future status of Kirkuk (International Crisis Group 2006, 3). Their narratives are based not only on historical and geographical attachments, but also on some sentimental elements. Iraqi President Jalal Talabani, a Kurd, even calls Kirkuk "*our Jerusalem*" (International Crisis Group 2006, 3). But at the same time, for the Assyrians, Arabs, and the Turkmens, Kirkuk is and has been throughout history essential to their national awareness and identity (International Crisis Group 2006, 3).

For the Turkmens, "vilayet Mosul [including Kirkuk] was a Turkoman, not a Kurdish, Arab, or mixed region. They consider Kirkuk and other towns in the mixed population belt as originally Turkoman towns that also house other communities" (International Crisis Group 2006, 5). The native Arab and *wafedeen* (new comers to the city as a result of Arabization policy, mainly poor Shiites from the south) narrative, sharing many similarities with the Turkoman narrative, perceives Kirkuk as a multi-ethnic city and holds the Kurdish governance responsible for the recent Kurdish influx into Kirkuk. For them, this is not of the returning of displaced people (International Crisis Group 2006, 6).

Denial of social, cultural, and political rights is a common problem of this protracted ethnic tension on both sides of the border. Each behaves in the mirror image of the other; for example, where one denies a cultural right the same denial is reflected back across the border. In this way, each side is not acting, in fact, differently but the same as the other. The Turkish government fears the Kurdish identity, assuming that it will bring down the ideologically constructed indivisible nature of the Turkish nation. General Aytaç Yalman says, "We were told in our training that there was no such thing as Kurd. We used to see Kurds as part of the Turkish race. We were told the term Kurd emerged because the footsteps of people traveling in the snowy mountainous terrain sound-ed like that."[129] Because of this ideological fantasy of an indivisible nation, every Kurdish demand, regardless of its rightness or socio-cultural nature, has been refused. In due course, these demands for the recognition of Kurds have greatly politicized and polarized Kurdish people.

Gülen's Ideas on the Concept of "Otherness" and Fezalar Education Institutions in Northern Iraq

The Carnegie report, as an ethnic conflict prevention method, claims that, "education is a force for reducing intergroup conflict by enlarging our social group identification beyond parochial ones in light of common human characteristics and super ordinate goals – highly valued aspirations can only be achieved by intergroup cooperation" (Hamburg and Cyrus 1997, 120). As an Islamic scholar and activist, Gülen is well-known for his thoughts on interfaith dialogue, democracy, pluralism, and tolerance (Yılmaz 2003; Yılmaz 2005a; Yılmaz 2005b).[130] While he strongly rejects the concept of the "clash of civilizations," he believes in communal peace which "lies in respecting all differences, considering these differences to be part of our nature and in ensuring that people appreciate these differences. Otherwise, it is unavoidable that the world will devour itself in a web of conflicts, disputes, fights, and the bloodiest of wars, thus preparing the way for its own end" (Mihai 2007, 425). Gülen accepts social, cultural, and political differences as a natural part of human existence, instead of erasing those difficulties and forcing them in more homogeneous structures.

In order to form this collective and common understanding, we must "be a human being among other human beings" (Gülen 2005, 76). He suggests that we should acknowledge others as dif-

---

129 Ekrem Dumanlı. "This shirt does not fit society." September, 5, 2008, www.todayzaman.com (accessed on 11.27.08).

130 Fethullah Gülen came on top in *Foreign Policy*'s 2008 poll on world's top public intellectuals. See www.foreignpolicy.com/story/cms.php?story_id=4349.

ferent but without changing them or forcing them to confirm to our standards. He believes that cooperation and collectiveness should be based on non-discriminatory forms of inclusiveness and further points out that "the Islamic social system seeks to form a virtuous society and thereby gain God's approval. It recognizes rights, not force, as the foundation of social life. Hostility is unacceptable. Relationships must be based on belief, love, mutual respect, assistance, and understanding instead of conflict and realization of personal interest" (Yılmaz 2003, 230). Therefore, his understanding of dialogue serves only to introduce these different cultures to each other without imposing one culture on another or simply assimilating a minor group within a dominant community. It is a kind of unconditional admittance and recognition of the other as different from us without having any judgment.

This is a very difficult task particularly when considering isolated antagonistic groups that have strong prejudices about their own minorities.[131] In fact, many writers emphasize that there are a growing number of young people in Iraqi Kurdistan who are not able to speak Arabic. The lack of a common language in Northern Iraq seriously challenges any effective dialogue process. Olson states that "many Kurds under 20 did not speak Arabic, although some acknowledged they would have to learn it" (Olson 2005, 42). Unlike the standard Kurdish schools, the curriculum in all FEI schools includes the study of four languages: Turkish, Arabic, Kurdish, and English in the first year, thus improving the opportunities for effective dialogue. This policy clearly demonstrates how Gülen's inclusiveness and his movement work within fragmented societies: by valuing each group and by constructing the desired society model in the schools. Schools are the best places to transform individuals into members of a more tolerant and peaceful soci-

131 According to Olson "growing Kurdish nationalism was clearly evident, especially among young people, most of them when asked, said they wanted an independent state: 'we never want to mix with Arabs again; they [Arabs] were raised on fighting and cruelty; we have different colour skin etc," Olson 2005, 42.

ety. There is no doubt that Gülen schools fill an extremely important gap in terms of creating the space through which all ethno religious groups can present culture and communicate with each other. By including all regional languages in their curriculum, they not only value the academic significance of each language in proper communication, but also provide a channel for solution-focused political activity, a truly public form of diplomacy by which they can create a cohesive, cooperative community.

In addition to constructing the conditions for possibilities on site, each year the Gülen schools organize a series of school trips which involve activities in Turkish cities and Turkish schools in order to introduce the Turkish culture to students and to enable Turkish people to experience Kurdish culture first hand.[132] The Gülen Movement takes every opportunity to expand and foster its core ideas of tolerance, dialogue, and collective cooperation in hopes of upward social movements; for instance, during the last "feast of sacrifice Eid," the Gülen Movement distributed meat to around 62,000 socially deprived Kurdish families and organized free health checks throughout southeastern Anatolia, including Northern Iraq (Kirk 2008). This kind of charity is unique compared to other charitable organizations. First, the number of families reached by the Gülen Movement is incomparably enormous, even for state organized charities. Second, their aim is not just simply giving to the poor, but also showing them they are cared for and thought about by the charity's founders (Kirk 2008). Unlike many other organizations, the Gülen Movement followers have preferred direct contact and delivery methods by donors rather than using professionals or other volunteers, which means that wealthy businessmen and professionals living in the western part of Turkey spend the entire festive period engaging in charitable activities by distributing and visiting people in the region (Koç 2008). This method has proved the movement's sincerity and genuineness in

---

132 For full article: http://www.haberegitim.net/news_detail.php?id=1844&uniq_id=1224858860 (accessed on 10.10.2008).

creating spiritual bonds of brotherhood between communities. Third, their aim was not only to deliver meat and goods to the people in need but also to show that there is a hope for peaceful coexistence through understanding and respecting each other's rights (Kirk 2008). Finally, but by no means least importantly, charity aids are administered through the most possible transparent and objective non-discriminatory principles, which achieves the highest level of inclusiveness (Koç 2008).

Fethullah Gülen sees education as the best instrument to achieve this goal in a practical sense. In his interview with *Foreign Policy*, he explains: "We must acknowledge that we are all human beings. It is not our choice to belong to a particular race or family. We should be freed from fear of the other and enjoy diversity within democracy. I believe that dialogue and education are the most effective means to surpass our differences."[133] In his understanding, schools constitute a mini-prototype for his vision and the values he is advocating for. The schools that were inspired by Fethullah Gülen are considered a living sample of a pluralistic society in which all moral values, such as tolerance, are exercised at every stage of the process from the level of administration to teaching. In other words, Gülen schools have not only proved to be academically successful, but at the same time they reduce, if not eliminate, the fear of the other and sustain the hope for peaceful coexistence and democracy in multi-ethnic societies.

Unlike conventional preventative methods, educational institutions focus primarily on individuals. From the individual to all parts of the community, this kind of education targets a slow but stable and strong change of values, perception, and understanding, and in conclusion, it helps construct a democratic, tolerant, and morally strong society which will enjoy pluralist enrichment. Let me present a counter logic to clarify my argument. Let us assume for a

---

133 Full interview available on the web: www.foreignpolicy.com/story/cms.php?story_id=4408 (accessed 08.2008).

moment that the Turkish government and the KRG administration have amicably settled all the issues. They agreed on how to share oil revenues and govern Kirkuk. The PKK is eliminated by military means. Will all these agreements at the level of politicians change the Kurdish people's perception of Turkey and independence or Turkish people's fear of the KRG's hidden agenda? How sustainable can this peace be? I argue that such a solution for peace will not be sustainable and durable due to a lack of public support.

The FEI's mission is to bring people together from different beliefs, thoughts, and nationalities, people respecting each other, loving, living together in peace without any fighting and conflict.[134] Because of high academic success and humanitarian aims, the FEI "often has legitimacy and operational access that do not raise concerns about sovereignty, as government activities sometimes do" (Hamburg and Cyrus 1997, 120). Indeed, very recently the Iraqi Kurdish Regional government has granted a license and land to FEI to open a new University. Significantly, there was a serious military confrontation risk at that time as the Turkish army crossed the border into Iraqi territory fighting against PKK forces. Even during the civil war (1994–1998), the FEI schools expanded by opening branches in both the KDP and the PUK controlled areas; Nilufer Private College for girls was opened in 1996 in Arbil, which was under the control of the KDP, and Salahaddin Ayyubi College was opened in 1997 in Suleymaniye, which was controlled predominantly by the PUK administration.

If educational institutions are expanding during a civil war, such as the college in Suleymaniye, then this demonstrates that education is trusted, valued, and considered capable of neutrality. I was provided with evidence of this during my visit to Iraqi Kurdistan at the time of national elections on March 7, 2010.[135] Letters between the Turkish government and the FEI schools, and between the

---

134 www.fezalar.org/articles.asp?cat=42 (accessed on 08.25.2008).

135 Mr. Büyük provided these letters during my interview that took place on the 6th of March 2010 in Erbil.

PUK political bureau and the Turkish government, demonstrate that these groups trusted and believed in the FEI schools' ability to be neutral. In these letters, the following points are significant:

The PUK letter dated February, 2 1997 (see appendix 2) addressed to the Turkish Foreign Office requested that through their (the Turkish government's) direction, Fezalar Schools set up a school in Suleymaniye. In addition to the request, the PUK pledged land and materials for construction of the school. Although the FEI is an NGO operating independently, the PUK clearly perceived their role as unofficial representatives of the Turkish government and made their request through official channels. Upon receiving this letter through the Turkish Foreign Office, the FEI sought official advice from the Turkish Ministry. In a letter dated May 7, the Turkish Ministry of Foreign Affairs replied to the FEI application for permission to build (see appendix 1). In this letter, Ambassador Tuzel stated that "there is no objection for opening a school in Suleymaniye." He also expressed his concern about the "timing due to the political vacuum in Iraq." It is very clear that the FEI activities in Iraqi Kurdistan pluralized the existing diplomatic relations and communication channels, which were predominantly constituted and dominated by the Turkish army.[136]

The initial FEI schools were built in areas with KDP strongholds; however, because they value the importance of the schools, the PUK is quite happy for the same school provider to set up in their area, too. Even for antagonistic parties in an ethnic conflict, these educational institutions are considered neutral and trustworthy.

In order for the country to progress, there is now a need on the ground in Iraq for strong cooperation and an officially acknowledged agreement, not only in education but in all aspects of the social and political life (Kirisci and Winrow 1997, 199-201). On

136 Makovsky and Sayari states that "the military, of course, is often a dominant player in Turkish foreign policy...it is widely assumed, for example, that the military takes the lead in decision regarding Turkish policy in northern Iraq and the fight against the PKK," Makovsky and Sayari 2000, 4.

this point, I believe that the FEI schools have created, and are continuing to create, the conditions in which all parties may overcome the fear of otherness. More importantly, the FEI schools have the potential to reduce the risk of ethnic confrontation by developing strong ties between Turkey and the KRG. By transferring academics and resources from Turkey to Iraq through opening a university, the FEI offers itself as an alternative organization, building confidence and cooperation between the conflicting parties. Gülen-inspired Turkish schools have also created, and continue to create, de facto conditions which provide both parties with unique opportunities to improve their relationship.

Gülen-inspired Turkish schools are spreading the concept of tolerance, dialogue, democracy, and pluralism in Kurdish communities through education. They are promoting non-violent conflict resolution by showing how to approach social problems through collective cooperation. Expansion of FEI educational activities open up a political and social space for an alternative approach to the prevention of ethnic conflict. More importantly, they present an alternative way of thinking about ethnic conflict resolutions based on an increasing level of social, cultural, and trade contacts between conflicting parties. Another example of this type of activity is the Gülen-inspired organization called "Abant Platform," which by gathering diverse groups of intellectuals, academics, and representatives of the civil society organizations, organized a meeting to predominantly engage the question of the Kurdish issue. In the declaration statement for the meeting (February 15–16, 2009, Arbil), they stated: "The aim is to have sound and dynamic channels of communication in order to put an end to the lack of dialogue rather than trying to convince the parties to come to terms around a solution program. As a chief principle, we defend the free expression and discussion of any sort of ideas unless they contain open calls for violence, and we expect everyone to respect the right of all people and groups to express their various thoughts and ideas… Kurds, alongside all groups in Iraq, are our brothers. We see it a compulsory move to develop friendly ties with the Federal Kurdish Administration. Sustaining the democratization process in Turkey is also compulsory for solving the Kurdish problem."[137] On this issue, the FEI stands out as the only strong and well-organized NGO with the potential to establish stronger social, cultural, and economic ties between Turkey and Iraqi Kurds.

Despite all of the above claims, many still argue that the FEI educational activities will need a longer period of time to demonstrate their full effect in helping to resolve the conflict. I believe that in providing a viable strong and alternative approach to other conventional conflict mechanisms, through the opening of 15 schools and a university during the last 17 years in the war-torn region of Northern Iraq, these schools have proved that they have the potential to play a vital role in understanding the different parties in this ethnic conflict. I believe, just as the Director of the FEI schools, Mr. Büyük, claims that "we do not need to wait for 20–30 years to see the results of our educational investments in Northern Iraq."[138] More importantly, as it has been stated, the whole purpose of the NGOs in the ethnic conflict prevention process is not to solve conflict but to prepare the conditions for more constructive negotiations between conflicting parties by creating social and political facts on the ground and expanding political space. Gülen-inspired Turkish educational institutions perform this particular task efficiently. In addition to this long term projection, the FEI has also managed to achieve an important milestone in the delicate relationship between Turkey and the Iraqi Kurdish Regional government by bringing official political representatives together in one particular event. Prior to this event, Iraqi Kurdish government officials

137 For full statement, see http://www.gyv.org.tr (accessed on 10.10.2008). The closure statement of the meeting is also available at http://www.abantplatform.org/index.php/main/component/option/frontpage/section/1/category/453/content/2806

138 Translated by the author. The original text appears as "Irak-Türk Okulları Genel Müdürü Talip Büyük, Kuzey Irak'a yönelik kapsamlı bir eğitim hamlesinin sonuçları için 20-30 yıl beklemek gerekmediğini söylüyor." Available at http://www.aksiyon.com.tr/detay.php?id=29041 (accessed on 10.14.2008).

could only talk through military personnel or MIT (National Intelligence Service) secretly. But for the first time, they shared an event together publicly and gave their message to each other openly. This was followed by the ministers of the Turkish Foreign Office's visit to Erbil in 2009 after which the Turkish government appointed its first consul general to Erbil, Mr. Mehmet Aydın Selcen, in March 2010.[139] This demonstrates the gradual improvement of the political relationship between the Kurdish federal region of Iraq and the Turkish government, beginning with the setting up of the FEI schools.

At the opening ceremonies of the Ishik University, the president of the KRG, Mr. Nechirwan Barzani delivered a speech that focused on the importance of FEI and its activities in strengthening its relationship with Turkey. He said, "I hope that Ishik University will become a centre where both the academic aspirations of our students and the aspirations of our government for a strong relationship with Turkey are realized."[140] It is very clear that the Iraqi Kurdish administration perceives the university and the Gülen Movement in general as a golden opportunity to improve its relationship with Turkey for a number of reasons. First, growing tension with the Iraqi central government regarding disputed territories (not only Kirkuk but Diyala and Khanaqin) and Obama's victory in the American presidential election, which signaled the pull out of American military personnel by the end of 2011, grossly concerned Kurdish politicians with regard to their short and long term political future in Iraq. Turkey is the best available strategic option for Kurdish politics as has been proved in the immediate aftermath of the first Gulf War in 1991 when almost half a million Iraqi Kurds became refugees in Turkey to avoid Saddam's ethnic cleansing campaign. Second, the FEI provides crucial public servic-

139 For the KRG's press release please see http://www.krg.org/articles/detail.asp?lngnr=12&smap=02010100&rnr=223&anr=34244 (accessed on 03.25.2010).

140 For the full report, see "Prime Minister Barzani and Turkish MPs attend the opening of Ishik University in Erbil" at http://www.krg.org/articles/detail.asp?rnr=223&lngnr=12&smap=02010100&anr=2663(accessed on 19 April 2010).

es including education, health care, and business to the Kurdish community which suffers from a high rate of unemployment,[141] illiteracy,[142] and a lack of general health care.[143] Modernizing the educational system, creating jobs and business opportunities, and improving health care services are the most urgent needs for a deprived Kurdish society. Therefore, Turkey and the FEI are not only a strategic option for a safer and sustainable administration for Kurdish politics but also the most effective way to modernize the Kurdish community in Northern Iraq.[144]

In the opening ceremony of Ishik University, alongside high ranking KRG officials, Turkey was represented by the vice-consular of Mosul, some MPs, the general director of higher education, and some 200 Turkish businessmen. In the opening ceremony Vice-Consular Ahmet Yıldız read a congratulatory letter written by For-

141 Although there is no reliable statistical data referring to unemployment rates, experts claim that it is high and hidden as the KRG administration has stopped taking new employment in 2007. The total number of employees working in the public sector according the KRG is around 1,100,000, which is extremely high for the total 4.5 million population. See the full report by Victoria Player "Unemployment in Kurdistan." http://iraqnewsmonitor.blogspot.com/2007/09/unemployment-in-kurdistan.html; See also Michael Rubin, "Is Iraqi Kurdistan a good ally" at http://www.aei.org/publications/pubID.27327/pub_detail.asp (accessed on 11.24.2008).

142 According to WADI (German-Iraqi NGO operating in Kurdistan since 1993 promoting human rights and supporting the developments of civil society), the projected current illiteracy rate is more than 50% in Iraqi Kurdistan. See the full activity report at http://www.wadinet.de/projekte/frauen/khanzad/women-brief.htm (accessed on 11.25.2008).

143 The latest cholera outbreak in Suleymaniye and Kirkuk cost several lives in Iraqi Kurdistan and triggered a public debate and strong criticism of general health care services in the area.

144 Ms. Bayan Sami Abdul Rahman, who is the high representative of the KRG in Britain, acknowledged these facts and problems presented above. She also acknowledged some of the critics of Kurdish politics such as nepotism, corruption, and the lack of transparency. However, she stated that "instead of denying these problems, we are facing and dealing with them. We cannot change our culture overnight. We are training and educating our civil service to raise their standards and it will take time." A seminar organised by SOAS (University of London) Kurdish Studies and Student Organization (KSSO), "Kurdistan in Iraq – Progress and Challenges" on March 20, 2010.

eign Office Minister Ali Babacan, which again strongly emphasizes the role of Ishik University in future relations between Turkey and the Iraqi Kurds.[145] This simply and obviously shows that the general attitude of the Turkish government and its problematization have been changing from a military discourse to one that is more civil and more democratic. By appointing a general consul in Erbil, the Turkish government has marked this transition officially and has opened up a new communication channel with Iraqi Kurds for further constructive dialogue. The argument of this paper claims that the FEI can function in a way that encourages both parties to build confidence in order to make progress at the negotiation table. By providing such a common platform for officials and politicians to express their thoughts and give messages to each other, the FEI already proved itself as an alternative form of public diplomacy.

Conclusion

In this study, I attempted to challenge the common theory of potential ethnic conflict prevention, which can be summarized as: more contact, particularly the growth of commerce between antagonistic parties, is likely to increase confidence and positive relationships, which lead to successful conflict management. I analyzed the nature of contact and showed that it can be perceived differently or misinterpreted by different actors. In comparison to the conventional ethnic conflict mechanisms—diplomacy, economic measures, and the use of force—I offer NGOs as an alternative mechanism. As it has been argued above, at present time the application of conventional ethnic conflict prevention tools are not an effective instrument in preventing ethnic conflict between Turkey and the Iraqi Kurdish administration. However, one fact relating to the real politics of the region is that neither of the conflicting parties are able operate their own

145 For the full report, see Yusuf Acar, "The First Turkish University in the Middle East" at http://www.zaman.com.tr/haber.do?haberno=763285&title=ortadogunun-ilk-turk-universitesi-resmen-acildi (accessed on 11.23.2008).

policies without the other's cooperation. In the current situation, it is almost impossible for the Turkish government to engage with the PKK issue by itself, and vice versa, it is also impossible for the KRG administration to sustain a strong and stable political administration without Turkey's active support and cooperation. In the words of the governor of Arbil, Nevzat Hadi: "We do not think of any strategic move that does not involve Turkey's concern."[146] There is a strong consensus among state elites, including the chief of general staff, political parties, and intellectuals, that the PKK issue, or in a wider perspective Kurdish issue, cannot be solved by military activities alone. We need more comprehensive approaches including socio-cultural and political efforts.[147]

I claimed that within the specific historical and political context of the relationship between Turkey and Iraqi Kurds, Fezalar Education Institutions have more potential to reduce ethnic conflict and establish healthy communication channels between communities than the conventional methods. In the long term, I believe that they can be more successful and constructive instruments for regional peace and stability. In conclusion, the most significant testimony towards a successful ethnic conflict resolution is that, in direct opposition to prevailing political trends (since 1993 Iraqi Kurdistan has had significant difficulties in implementing a functional institutional democracy), Fezalar Education Institutions have managed to establish 15 successful schools and a university where ethnic differences are valued and celebrated. More importantly, these institutions have always been supported by all parties and have not experienced any resistance or objection. However, unlike the popular claims that economic growth will bring peace and sta-

146 Translated by the author from Turkish original, "Biz içinde Türkiye'nin olmadığı hiçbir stratejik adım düşünmüyoruz. Bu iyi anlaşılmalı," in Nasuhi Güngör's article "Northern Iraq Notes" in *Star* newspaper 22.09.2008 available from http://www.stargazete.com/gazete/yazar/kuzey-irak-tan-notlar-129513.htm (accessed on 10.10.2008).

147 For further information and the full press release of the general Başbuğ on 09.05.2008, see http://www.tsk.mil.tr/10_ARSIV/10_1_Basin_Yayin_Faaliyetleri/10_1_7_Konusmalar/2008/org_ilkerbasbug_diyarbakir_05092008.html (accessed on 10.10.2008).

bility in to the region, I critically argued that this may not always be the case, and it may even prove otherwise. Gülen's dialogical approach based on unconditional and inclusive acceptance of "other" is more powerful and has more potential towards peaceful coexistence. I believe, therefore, that the way forward in the region will be through educating the masses so that they can understand the needs of the other ethnic groups and, more importantly, so that all ethnic groups in Iraqi Kurdistan can enjoy cultural diversity while preserving their own identity. The clash of ethnic groups in Iraq is an inevitable fate of the communities unless they develop strong and effective communication channels. At present, the FEI are providing the only instruments to act as neutral and effective mediators between antagonistic parties.

References

Barkey, J. H. and Graham E. F. 1998. *Turkey's Kurdish Question*. New York: Rowman & Littlefield.

Bruinessen, M. V. 1992. *Agha, Sheikh and State: The Social and Political Structures of Kurdistan*. London: Zed.

Campbell, D. 1998. *National Deconstruction: Violence, Identity and Justice in Bosnia*. Minneapolis: University of Minnesota Press.

Ferris, E. and K. Stoltz. 2008. *The Future of Kirkuk: The Referendum and Its Potential Impact on Displacement*. Brooking Institute: University of Bern.

Forbes, H.D. 1997. *Ethnic Conflict Commerce, Culture and the Contact Hypothesis*. New Haven: Yale University Press.

Foucault, M. 1991. "Politics and Ethics: an Interview." *The Foucault Reader*. Edited by D. Robinow New York: Penguin. 373-380.

Gunter, M. M. 2006. "Federalism and the Kurds of Iraq: The Solution or the Problem." *The Kurds: Nationalism and Politics*. Edited by Faleh A. Jabar and Hosham Dawod. London: Saqi. 231-258.

Gülen, F. 2005. *Pearls of Wisdom*. New Jersey: The Light, Inc.

Hamburg, D. A., R. Cyrus. 1997. *Preventing Deadly Conflict*. New York: Carnegie Corporation.

Helmut, A. 2001. "Introducing Global Civil Society." Helmut Anheier, Marlies Glasius and Mary Kaldor (eds.) *Global Civil Society*. Oxford: Oxford University Press.

Human Rights Watch. 2004. “Claims in Conflict Reversing Ethnic Cleansing in Northern Iraq.” 16:4 E (August, 2004).

Human Rights Watch. 2007. “Caught in the Whirlwind Torture and Denial of Due Process by the Kurdistan Security Forces.” 19:2 E (July, 2007).

International Crisis Group (ICG). 2006. “Iraq and the Kurds: The Brewing Battle over Kirkuk.” *Middle East Report 56*.

International Crisis Group. 2007. “Iraq and the Kurds: Resolving the Kirkuk Crisis.” *Middle East Report* 64 (April 19, 2007).

Kirisci, K. and Winrow G. G. 1997. *The Kurdish Question and Turkey: An Example of a Trans-state Ethnic Conflict*. London: Frank Cass.

Kirk, A. M. 2008. “Seeds of Peace: Solidarity, Aid and Education Shared by Gülen Movement in South Eastern Turkey.” Presented at the conference, Islam in the Age of Global Challenges: Alternative Perspectives of the Gülen Movement, Washington D.C., USA, November 14–15, 2008.

Koç, D. 2008. “Generating an Understanding of Financial Resources in the Gülen Movement: ‘Kimse Yok mu’ Solidarity and Aid Association.” Presented at the conference, Islam in the Age of Global Challenges: Alternative Perspectives of the Gülen Movement, Washington D.C., USA, November 14–15, 2008.

Kramer, H. 2000. *A Changing Turkey: The Challenge to Europe and the United States*. Washington D.C.: Brooking Institute Press.

Lundberg, A. 2000. *The Unwelcome Neighbour: Turkey’s Kurdish Policy*. London: I.B. Tauris.

Makovsky, A. and S. Sayari. 2000. *Turkey’s New World*. The Washington Institute for Near East Policy: Washington, D.C.

McDowall, D. 1992. “The Kurdish Question: A Historical Review.” *The Kurds: A Contemporary Overview*. Ed. Kreyenbroek, Philip G. and Stefan Sperl. London: Routledge, 1992. 10–33.

———. 2004. *A Modern History of the Kurds*. London: I.B. Tauris.

Mihai, I. V. 2007. “Giving Precedence to Common Points: The Limits of the Otherness. Fethullah Gülen’s Dialogic Methodology for Interfaith Encounters.” İhsan Yılmaz et al. (eds.) *Muslim World in Transition: Contributions of the Gülen Movement*. London: Leeds Metropolitan University Press. 419–427.

Natali, D. 2005. *The Kurds and the State*. New York: Syracuse University Press.

Olson, R. 2005. *The Goat and the Butcher: Nationalism and State Formation in Kurdistan-Iraq since the Iraqi War*. California: Mazda.

———. 2005. "Turkey and Kurdistan–Iraq Relations: The Consolidation of Iraqi Kurdish Nationalism: 2003–2004." *The Kurdish Question and the 2003 Iraqi War*. Ed. Mohammed, M. A. Ahmed and M. M. Gunter. California: Mazda Publishers. 97–123.

Romano, D. 2006. *The Kurdish Nationalist Movement: Opportunity, Mobilization and Identity*. Cambridge: Cambridge University Press.

Ross, M. H. and J. Rothman, eds. 1999. *Theory and Practice in Ethnic Conflict Management*. London: Macmillan.

Tosh, C. and Z. Ahmed. 2008. "Kirkuk Dispute Close to Boiling Point." *IWPR*. 250.

Türköne, M. 2005. "NGO Olarak Türk okulları." *Barış Köprüleri Dünyaya Açılan Türk Okulları*, Ed. T. Ateş, E. Karakaş, and İ. Ortaylı. Istanbul, Da Yayıncılık. 145–161.

Vesely, M. 2004. "Iraq's Oil Wealth Fuel Fires of Discontent." *Middle East*. 351:30.

Yavuz, M. H. 2005. "Turkey's Kurdish-Centered Iraqi Policy." M.A Mohammed Ahmed and M. Michael Gunter (eds.) *The Kurdish Question and the 2003 Iraqi War*. California: Mazda. 163–174.

Yıldız, K. 2004. *The Kurds in Iraq: The Past, Present and Future*. London: Pluto.

Yılmaz, İ. 2003. "*Ijtihad* and *Tajdid* by Conduct: The Gülen Movement." M. H. Yavuz & J. L. Esposito (eds.) *Turkish Islam and the Secular State*. New York: Syracuse University Press. 208-237.

———. 2005a. "State, Law, Civil Society and Islam in Contemporary Turkey." *The Muslim World*. Vol. 55, 385–411.

———. 2005b. *Muslim Laws, Politics and Society in Modern Nation States*. Aldershot, UK: Ashgate

Wimmer, A., J. R. Goldstone, L. D. Horowitz, U. Joras, and C. Shetter. 2004. *Facing Ethnic Conflicts toward a New Realism*. Oxford: Rowman&Littefield.

APPENDIX-1

Ek-1

T.C.
DIŞIŞLERİ BAKANLIĞI
Yurtdışında Yaşayan Türkler Genel Müdürlüğü

07 Mayıs 1997

SAYI : YBGY-330.100-2190
KONU : Okul açılması

FEZALAR EGITIM LIMITED ŞIRKETINE

Kuzey Irak'ın Süleymaniye kentinde bir özel okul açma talebiniz incelenmiştir.

Sözkonusu okulun açılmasında herhangi bir sakınca görülmemekle beraber, bu bölgede halen mevcut otorite boşluğu, belirsiz durum ve güvensizlik ortamı gibi olumsuz şartlar dolayısıyla zamanlama konusunda dikkatli davranılmasının uygun olacağı mütalaa edilmektedir.

Bilgilerine saygı ile sunarım.

Erdim TÜZEL
Büyükelçi
Bakan a.
Yurtdışında Yaşayan Türkler Genel Müdürü
(YTGM)

APPENDIX-2

Patriotic Union of Kurdistan

Politburo

No.: 10
Day: 11.2-1997

الاتحاد الوطني الكردستاني

المكتب السياسي

العدد: ١٠
التاريخ: ١١/٢/١٩٩٧

الى وزارة الخارجية فى الجمهورية التركية

م/ فتح مدرسة ثانوية

ننتهز هذه الفرصة لنقدم لكم ازكى التحيات متمنين تطوير وتمتين العلاقات الاخوية بيننا .
وفى الوقت نفسه نرحب بقيام شركة (فزالر للتربية والتعليم) بفتح مدرسة ثانوية في مدينة السليمانية اسوة بالثانوية التي فتحت في اربيل قبل ثلاث سنوات ، ونحن مستعدون لتهيئة البناية الملائمة والمستلزمات الضرورية الاخرى .

مع التقدير

المكتب السياسي

CONCLUSION

John L. Esposito and İhsan Yılmaz

As we have seen, Fethullah Gülen's pluralistic, inclusivist and peacebuilding ideas have enabled the Gülen Movement to successfully turned its moral, spiritual, intellectual, financial and human resources into effective social capital and utilized this social capital in establishing educational institutions from primary school to university levels.

As discussed throughout the book, the Movement's stance toward pluralism, diversity, tolerance, acceptance, civil society, secularism and democracy shows that the Movement generates a bridging social capital, extremely helpful for peacebuilding and establishing sustainable peace.

The Gülen Movement is not a political movement, but with its projects and achievements it is paving the way for conditions required for a pluralist democracy. Dialogue activities, fostering tolerance and acceptance, educational projects, indirectly helping to raise socio-economic standards of a community, encouraging local communities to cooperate around charity and educational projects and lastly poverty alleviation programs of the movement obviously are helpful for the establishment of pluralistic societies and the sustainability of democracies. As it is a faith-based movement, it would methodologically be wrong to compare the Movement with political ideologies. But if individualism, freedom, rationality, equality, tolerance, and consent—not in the Gramscian sense—are some of the characteristic of social and political liberalism, then it could be said that all of the movement's projects foster these attributes, attitudes and characteristics. Yet, it must also be noted that the

Movement emphasises the vitality of voluntary communitarianism and its discourse and praxis discourage atomistic individualism.

The Gülen Movement's bottom-up approach and focus on comprehensive civic and social activism is also important given that peacebuilding efforts of many civil society organizations have been criticized by scholars of being project-oriented and top-down, rather than mass-based. Moreover, the fact that the Movement does not boast that it is engaged in peacebuilding (peacebuilding and conflict prevention by conduct) and tries to reach all members of society from preschool students to university youth as well as their parents, makes the Movement's peacebuilding more resistant-proof and long term.

INDEX

A

D

E

H

I

J

W

Y

Z